The World Turned
Upside Down

The World Turned Upside Down

America, China,
and the Struggle
for Global
Leadership

Clyde Prestowitz

Yale UNIVERSITY PRESS
New Haven & London

Yale University Press books may be purchased in quantity for educational, business, or promotional use. For information, please e-mail sales.press@yale.edu (U.S. office) or sales@yaleup.co.uk (U.K. office).

Set in Galliard and Gotham types by IDS Infotech Ltd. Printed in the United States of America.

Library of Congress Control Number: 2020940160
ISBN 978-0-300-24849-4 (hardcover : alk. paper)

A catalogue record for this book is available from the British Library.

This paper meets the requirements of ANSI/NISO Z39.48-1992 (Permanence of Paper).

10 9 8 7 6 5 4 3 2

Contents

The World Turned
Upside Down

The U.S.-China Balance of Power.

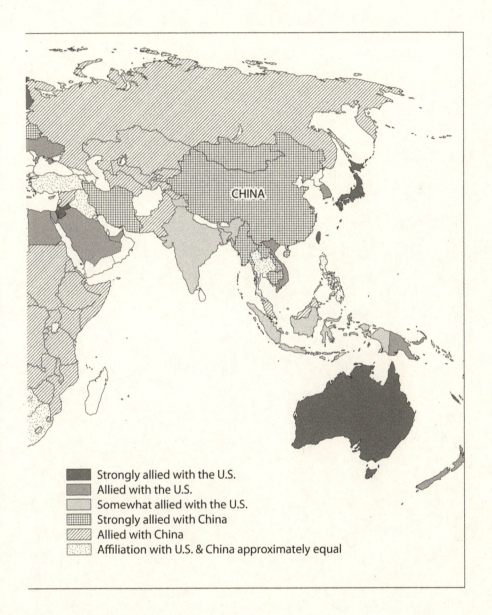

Strongly allied with the U.S.
Allied with the U.S.
Somewhat allied with the U.S.
Strongly allied with China
Allied with China
Affiliation with U.S. & China approximately equal

CHINA

Introduction

> When the facts change, I change my opinion. And what do you do, sir?
> —*John Maynard Keynes*

In 1991, having emerged triumphant from the Cold War, America and the free world countries experienced a wave of euphoria. The classic expression of the era's geopolitical mood was Francis Fukuyama's book *The End of History and the Last Man*, which reported that the conquest of the world by democracy and free market capitalism was irresistible and permanent.[1]

China did not appear to be an exception. It was still ruled by the Chinese Communist Party (CCP), and thus continued to call itself a communist country. But the CCP was led by the pragmatic Deng Xiaoping, who famously commented that "it matters not whether a cat is black or white, so long as it catches mice." True, Deng had ordered the massacre of hundreds and perhaps thousands of students and workers demonstrating for democracy in Beijing's Tiananmen Square and throughout the country on June 4–5, 1989. (An estimate from the U.S. embassy in Beijing put the number of deaths at five hundred to twenty-six hundred.[2] Most casualties were reported to have occurred on Changan Avenue, outside the square.) But he assured global leaders that this was just domestic politics, and it should in no way deter them from taking advantage of China's ultra-low wages by using it as a production location from which to export to world markets and to sell into the growing China market.

One of the first to do so was Robert Galvin, the CEO and chairman of Motorola and the son of its founder. He once told me that the Tiananmen Square incident had created a great opportunity for his company. The Chinese, he said, desperately needed investment and technology, and because of all the bad press they were willing to make significant concessions to attract foreign companies. He hurried to Beijing, where he offered to put Motorola factories in China on the condition that Motorola retain 100 percent ownership of the business. Standard Chinese policy had been to require joint ventures with Chinese partners, but as Galvin had anticipated, Deng and company made an exception for Motorola, which hastened to begin offshoring its production from the United States to China. Other U.S. and global CEOs soon followed suit.

Nor was there any pushback from Western governments—quite the opposite. President William Clinton called for "engagement." Regarding China's possible censorship of the then new internet, Clinton scoffed that "that would be like trying to nail Jell-O to the wall." In this he was supported by U.S. trade representative Charlene Barshefsky, who said it was a "no brainer" that the internet would lead to China's liberalization. "The government is not going to be able to control content. It is not going to be able to control access. The Net is going to have the single most profound change on China, engendering tremendous pressure on the Chinese leadership."[3]

In 2001, the U.S. government backed China's entrance into the World Trade Organization (WTO). A key argument in favor of this move was that the greatest potential danger to the world would not be a rapidly developing China but rather an economically failing China. This kind of assessment was often followed by another, expressed by former deputy secretary of state Robert Zoellick, who asserted that the United States and its allies wanted China to be "a responsible stakeholder in the global system."[4]

I was reminded of this when my chief research assistant, Joel Fischl, was tardy in responding to my request for information during his tour of southern China in the spring of 2019. When he finally emailed me from Manila, he began, "I wanted to write a version of this email to you while I was in China, but I was nervous about doing so. I self-censored myself for fear of writing anything critical of China while I was in the country. Maybe this is paranoid, but that's what I was thinking. Although the likelihood of being detained while in China for writing this was low, it was high enough in my considered opinion to prevent me from doing it."

A Mandarin speaker with twenty-five years' experience living in Asia (twenty of them as a U.S. commercial diplomat, including five years in Beijing and Shanghai and six years in Hong Kong and Taipei), Fischl added that the CCP has succeeded in teaching 1.4 billion Chinese people—one-fifth of humanity—an alternate version of history by creating an alternate internet and establishing an alternate to the reality seen by the rest of the world. The Chinese people, he wrote, "can only get the 'facts' that are approved by the CCP. Few, if any young people have any knowledge of the Tiananmen Square incident. Few are aware of the true nature of the reeducation camps established for the Muslim Uighur people in Xinjiang province or . . . that the CCP has virtually succeeded in wiping out the entire Tibetan culture. The most frightening thing is their ability to spread and sell their authoritarian model of government not just to other dictators and oppressive regimes, but to countries such as Thailand and Ecuador who like the idea of security cameras, facial recognition software etc. to help maintain political power. China—slowly but surely—is reordering some parts of the world in its own image."

When China joined the WTO in December 2001, it was an authoritarian state with an $80 billion trade surplus (technically a current account surplus) with the United States and a $1.3 trillion annual GDP. This was a bit more than one-tenth the U.S. GDP of $10.5 trillion. The United States was the world leader in a wide variety of high-technology industries like telecommunications, avionics, and semiconductors, while China was concentrating on producing shoes, textiles, steel, and concrete. Top U.S. officials like U.S. trade representative Barshefsky and commerce secretary Mickey Kantor told Congress that admitting China to the WTO would cut the U.S. trade deficit in half because China's high tariffs would be greatly reduced while the low U.S. tariffs wouldn't change. In other words, it seemed China was making all the concessions. The result, they said, would be millions of new high-paying U.S. jobs.

Over the next twenty years, that forecast proved embarrassingly false. The U.S. trade deficit with China hit nearly $400 billion in 2018 and was accompanied by the loss of 5 million jobs.[5] Indicative of what was happening was the example of General Electric's avionics division. In November

2009, GE announced it was merging this division into a joint venture with the Chinese state-owned Aviation Industry Corporation (AVIC) and moving operations to a headquarters in Shanghai. At first blush, this seemed like a strange decision on two counts. First, avionics are not a labor-intensive product and China had no previous avionics production experience. This was the kind of product that economists said should be made in capital- and technology-rich countries like the United States, rather than in low-wage countries like China, because very few worker hours were necessary to make avionics products. Second, GE's CEO and chairman Jeff Immelt was also at that time the chairman of President Obama's Commission on Jobs and Competitiveness. It seemed odd that a person in that capacity would want to be seen sending high-tech, high-paying jobs out of the United States.

But there was a method to this madness. In the eight years since 2001, China's GDP had quadrupled. Demand for air travel was soaring and China had decided to develop its own aircraft industry. The Chinese government and the CCP had made it clear to Immelt that he'd have a better chance of selling avionics in China if GE made them in China. This was, of course, contrary to the dominant neoclassical free trade theory, to the rules of the WTO, and to the expectations of Anglo-American economists, journalists, and trade officials—but it was easily understood by those who had watched Japan, Korea, Taiwan, and Singapore get rich. They had done so through industrial policies that protected and subsidized investment aimed at developing indigenous capacity in industries characterized by economies of scale and rapid technological advances in the context of potentially large export markets.

In June 2012, China seized Scarborough Shoal. It lies in the South China Sea about 137 miles from the Philippines, which claims that the reefs making up the shoal are longtime Philippine fishing grounds and rightfully lie within its territorial waters. (This claim was later confirmed by the International Court of Arbitration in The Hague.)[6] In the absence of any international response, the giant Chinese dredger *Tianjin* was sent to Cuarteron Reef in the Spratly Island chain during September 2013, and then to Fiery Cross reef, also in the Spratly chain. When none of these visits elicited any U.S. reaction, the *Tianjin* began China's first artificial island–building project at Johnson South Reef, another Spratly island, in the fall of 2013. By the time Chinese president Xi Jinping visited President Barack Obama in September 2015, China had built seven artificial islands in the South China Sea, complete with airstrips, suggesting possible military use. In response to Obama's direct request, Xi promised that China would not militarize the Spratly Islands. Rather, he said, they would be used only for civilian and disaster relief purposes. By mid-December 2016, however, military units were in fact deployed on the islands and China's Ministry of Defense was saying that such deployment was perfectly legitimate.[7]

In the 1980s, the United States partnered with Israel to develop a new fighter plane based on the F-16. As costs rose, however, Washington abandoned the project, leaving Israel's "Lavi" fighter unfinished. Some years later, Israel sold the plans for the plane to China, which introduced what it calls its J-10. The J-10 looks amazingly like an F-16. In 2011, China introduced a J-20, which closely resembles the U.S. F-22 because its design was stolen by a Chinese national named Su Bin, who subsequently served forty-six months in federal prison for the theft. Then, in 2014, China's J-31 appeared, looking a lot like the U.S. F-35 because Su Bin had also stolen F-35 data.[8] Beyond Su Bin, cyber hacking has also been a major area of Chinese theft, not only of plans for military equipment but of data on federal personnel and much else.

As articulated by Xi, the Chinese dream is not to become a "responsible stakeholder" in the "global, rules-based system" created and sustained by the United States in the wake of World War II and the Cold War. It is instead to return to the grandeur of China's past. In this dream, China is the heir of a five-thousand-year-old civilization that was the supreme world leader—militarily, culturally, technologically, administratively, and artistically—until the mid-nineteenth century, when the Opium Wars initiated "a hundred and fifty years of humiliation." In written Mandarin, the characters for "China" literally mean Middle Kingdom. And the dream evokes the notion of restoring a globally dominant country surrounded by vassal states and barbarians from whom tribute may be exacted. This, of course, means displacing the United States as the world's leading power, an aim first enunciated by Mao Zedong and strongly implied by Deng Xiaoping's injunction to "hide your light and bide your time."[9]

But the United States is too powerful to be easily or directly displaced. It must be approached indirectly. Doing so has been a part of Chinese grand strategy for many years now.

At 4 p.m. on a warm January afternoon in 2019, I had drinks in Singapore with an old friend who had long been a top official of the Singapore government. We talked about China's growing power and influence in Asia and what the response should be from the countries of the region as well as from the United States.

A committed friend of America, my host explained that he and most of Singapore's leaders want the United States to maintain a strong military presence in the East China Sea, the South Pacific, and the Indian Ocean as well as in the South China Sea. He also wished that the United States would find a way to become more economically invested and integrated into the region. He noted that Singapore makes its harbors and shipyards available to the U.S. Navy for re-provisioning and repairing its ships and supports U.S. efforts to maintain freedom of navigation for all shipping in the South China Sea, against Chinese claims of sole sovereignty.

"You know we love you," he began.

> But you must also understand that doing so is becoming more and more difficult. Look at our economy. We live by exporting. Our single biggest export is tourism, and the tourists are mostly Chinese from Mainland China. Our second-biggest export is education for students, who come from all over the world here to Singapore to earn their university and advanced degrees. Most of these students are Chinese. Our third-largest export is advanced electronics and technology gear, and the biggest market for these products is China. Thus, you can see that we, as a country, are heavily dependent on China.
>
> In the case of most countries, that would not pose a serious consideration, but China is not like most countries. We know the Chinese government under the direction of the Chinese Communist Party can weaponize its imports. Do you remember that Lotte's (a Korean conglomerate) sales to China evaporated overnight when land owned by Lotte in Korea was used to build the U.S. THAAD

anti-missile battery? We know that if Beijing were to become too upset with us, the flows of Chinese tourists and students to Singapore could dry up overnight. And we'd be in a first-class pickle. So that is why we don't want to be forced to choose between the United States and China. Of course, in our hearts we favor the United States. But for the sake of our pocketbooks and our stomachs, we must be careful about how we handle China.

From Singapore, I flew to Sydney, Australia, where I met with the head of one of Australia's major banking firms. "Look," he said, "we [Australians] were with the Brits in World War I, especially at Gallipoli, where Australia suffered more than twenty-six thousand casualties, and with your lot in World War II as well as in Korea, Vietnam, Afghanistan, and Iraq. But if there is any dust-up over Taiwan, don't look for us on the beach."

He preempted the obvious "Why not?" question: "Our biggest exports are iron ore and coal, and the best part of that goes to China. Our third-largest export is education, and the students mostly come from China. Our fourth-biggest export is tourism, and the tourists are mostly Chinese. So you can, perhaps, see why we are anxious not to upset China."

Nor does that concern affect only businesspeople and government officials. Clive Hamilton is a professor at Charles Sturt University in Canberra. In April 2008, as the Olympic torch for the games to be held later that year in Beijing was passing the lawns outside Parliament House, Hamilton saw large numbers of Chinese students mob and abuse a small group of pro-Tibet protestors standing along the way. Eight years later, when a political corruption case demonstrated that a handful of rich Chinese had become the largest donors to Australia's major political parties, Hamilton felt that China and Australian democracy were colliding. He decided to write a book on the topic. Initially, his usual publisher, Allen & Unwin, was enthusiastic and contracted with Hamilton to publish the book. But a year later, as the revised manuscript was about to be sent for typesetting, Allen & Unwin told Hamilton it was canceling the contract out of fear of retaliation by Beijing or by people in Australia acting on the CCP's behalf. Fortunately for Hamilton, publisher Hardie Grant had more stomach.[10]

The book, *Silent Invasion*, dramatically reveals a CCP strategy to penetrate Australia and decouple it from its ally the United States—a strategy that has had some remarkable successes. The plan was revealed to the staff of the Chinese embassy in Canberra as early as February 2005. The idea was to include Australia in China's overall periphery and initially secure it as a reliable and safe supply base for China. Longer term, the idea was to "drive a wedge into the America-Australia alliance" and to achieve "comprehensive influence over Australia economically, politically, culturally, in all ways."[11] Eventually, China would use economic tools to force Australia into making concessions on a wide range of economic, military, and human rights matters. This is all known to be true because Chen Yonglin was at the staff meeting and read the documents. At the time, Chen was first secretary for political affairs at the Chinese consulate in Sydney. Four months later, he defected and sought political asylum in Australia. This is when he revealed what China had in mind for his adopted country.

As Chen says: "In accordance with their fixed strategic plans, the Communist Party of China had begun a structured effort to infiltrate Australia and New Zealand in a systematic way because they were seen as the weak link of the western camp."[12] The idea was to test methods of infiltration and subversion in a country characterized by openness, a relatively small population containing many immigrants from China, and a commitment to multiculturalism: all attributes that could weaken its capacity to recognize and defend against Communist Chinese penetration.[13]

China's One Belt One Road (OBOR) project aims to use the $3 trillion of foreign currency reserves accumulated by China's trade surpluses (mainly with the United States) to fund a gigantic global infrastructure project that will link China to all the major parts of Asia, Europe, and Africa, and even Central and South America. Chinese state-owned companies already own, partially own, and/or operate a wide array of ports, electricity-generating operations, pipelines, and telecommunications infrastructure around the globe. These include the Greek port of Piraeus, the Israeli port of Haifa, the Australian port of Darwin, the major electricity generator in the Philippines, a host of properties in Panama bordering the Panama Canal, and many others.

These investments are already affecting the European Union. To take a formal position on a key global issue, the European Union requires unanimity among its members. Recently, key member states such as Germany and France wanted the European Union to make a statement in the United

Nations criticizing China's human rights abuses. But they could not get unanimous agreement among the member states. Greece, whose port of Piraeus is owned by a Chinese state-owned company, demurred.[14] Mercedes Benz recently issued an apology to the Chinese people for including a quote from the Dalai Lama in a post on Instagram for its cars.[15] Or let's jump to Australia, the major supplier of iron ore, coal, and other minerals to China. Chinese investment has been especially heavy in Australia. In the wake of Canberra's request in May 2020 for an international inquiry into the origin of the COVID-19 virus, China, in complete violation of its agreements as a member of the World Trade Organization, suddenly and dramatically reduced its imports of Australian beef and barley.[16]

On March 1, 2018, the widening gap between the assumption that globalization would liberalize China and the reality that it was not doing so led the *Economist*, long a staunch supporter of liberalization via globalization, to run a cover story entitled "How the West Got China Wrong." This was followed in March/April 2018 by a similar article in *Foreign Affairs* by former assistant secretary of state Kurt Campbell, also once an advocate of liberalization through trade.[17] These articles show how badly the intellectual foundations of the West's foreign policy establishment have been shaken.

Even more jarring have been the events that began in Wuhan, China, on November 17, 2019, when the first case of a person suffering from Coronavirus 19 was discovered.[18] By December 15 the total number of infections stood at twenty-seven and then grew to sixty by December 20. On December 30, Dr. Li Wenliang sent a message on WeChat to a group of doctors warning them to use protective clothing to avoid becoming infected. On January 3, 2020, he was summoned to the Public Security Bureau and told to sign a letter that charged he had "severely disturbed the social order." It went on to say: "We solemnly warn you: If you keep being stubborn, with such impertinence, and continue this illegal activity, you will be brought to justice—is that understood?" Underneath, in Dr Li's handwriting, is written: "Yes, I do." He was one of eight people who police said were being investigated for spreading rumors. For the first few weeks of January officials in Wuhan were insisting that only those who had had contact with infected animals could catch the virus.

No guidance was issued to protect doctors. On January 10, Dr. Li began coughing; the next day he had a fever, and the day after that he went into a hospital. By the end of January, he was very sick and, perhaps anticipating his own death and feeling that he had nothing to lose, he posted the Security Bureau letter he had had to sign on Weibo, one of China's largest public messaging websites. That was how the Chinese public eventually became aware of the epidemic facing it. Finally, on January 23, the authorities began locking down Wuhan and neighboring Hubei province. Of course, by then the virus was already well on its way to becoming the pandemic it is now.

Many countries, including first and foremost the United States, have not responded well to this killer virus. But there might have been no need to respond at all if instead of threatening severe punishment for Dr. Li's disclosures, the Chinese system had been willing to listen to the truth from the beginning.

As a result of all these developments, what for a very long time was considered holy writ on U.S. policy toward China is no longer holy, or, at least no longer worshiped so devoutly. But as of this moment, no coherent new strategy has emerged.

The purpose of this book is to suggest one.

PART

I

Know the Other
—Sun Tzu

1

Origins of the Chinese Dream

Tianxia—All lands under the sky, all peoples agreed, in a universal Order.

At the zenith of the splendor of the Qing Empire in 1757, the Qianlong emperor made an odd and, in retrospect, perhaps telling decision. British, American, Portuguese, Dutch, and other voyagers from the West had begun to arrive regularly in Chinese ports looking for trade. Apparently fearing that a possibly disadvantageous transformation of his Celestial Empire might result from the unrestricted access of foreigners to China, Qianlong imposed what came to be known as the Canton System on China's trade with foreigners, especially those from the West. Under this arrangement, all formal trade was required to pass through a guild of thirteen trading companies, known as the Hong in the area of present-day Guangzhou, which British merchants at the time called Canton. Beyond this restriction, the emperor's subjects were also not permitted to teach the Chinese language to foreigners, and foreign traders were not allowed to bring women with them to China in any capacity.

Since this was a major change from past practice, the obvious question is why the big policy shift?

From ancient times, for more than twenty-five hundred years, China had been the dominant state of Far East Asia and, in its own mind, the dominant state of the entire world. It was the oldest of living empires and had enjoyed an unbroken history of unsurpassed technological and cultural achievements. It had been there when Rome was the great empire of the

West and had remained after Rome, Byzantium, the Holy Roman Empire, and Napoleon were long gone. There had been no trade restrictions when Marco Polo had been invited to enter the service of the Great Khan in Cambulac (Beijing) in 1275. Perhaps this was because Polo had obviously been in awe of the size, sophistication, power, and technological advances of China at the time of the Yuan Dynasty under Genghis Khan when, as part of the great Mongol Empire, China had reached the greatest extant of its history, with borders on the North Pacific, what would become St. Petersburg in Russia, northern India, the Arabian Peninsula, the Mediterranean Sea, the Black Sea, and Poland. Polo had never seen anything as great in Europe or elsewhere in Asia during his travels.

The Middle Kingdom

Perhaps the best indicator of China's perspective was the name it gave itself—the Middle Kingdom. By using this sobriquet, the Chinese meant that their kingdom was the most powerful and the most important in the world, located at the exact center of the universe with authority radiating out in all directions over Tianxia (all under heaven). Interestingly, the two dynasties of China's greatest extent and power were the Yuan, which had been ruled not by Chinese emperors but by Mongol khans, and the Qing, which was run by non-Chinese Manchu emperors. In other words, during its two greatest dynasties China had been ruled by foreign leaders. On the other hand, the power of Chinese civilization was such that both the Mongols and Manchus became Sinified, adopting Chinese customs and often the Chinese language, and ruling through the age-old traditional Chinese bureaucracy chosen from the winners of the annual scholarly bureaucratic examination. Thus, the conquerors became the conquered in a civilizational and bureaucratic sense. In addition to these factors was the fact that China had long been the global leader in technology. It had invented such key items as the magnetic compass, paper, gunpowder, paper money, printing, a postal system, and much else long before the West. Indeed, the early fifteenth-century eunuch Admiral Zheng He had sailed fleets of Chinese junks that dwarfed the later likes of Columbus's *Niña, Pinta,* and *Santa Maria.* And Admiral Zheng had gotten to the real India and to Africa and perhaps even to Australia, rather than to an imagined India in the Caribbean Sea, as Columbus had done.

In the Chinese Middle Kingdom, located in the center of the world and ruling "all under heaven," some peoples were ruled more directly than others. Those close by were closest to the emperor's enlightenment and thus the most civilized. Enlightenment became more tenuous for those farther away, and didn't exist at all for those who were considered barbarians by dint of their distance from the center of enlightenment in Beijing. But in principle, they were all ultimately considered subjects of the Son of Heaven ruling in Beijing.

Over the centuries, the dynasties of this Celestial Empire alternated between two guiding pole stars at opposite ends of a philosophical continuum. The first was Confucianism, as conceived and preached by the ancient philosopher Confucius during the Zhou Dynasty around 500 BC, which was known as the Spring and Autumn Period. He called for leading by example, honoring elders, not doing to others what you would not want done to yourself, putting family before state, privileging moral values over material values, and governing by ritual and education rather than reward and punishment. While this sounds eminently enlightened, it should not be understood as affirming any kind of human rights or democracy. The Book of Odes (the Shih Ching, 305 poems from 1000 to 600 BC) notes, "All land under heaven belongs to the King, and all people on the shores are subjects of the King." The term "Son of Heaven" arose during this period and was effectively a claim of power over all the earth.[1]

But over time the king's power waned and the country entered what came to be known as the Period of the Warring States (475–221 BC). As fighting became continual and ever more ferocious, the chivalry of the past gave way to barbarity and mass slaughter. Eventually, King Qin Shihuang conquered the last independent states and established the Qin Dynasty as the founding dynasty of a unified Chinese state under centralized power in 221 BC. Although it lasted only fifteen years with but two emperors, the Qin Dynasty inaugurated the Chinese imperial system under which China would be ruled (with some interruption and adaptation, to be sure) for the next 2,132 years. It established the absolutist, autocratic model that has endured in China down to the present day.

The emperor Qin Shihuang had no time for Confucius, instead following the doctrine known as Legalism. This was a philosophy based on the notion that humans are more likely to do wrong than right because they act purely out of self-interest. Therefore, they must be controlled by the threat of severe punishment, and the ruler must have absolute power over essentially everything, even over every thought. The emphasis was on gaining wealth and power for the state. This was the antithesis of the older doctrine of Confucius.[2] Particularly regarding warfare between states, the new Legalist doctrine called for total war. The Legalist credo held that "a wise prince doesn't ask his subjects to behave well—he uses methods to prevent them from behaving badly." Thus, Emperor Qin made the private possession of weapons illegal. He undercut aristocrats and landowners and gained direct control over the peasantry who, after all, constituted the major part of the population and labor force. Severe punishment was meted out for any infraction of the emperor's directives. The books and writings of previous periods were reviewed, and those the emperor found not useful were burned—and many of the scholars who wrote them were executed.

Succeeding dynasties mixed the two philosophies according to what they thought their situation required—gentle guidance or the iron fist. As Emperor Han Xuan (73–49 BC) noted, "The Han dynasty has its own institution. It is a blending of the Way of the Hegemon [Legalism] with that of the Sage-King [Confucianism]. How can we rely solely on one teaching?"[3]

In any case, the two teachings were at one regarding the situation of China and its role in the world. Legalists believed that "power of all kinds was concentrated in the hands of the emperor and flowed out from His Radiant Highness."[4] His benevolence shone in a pattern of concentric circles. The light was of course brightest at the very core: in the emperor's palace and in China itself. But even in China, those who lived in distant provinces were assumed to be inferior to the cosmopolites of the capital. Outside China was an inner circle of vassal states that paid tribute for the "gift" of the emperor's benevolence and the privilege of doing business with his subjects. At the next concentric circle were unruly states that needed to be disciplined from time to time. Then, beyond that circle, was the outer circle of barbarians.

Confucius had first spoken of the Grand Unification, also called the Grand Uniformity or Great Harmony (Datong) in the Book of Rites. He emphasized, "Just as there are not two suns in the sky, so there cannot be two emperors on earth." Confucius taught that rulers should educate their subjects in virtue and provide a moral example. He suggested that leaders should be "like the North Star which keeps its place while all others turn towards it."[5] But like the Legalists of the Qin Dynasty, he never suggested that the people had any role other than submission to their emperor. The only question was whether the emperor had to beat the people into submission or whether they strove of their own free will to follow his guidance.

A New Hegemon

Whether consciously or subconsciously, the Qianlong emperor's imposition of the Canton System signaled a new, perhaps worrying, element in the universe. Despite the haughty tone of the order, it betrayed weakness rather than strength. The new element was opium as the possible solution for a peculiar problem that afflicted all those who traded with China. It was really a very simple matter. The Chinese refused to sell their silk, tea, and porcelain in exchange for almost anything except silver. To be sure, the Western countries stripped the U.S. West Coast of sea otters, the Hawaiian Islands of sandalwood, and the Appalachian Mountains of ginseng in their efforts to find something the Chinese would buy, but ultimately the only thing the Chinese could be counted on to accept as payment for their exports was silver.

As a result, the global supply of silver began to fall while its prices rose. Not only could the Westerners not gain much from this trade, the Western countries were running out of the silver necessary to sustain any of it. The British government and traders in particular were growing concerned over Britain's ever-mounting trade deficit and payments imbalance with China and began trying to obtain greater trade rights as part of an effort to find something for which the Chinese would actually trade. Britain was then importing increasingly massive amounts of tea as well as porcelain and silk. The British East India Company was required to pay for the Chinese goods with silver, and it was running out of silver. It needed to find something it could sell in quantity to the Chinese.

A second element of the situation was that the ships and equipment involved in the trade were almost entirely from the West. To a close observer, it would have been clear that the ships, navigation technology, maps, charts, and other standard sea gear involved in the trade were more advanced on the Western side than the Chinese. The ships carrying Chinese goods to Europe and America and the charts used to guide them were not Chinese. For the first time in their history, the Chinese were not number one in some key areas of knowledge. This was something new for China and perhaps the Qianlong emperor, despite his condescending tone, had begun, subconsciously, to sense a weakness on his own side.

The Macartney Mission

Wishing to solve its trade deficit with China, the British government sent George Macartney, former governor of Madras (present-day Chennai), India, to persuade the Chinese emperor to direct his subjects to buy something—anything—from the rich offerings of Britain's emerging industrial revolution. The East India Company had been experimenting with opium since the early eighteenth century. It produced opium in India and shipped it to China, where it could readily be sold to opium dens in the Chinese port cities. Initial marketing probes indicated a potentially hungry market. But Macartney was not sure selling the drug was a good idea. He preferred to find something else, like rice or manufactured goods. In any case, he was instructed to establish a direct line of communication between the British and Chinese governments (thereby cutting out the Cantonese merchants), establish a permanent embassy in Beijing, and gather intelligence on Chinese government and society with an eye toward discovering what they might want to buy and how they might buy it efficiently without the interference of the Hong and its merchants.

A final major goal of the mission was to demonstrate the utility of British science and technology. Macartney brought a variety of gifts, including clocks, telescopes, weapons, textiles, and other products representative of the high technology of the day. These were meant both to impress the Chinese with the state of Britain's technology and to whet its appetite for mutual trade rather than merely for sale of Chinese goods in return for silver.

His delegation departed Portsmouth in three ships on September 26, 1792. By early October, the convoy was in the Canary Islands and from there was forced by adverse winds to sail all the way to Rio de Janeiro, where Macartney suffered an attack of gout that laid him up for a month. The mission left Rio on December 17, rounded the Cape of Good Hope on January 7, 1793, and then, after stops in Batavia (present-day Jakarta) and Macau, reached Beijing on August 21. From there the group traveled overland to Chengde, where the Qianlong emperor resided.

The first negotiation involved the kowtow genuflection (kneeling with both knees on the ground and touching the forehead to the ground). The Chinese demanded that Macartney perform the kowtow, but he countered with a proposal to bow as he would when presenting gifts to his own sovereign. The Chinese responded that this was not about gift giving but about paying tribute. In no way did they accept any notion of equality between the barbarian British king and the Son of Heaven emperor. Eventually it was agreed that Macartney would genuflect, and the audience took place on September 14. Asked the reason for his visit, Macartney replied that the king of England wished for more commerce between their nations.

The emperor's response was a classic of proud misunderstanding. After a week or so of formal gift giving, dinners, and entertainment, he declared, "Our Celestial Empire possesses all things in prolific abundance and lacks no product within its borders. There is therefore no need for us to import your manufactures in exchange for our own produce."[6] In a letter to King George III after the audience, the emperor referred to Europeans as barbarians and indicated that all nations of the earth were subordinate to China. His final words commanded the king to "tremblingly obey and show no negligence," this being the standard imperial sign-off.

Ships Passing in the Night

The emperor's hauteur is easily understood. For most of the past two thousand years China had been the biggest, most populous, richest, and most technologically advanced country in the world. As far as the Chinese were concerned, the world had always been organized that way. Of course, at one time, there had been a great empire in the West known as the Roman and later the Byzantine Empire, but it had not impinged on China except as a distant customer for the silk and other commodities carried from the Celestial Empire to the West over the ancient Silk Road. In its own neighborhood, China, as noted above, had twice been conquered by the Mongols and the Manchus, but by dint of cultural jujitsu had absorbed the outsiders and remolded them into just another extension of China. Certainly, there had never before arisen a force in Asia that could ignore the wishes of the Son of Heaven with impunity while forcing him to bend to its will.

The first Western traders, such as Marco Polo in the late 1270s and early 1280s, had been astounded by the size, order, wealth, technology, and cultural development of China, which far surpassed anything they had seen in the West or Middle East. As for the Chinese, expressions and concepts regarding the world beyond China had been very vague. After all, Tianxia means "everyone under Heaven," implying that China was the world or that the world belonged to China. As Carnegie Endowment Asia scholar Ashley J. Tellis notes: "China's grand strategy has never been explicitly presented in any comprehensive statement by its rulers." Historians of the Han Dynasty declared that "the power of the Han has no borders," and an edict of the Tang Dynasty claimed, "The height of the emperor is as great as that of Heaven, his width is as huge as the earth. His radiance matches that of the Moon and Sun, his honesty and faithfulness is equal to that of the four seasons." Another Tang Dynasty document emphasizes, "Any creature, so long as they exist in the world, must receive the emperor's nurture."[7]

So the concept of boundaries has always been rather vague in China. The chaos that prevailed so long in ancient China instilled a great fear of disorder. In the old and long-enduring Chinese view of the world, such disorder could be avoided only by organizing vassal and tributary states around the main axis of power. Such an axis would be a hegemon (Ba), and because there could not be "two Suns in the Sky," the tendency of the hegemon would inevitably be to expand its power to the maximum possible extent.

It was this Middle Kingdom China that had overwhelmed Marco Polo when he visited Cambulac in 1275 at the height of the Yuan Dynasty established by Kublai Khan. It included most of present-day China plus Outer Mongolia and southern Siberia. At the same time, Yuan Dynasty China was loosely part of a greater Mongol Empire (that originally established by Genghis Khan) that incorporated most of present-day Siberia, China, central Asia, Pakistan, Afghanistan, Iran, Iraq, Turkey, Ukraine, part of Poland, Rumania, Korea, Tajikistan, Kyrgyzstan, Moldova, Kuwait, Uzbekistan, Azerbaijan, Georgia, Armenia, and Russia. It was the largest empire the world had ever seen (or has seen since), and Kublai Khan was nominally its ruler as well as the founder and ruler of the Chinese Yuan Dynasty.

As Polo reported, China had invented paper money, silk cloth, tea culture, the magnetic compass, gunpowder, the use of coal for heating, kites, and deep drilling. Its cities were a magnitude larger and incomparably better organized than those in any other part of the world. The culture was, in a word, magnificent. And it would soon go on to send its naval fleets to Africa, Arabia, India, Indonesia, and perhaps even to Australia, long before Columbus was born.

The Last Dynasty

Eventually the Yuan Dynasty splintered as Genghis Khan's sons fought and divided territories among themselves. The Ming Dynasty of Chinese rulers arose from the Mongol ruins and controlled not so much an empire as the territories of ancient China from about 1368 to 1644. Then the non-Chinese Manchu cavalry from the region north and northwest of China invaded.

The Manchus did not complete their conquest of China and declare the Qing Dynasty until about 1683. They then went on under the Qianlong emperor to extend Qing control into inner Asia, forming the fifth-largest empire in history. By 1796, it covered China, Tibet, Inner and Outer Mongolia, and Russia almost to Lake Baikal. It went well north of the Amur River (the current boundary between Russia and China) far into Siberia, and in the west it extended nearly to Tashkent and to the borders of Kashmir and Nepal. China had been bigger only during the Yuan Dynasty of Kublai Khan. Its population, at 400 million, was the largest in the world and more than double what it had been under the Yuan Dynasty. On paper, it was formidable. In the real world, however, it was in trouble.

In retrospect, the Qianlong emperor's 1757 decision to restrict and carefully control trade with the outside world, and to limit the number and activities of foreigners in China, betrayed a celestial unease arising perhaps from as yet ill-defined fears that China and the long, distinguished reign of the Qing Dynasty might soon face unexpected difficulties.

Indeed, Macartney may have deftly put his finger on the problem in a note he recorded in his diary after leaving China: "The Empire of China is an old, crazy, first-rate Man-of-War, which a fortunate succession of able and vigilant officers has contrived to keep afloat for these one hundred and fifty years past, and to overawe their neighbors merely by her bulk and appearance, but, whenever an insufficient man happens to have the command upon deck, adieu to the discipline and safety of the ship. She may perhaps not sink outright; she may drift some time as a wreck and will then be dashed to pieces on the shore; she can never be rebuilt on the old bottom."[8]

The Qianlong emperor's sign-off thus signaled the confidence of a man who ruled the oldest, longest-lived empire in history—an empire that, in the view of everyone important to him, was synonymous with civilization. Yet he seemed to feel the future creeping up on him.

Opium Reigns

In lieu of any new deal, the British traders put all their energy into shipping ever more opium to China. At the time of Macartney's visit, they had been sending four thousand chests, 170 pounds each, of opium to the China market annually. By 1833 that number had increased to thirty thousand chests, and the number of Chinese drug addicts was estimated to be between 4 million and 12 million.[9] Many of China's large coastal cities were devastated. In 1839 the son of the Qianlong emperor (who had died in 1799), Emperor Daguang, wrote to Queen Victoria pleading with her to halt the opium trade. That there was no reply only demonstrated the depths to which the prestige of China's emperors had fallen and confirmed what must have been the hidden, fearful suspicions of the Qianlong emperor.

With no response from London, in desperation, Emperor Daguang ordered the seizure of all the opium in Canton, including that held by foreign governments. China tried to persuade the trading companies to take tea in exchange for turning their opium over to the Chinese government authorities, but when that failed, the Imperial Court ordered confiscation of all supplies and a blockade of foreign ships to make them surrender their stores.

Great Britain's Royal Navy responded by sending a flotilla up the Pearl River to capture Canton and then Nanking. The battle was no contest. The Qing army was outfitted with shotguns that had a range of 130 yards and a firing rate of one to two shots per minute. It also used spears and crossbows. The range of the British guns was 260 yards and the firing rate two to three times per minute. The British did not use spears or crossbows.

The sailing war junks of the Qing navy were brushed aside by the steam-powered British gunboats and crushed to splinters by their heavy cannons. For the Qing forces, this was a major war. For the British, it was more like a training exercise. The war ended in 1842 with the signing of the Treaty of Nanking, which forced China to cede Hong Kong Island in perpetuity to the United Kingdom and to establish five treaty ports for Great Britain: at Shanghai, Canton, Amoy, Ningbo, and Fuzhou. A second treaty the following year granted the United Kingdom most-favored nation (MFN) status and added provisions for extraterritoriality (meaning British citizens in China would be subject not to Chinese law but only to British law). France secured similar concessions in 1843 and 1844.

The Second Opium War, lasting from 1856 to 1860, resulted from continuing British efforts to achieve general legalization of the opium trade to all of China and an exemption from any import or transit duties. This was simply imposed on the Qing Empire by the British, French, and other foreign powers—because they could. They had power and the Qing forces did not. Some eighty treaty ports were opened to the opium trade, and the citizens of all foreign powers had rights to travel throughout China and rights to extraterritoriality. These agreements became known to history as "the Unequal Treaties," and China has long cited them as the source of great humiliation to China and its citizens, which it undoubtedly was.

Yes, unlike the Mongols and the Manchus, the Europeans did not conquer and rule over China. The Qing Empire remained one of the largest empires in world history, and the Qing emperors remained on the throne until 1912.

Nevertheless, the Blessing of Heaven seemed to be receding from the throne. The Taiping Rebellion (1850–64) and the Dungan Revolt (1862–77) brought not only civil war but famines; combined, they left 20 million dead. In the 1860s, Russia occupied all of Siberia and part of Manchuria. The problem wasn't just the arrival and interference of foreign barbarians: the imperial system itself was increasingly not working, and the empire could feel itself slowly rotting from the inside, as Macartney had forecast.

Through great soul-searching, China's leaders struggled to find a way to catch up technologically with the West while maintaining traditional doctrines and the old examination-based bureaucratic rule. The so-called Self-Strengthening Movement, launched in 1861 in response to the emperor's agreement to purchase foreign weapons, emphasized learning Western technology and ways of warfare. Perhaps the most important element was the rebalance away from the Confucianism that had come to permeate the imperial bureaucracy toward a new doctrine reminiscent of the ancient Legalism on which the initial Qin Dynasty had been founded. Great emphasis was placed on wealth and strength, on creating a rich country and a strong army.

Phase 1 focused on adoption of Western firearms, machinery, and scientific knowledge and on the training of engineers and diplomatic officials. Schools were established to teach foreign languages, astronomy, and mathematics, and foreign newspapers and books began to be translated into Mandarin. The first objective was the construction of military arsenals and shipbuilding facilities to strengthen the Chinese navy. But these industries, being largely sponsored by the government, suffered greatly from inefficiency and nepotism. Production of Remington-style breech-loading rifles began in 1871, but by 1873 only four thousand rifles had been produced. It was the same with shipbuilding: vessels built in China cost twice as much as similar ships made in Britain. Efforts to reorganize and retrain the army and navy met with similar results, as did suggestions to add scientific and mathematical elements to the annual imperial examinations.

Phase 2, beginning in the mid-1870s, focused on creating wealth. For an empire that had always relied economically on agriculture, the development of profit-making industries such as shipping, railroads, and telegraphy was a monumental shift. The imperial government established government-supervised merchant undertakings, including the China Merchants Steam Navigation, the Kaiping Mines, the Shanghai Cotton Mill, and the Imperial Telegraph Administration. In principle, these were profit-making enterprises owned by private investors, but they operated under the supervision of government officials and with the help of government subsidies. Moreover, the government did not hesitate to subsidize competition against foreign enterprises. With the aid of these subsidies, the China Merchants Steam Navigation Company expanded its fleet from four to twenty-nine ships, while Britain's privately held Jardine Matheson could manage just six.

A problem with phase 2 was that most Chinese officials looked down on foreigners and all things foreign. As Duncan MacPherson (a veteran of the Opium Wars) wrote: "Haughty, cruel, and hypocritical, they despise all other nations but their own; they regard themselves as faultless. Next to the son of heaven, a true Chinaman thinks himself the greatest man in the world, and China, beyond all comparison, to be the most learned, the most fruitful, the most ancient, in short, the only country in the world."[10]

Phase 3 saw efforts better to coordinate military modernization, reduce government interference in business, and promote light industry such as textiles. But by this time, 1885–95, much of the early enthusiasm had evaporated. The war with France over Vietnam in 1883–85 had gone badly. In 1895, the Japanese destroyed the new Chinese navy's fleet and incorporated Taiwan, the Liaodong Peninsula, and Penghu into the Japanese Empire, while Korea was transferred to Japan's sphere of influence.

It had been humiliating enough to lose the Opium Wars to the barbarian British. But to lose to the "dwarves," as the Chinese termed the Japanese, was absolute devastation, especially after all the Self-Strengthening. Any pretense of Chinese superiority over all under heaven had completely evaporated. The pressing question became not whether China could adopt Western technology and methods of creating wealth, but whether there needed to be some fundamental change in China's system of governance, or even in the character of its people. That these questions could even be asked indicated a subtle but powerful and important new psychology.

Recall that the Mongols and Manchus had both conquered China, and that the Qing Dynasty had even existed under Manchu rule. One might think that being conquered would be humiliating. But the word *humiliation* is never used in connection with the Yuan and Qing dynasties. While they were superior militarily, the Mongols and Manchus were not stronger as societies and cultures. They ended up adopting the Chinese system. Chinese civilization was thus the ultimate conqueror, and the Chinese could feel superior to Mongols and Manchus even when being ruled by them. But now, in the late Qing Dynasty, the ancient system was no longer working, either internally or externally. This led to something far more devastating than humiliation. It led the Chinese to a complete loss of confidence in themselves, their ways, and their principles. Sun Yatsen (the first president of China) captured the feeling perfectly when he said that China is nothing but "a sheet of loose sand."[11]

In this regard, Macartney proved clairvoyant in the comments in his diary about the need for a completely new bottom of the ship of state.

Toward a New Bottom

Once China was dashed to pieces on the shore of the twentieth century, she could not be rebuilt on the old bottom. In the first half of the century, China was besieged by famine and natural disasters as well as continual political strife, rebellion, and war. An uprising in October 1911 led to the final fall of the Qing government, and the last emperor abdicated in early 1912. The provisional president of the newly declared Republic of China, Sun Yatsen, preached nationalism, democracy, and welfare of the people. But he also preached humiliation. "Despite four hundred million people gathered in one China," he wrote, "We are the poorest and weakest state in the world, occupying the lowest position in international affairs; the rest of mankind is the carving knife and the serving dish, while we are the fish and meat. Our position is now extremely perilous. If we do not earnestly promote nationalism and weld together our four hundred million into a strong nation, we face a tragedy—the loss of our country and the destruction of our race."[12]

Sun founded the Chinese Nationalist Party (Kuomintang), which gained a large representation in the National Assembly. But he died before being able to govern China in any significant way. His protégé Chiang Kaishek took up the leadership in 1925 and was able to overcome most of the warlords who had sprung up in the wake of the emperor's abdication to achieve a kind of quasi-reunification of the country in the early 1930s. Journalist Theodore White wrote of him: "With his people he shared, and shared personally, a century of humiliation that had cut him so sharply it etched every facet of his personality."[13] Of course, the Japanese invasion of Manchuria in 1931, World War II, and the civil war with the Chinese Communist Party undermined Chiang's ambitions and efforts. But in a fundamental way he and the CCP were fighting the same fight: for reinvention of the system.

The Communists Enter

The name Chen Duxiu means little to people today, even in China. But he was a rebel with a cause. As a young man he perceived China to be in a life-or-death struggle with other countries and believed it would perish if it could not quickly adapt. The weakness, he believed, literally began at home. "Chinese," he wrote, "care about family and do not care about their nation." Without a strong sense of patriotism, he believed, the nation could not defend itself. At first, he admired Sun Yatsen's idea of democracy, but he later became convinced that a new China could be brought into being only by an elite revolutionary guard. "China's governmental revolution in the next couple of years absolutely cannot effect a Western style democracy," he warned at a meeting in Shanghai on July 21, 1921.[14] This was the first congress of the Chinese Communist Party. At that same meeting was a young man named Mao Zedong.

While Josef Stalin, who headed the Communist International movement known as the COMINTERN, ordered the new CCP to focus on the working class in Chinese cities, according to standard Marxist doctrine, Mao had left Shanghai to return to his home in rural Hunan province. He was surprised to find that the most active and effective political agents weren't among the industrial working class—rather, they were the backward peasants who were spontaneously rising in anger to "overthrow the feudal power" by seizing the lands rented to them at onerous rates by usurious landlords. Mao instantly saw the peasants as potentially the main force of a Chinese revolution. In a report on the Hunan experience, he noted that "what Mr. Sun Yatsen wanted, but failed to accomplish in the 40 years he devoted to the national revolution, the peasants have accomplished in a few months." It was also here that he famously wrote: "A revolution is not like inviting people to a dinner, or writing an essay or painting a picture, or doing embroidery; it cannot be so refined, so leisurely and gentle, so benign, upright, courteous, temperate and complaisant. A revolution is an uprising, an act of violence whereby one class overthrows the power of another. . . . To right a wrong it is necessary to exceed the proper limits; the wrongs cannot be righted without doing so."[15]

As a youth, Mao had stumbled upon a pamphlet describing the dismemberment of China. He remembered reading its first words, "Alas, China will be subjugated," and feeling "depressed about the future of my country." He "began to realize that it was the duty of all the people to help save it," so he read extensively and became convinced by the ancient Legalist arguments that the way to save China was through strong, willful—even brutal and violent—leadership.[16] We know, of course, that in his remarkable career he succeeded in defeating Chiang, reconnecting most of the pieces of the

Qing Empire, and establishing the People's Republic of China. He certainly believed he had discovered the desperately sought answer to the question of the future of the Chinese system when he told the Chinese People's Political Consultative Congress in Beijing in September 1949, "The Chinese people, comprising one quarter of humanity, have now STOOD UP."[17]

One wonders if, in the bitterness of exile in Taiwan, Mao's defeated rival Chiang Kaishek had a moment of empathy.

Dream and Rejuvenation

In fact, however, China had not stood up. It had rid itself of unwanted foreign presences, but it remained a torn and extremely poor country, and Mao had not discovered a system that worked, either internally or externally.

It is repeatedly said, pridefully by the CCP and respectfully of the CCP, that it succeeded in lifting 800 million people out of poverty. This is very wide of the mark. In 1949, Japan was a war-torn wreck of a country with its capital city, Tokyo, still in ruins. Twenty years later, by 1969, it was the world's second-largest economy after the United States, and by 1979 it was beating the United States in many industries and technologies. Taiwan in 1949 was poorer than Mainland China. Thirty years later, it had become one of the "Asian Tigers." Korea in 1949 was among the twenty poorest countries in the world. Thirty years later, it was on its way to becoming a world-leading industrial nation.

Between 1958 and 1960, China embarked on the Great Leap Forward, which in fact was a great leap backward. By requiring the people to melt their household utensils, factory tools, and farm plows to make steel in backyard furnaces, it rendered itself unable to plant and harvest enough food for its population. It suffered great famines that killed by most estimates more than 40 million people—possibly as many as 50 million. It also went through the Cultural Revolution, in which Mao had tried to completely erase Chinese civilization in a great Legalistic spasm that tore apart the very soul of the country. If the CCP wanted to achieve prosperity, it had only to emulate Japan, Taiwan, and Korea. That it stubbornly refused to do so was an error of historic proportions.

But since the death of Mao in 1976 and the rise of Deng Xiaoping to the leadership of the CCP and of the country, China has essentially imitated its neighbors. By largely copying the formula of Japan and the other Asian Tigers, it has indeed enjoyed great success while finally lifting hundreds of millions of people out of poverty. But doing so has meant discarding Maoist ideology and engaging in quaint word games about something called "socialism with Chinese characteristics." Thus, despite its Marxist doctrine of class warfare and workers' rights, billionaire entrepreneurs like Alibaba founder Jack Ma are members in good standing of the Communist Party. In principle, there is nothing wrong with that, but it does raise the question of how the CCP can justify its stranglehold on virtually every aspect of Chinese life.

The Party's response is to point to the need to redeem past humiliation and recover past status and glory. Speeches and articles by Chinese leaders and media outlets are full of references to one hundred years of humiliation. But having finally stumbled upon a system that works both internally and externally and is widely admired, China has no reason to feel humiliation or to be in shock.

The cry of "humiliation" is a powerful emotional tool with which to justify a Legalist hold on power. Chinese President Xi Jinping has made realization of "the Chinese Dream" or a "Great Rejuvenation of the Chinese People" his country's main objective. Concretely, the dream calls for such policies as Made in China 2025, under which a variety of cutting-edge industries, such as aircraft, semiconductors, telecommunications, artificial intelligence, and biotechnology, would be led, if not dominated, by China. Development of these industries and technologies is being heavily subsidized and protected by the Chinese government which, according to the WTO, is also engaging in extensive theft of intellectual property, designs, and technology data in these and other industries. At the same time, Xi has emphasized the importance not only of Beijing regaining authority but of Sinifying all the territories and seas ever claimed by China. These include, of course, Taiwan, Tibet, the Uighur region of Xinjiang, and virtually the entire South China Sea, where China has established new military bases on artificial islands it has created around reefs and rocks that formerly rose above sea level only at low tide.

In short, under Xi, China seems to be determined to resurrect the old Middle Kingdom as the new world hegemon.

2

The Party Is Like God

> For truly I say to you, if you have faith the size of a mustard seed, you will say to this mountain, "Move from here to there," and it will move; and nothing will be impossible to you.
>
> —*Matthew 17:20*

As the Qing Empire tottered and fell, a stream of young people destined to become China's future leaders searched the world for some key or formula for restoring the empire to its former greatness. Sun Yatsen went to Japan and then to Hawaii and London. Liang Qichao, Zhou Enlai, and Chiang Kaishek all studied in Japan.

But perhaps the largest number of these young Chinese in search of their country's future wound up in France. These included Cai Hesen, Chen Yi, Li Fuchu, and Cai Chang, all friends of Mao Zedong. In August and September 1920, Cai wrote to Mao, then living in Hunan province, and urged him to prepare for a Russian-style revolution in China. Two others who showed up in France a bit later were Zhou Enlai and Deng Xiaoping. They were just a few of the approximately 130,000 students and workers brought to France between 1912 and 1927 by the Diligent Work–Frugal Study Movement, sponsored by a group of Paris anarchists who sought to make China aware of French science and social ideals. The Russian Revolution of 1917 was stirring young idealists everywhere, and communism was à la mode in Paris's salons, cafés, and universities. It was like the birth of a new religion.

Some saw a solution for China in the grafting of Western science and technology onto ancient institutions and ways. Others saw the answer in the adoption of democracy. Or they saw democracy as a necessary precursor to the science and technology. But as warlords jostled for power and China continued to deteriorate, many young people began to conclude that only some revolutionary, fundamental change could redeem the country. They began to believe that China would have to reinvent itself to save itself.

Before leaving for France, Zhou Enlai had been a member of a group in Beijing called the Awakening Society. This group included Li Dazhao, head librarian at Peking University (under whom Mao Zedong worked in the reading room) and Chen Duxiu, founding editor of *New Youth* magazine. In Paris, Zhou renewed his acquaintance with Zhang Shenfu, whom he had met at the Awakening Society in Beijing, and in spring 1921 Zhang recruited him to become a member of a French Communist Party cell consisting of Chinese expatriates. This preceded the formation of the Communist Party of China, which was jointly founded in Shanghai on July 1, 1921, by Li Dazhao and Chen Duxiu despite the fact that neither of them was able to attend the initial meeting of thirteen members (Mao was present but not a leader).

After helping to form the Party cell in Paris, Zhou moved to Berlin, where he became engaged with the Communist International (COMINTERN) to promote the spread of communist revolution globally. He returned to Paris in June 1922 and became a founding member of the European branch of the Chinese Communist Party. He helped draft the Party's charter and was elected to the three-member executive committee as director of propaganda. He also edited the Party magazine, *Red Light*, and hired a certain Deng Xiaoping, then seventeen years old, to operate the mimeograph machine.

The New Religion

In the background, as many Chinese youth moved toward the Red side, was a major announcement by the Soviet Union in July 1919. The deputy commissar for foreign affairs, Lev M. Karakhan, announced that Moscow was giving up all claims by czarist Russia to territories and special colonial privileges inside China. In sharp contrast to the allied leaders at the Versailles Peace Treaty negotiations, who had hinted that China would regain territories previously controlled by Germany but then had assigned them in secret to Japan, this announcement made the Soviet Union look like a savior to young Chinese struggling to find a future for their country.

The move also reinforced a quasi-religious faith and dedication within the young Chinese Communist Party. Marxism-Leninism went beyond political and social systems to provide what appeared to be a complete formula for life at all levels. It addressed core questions of human nature, good and evil, and the ultimate purpose and hopes of humanity. As well as being political, national, and international, it was also intensely personal. As we will see, it could engender a kind of devotion usually associated with religious figures such as St. Paul, the Jesuits and Franciscans of the Roman Catholic Church, or the founders of Protestantism such as Martin Luther and John Calvin. Communism promised salvation to those who believed. The salvation wasn't personal, but a kind of sociocultural earthly paradise arriving at some not-too-distant date. The Russian Revolution and the creation of the Soviet Union were powerful proof that if you believed strongly enough and acted in accordance with your faith, any miracle was possible. In fact, communism didn't need a miracle. It was scientific: Karl Marx had discovered the laws that move history. All that was necessary to achieve a new paradise was to interpret and correctly apply the laws and theorems of Marxism-Leninism. That is what the Chinese Communist Party set out to do. But just as the Apostle Paul found impediments along the way from his vision of Christ to his establishment of a few small churches scattered around the Roman Empire, so the Chinese Communist Party found boulders in its path.

From the beginning, the Party was heavily dependent upon the Soviet Union, which maintained representatives in Shanghai and elsewhere, provided funds and guidance, and often weighed in on matters of personnel. In the early 1920s, Moscow directed the CCP to join Sun Yatsen and Chiang Kaishek's Nationalist Party (Kuomintang, or KMT), which then had the strongest political support and military organization in China and was also receiving assistance from Moscow. The Soviets had helped establish the Whampoa Military Academy, a kind of Nationalist Party West Point. Chiang Kaishek had been appointed the first head of Whampoa, and because of Moscow's directives to the CCP to infiltrate the National-ist Party, one of Chiang's first hires was Zhou Enlai, who signed on to work in the Whampoa Political Department. There he hired several other young CCP members to assist him with the political indoctrination of Nationalist officers and trainees. At the same time, Zhou was made Com-munist Party secretary in the area of Guangdong and Guangxi, with the rank of major general.

In July 1926, Chiang led the "Northern Expedition," in which he de-feated many of the provincial warlords and roughly united China under one government for the first time since 1912. In 1927 he turned to further consolidating Nationalist Party power in the southern Chinese cities that had long been its main base. Chiang had studied in Russia before establish-ing Whampoa, and he had developed a strong dislike of the Soviet Union and of communists generally. He once remarked that "the Japanese are a disease of the skin, but the communists are a disease of the heart."[1]

The CCP tried to seize control of Shanghai three times after Chiang began his Northern Expedition: once in October 1926, again in February 1927, and again in March 1927. In April, Chiang retaliated with a bloody purge aimed at curing the "disease of the heart" by eliminating all Chinese communists. Over the next year he carried out a series of nationwide communist-suppression campaigns, forcing the CCP out of the cities and into the rural outback. This eventually turned out to be a blessing in dis-guise for the communists. Mao had noted in Hunan, early in his career, that peasants were rising up and carrying out land expropriation on their own, without incitement from the Party. It was then that he intuited the future communist takeover of China: not, as Marxist theory insisted, as an action of the urban proletariat, but as a revolt of poor peasants against landlords and better-off peasants. But that would happen later. Right then, in 1927 and 1928, the CCP literally had to head for the hills, for bandit country, where it could live off the land and the peasants, and where it declared the Chinese Soviet Republic.

In 1931, Chiang launched several communist-annihilation campaigns into the mountains and bandit country. The first two attempts failed, as Russian intelligence, money, and arms enabled the communist forces to lure the Nationalist forces into traps. But in July, Chiang himself led an army of three hundred thousand men on a third expedition. Within two months the Red base had been squeezed down to a few dozen square miles around Ruijin (Jiangxi province), and the CCP forces were on the verge of collapse.

Then they were saved. On September 18, Chiang set off by ship from Nanjing to Jiangxi to lead the final push against the trapped communist army. At 10 p.m. the same night, Japan invaded Manchuria. Chiang was forced to shift his attention and the CCP was able to survive and prepare to fight another day.

If you were a true believer, you might be excused for thinking that God or Marx was on the CCP side.

But the citizens of the Chinese Soviet Republic might be excused for imagining they had been pushed into the first circle of hell. The Red Republic, centered on Ruijin with a total population of 3 million souls and an area of twelve thousand square miles, became a place of public harangues, expropriation of food and land, purges of Party officials suspected of being spies or bourgeoisie, and the drafting of young men into the Red Army. One irony of the situation was that high CCP officials like Zhou, Mao, and Deng came from well-off families who owned land and sent their children to universities. They were exactly the kind of people who, were they not Party leaders, would have been targets of class warfare, expropriation, torture, and killing. They and many other CCP leaders had to find a way to justify to themselves the killing and maltreatment of people just like themselves. Whatever else might have been required, this certainly took supreme faith in the righteousness of the cause and the inevitability of victory. These men intended to move mountains—and they were confident they could.

Despite the Japanese intervention, renewed Nationalist pressure on the Red Republic made it too dangerous for the CCP to stay in Ruijin. In October 1934, eighty thousand members of the CCP set off with their families and retainers on what would become known as the Long March. They left southeast China, proceeded west almost to Tibet, and then turned north and northeast. Three hundred seventy days and six thousand miles later, about eight thousand people arrived in the mountain fastnesses and caves of Yan'an, which were safe from both the Nationalists and the Japanese, and close to the Soviet Union, whose support and supplies were essential. Even so, the CCP would again owe its survival to Japan. The invasion of China proper by Japan's Kwangtung Army on July 7, 1937, precipitated a rough and temporary ceasefire in the long-running Chinese civil war that enabled the decimated CCP forces to recover and replenish themselves.

Yet recovery, suggesting rest, would surely sound like a strange term to the veterans of the Yan'an years. Purges, spy hunts, self-criticism sessions, confession of error and even of treason, torture, and executions were the order of the day. The eighty thousand people who departed Jiangxi province on the Long March had been mostly uneducated peasants, soldiers, and laborers. Because the March was anti-egalitarian (Mao and other leaders were carried on litters, leaders received more and better rations, and they had better and warmer clothing), the remnant that finally arrived in Yan'an was heavily weighted toward the better-educated and wealthier leadership set of the CCP. Wishing to fight the Japanese or to create a better future for their country, about forty thousand young people, most of them full of idealism and better educated than those who had died on the March, made their way to Yan'an to bolster the exhausted Long Marchers.

Almost certainly their reception was quite different from what they expected. As a way of winnowing and disciplining them, most were treated as if they were suspected of being spies. Independent writings were not permitted. When thirty-five-year-old Wang Shiwei dared to write a criticism of the hierarchy of privilege existing in Yan'an, he was targeted by Mao, accused of being a Trotskyite, kept in solitary confinement for several years, and finally executed when the CCP evacuated Yan'an in 1947.[2] Virtually all the new arrivals had to spend days and weeks writing complete self-confessions of their own lives, telling in excruciating detail every small event they had experienced, every person they had met, and every thought they had ever had. Especially, they were urged to explicate every bad thought they had had of the CCP, and every negative aspect of their own characters and lives. If the overseers weren't satisfied, the writer had to do it again, and again, and yet again. Or they might be encouraged through sleep deprivation, hot wires to sensitive body parts, and the threat of death to remember and record yet more bad elements of their characters. People were also encouraged to inform on each other, a practice that prevented mutual trust and any spontaneous exchange of views. They thereby became perfect tools for the CCP machine.

Nor did this indoctrination and cultivation apply only to young people and newcomers. Leaders and cadres were expected to engage in repeated and extensive self-criticism, self-abnegation, and confession. Even Zhou Enlai, at one time the top CCP official, came under suspicion as a spy.[3] During a terror campaign in 1943, Mao charged that most communist organizations in Nationalist-controlled areas were spies for Chiang. Since Zhou was the overseer of these organizations and because Zhou himself was the CCP liaison with Chiang in the wartime capital of Chongqing as part of the common front against the Japanese, this comment suggested that Zhou himself might be a spy. On June 15, 1943, Mao ordered Zhou back from Chongqing, saying: "Don't linger . . . to avoid people talking." When Zhou returned in July, Mao's first words to him were: "Don't leave your heart in the enemy camp." Zhou was careful to sing Mao's praises at his welcome-back dinner and then at the Politburo meeting in November. He denigrated himself through five days of self-criticism in which he admitted to having "committed extremely big crimes."[4] He finished by saying it was Mao and only Mao who had saved the Party from himself (Zhou) and other wayward leaders.

Over his lifetime Zhou wrote out hundreds of self-criticisms. Peng Dehuai, commander of the Eighth Route Army, likewise went through a long series of harassment meetings. Liu Shaoqi, who eventually became number two to Mao, initially expressed doubts about the indoctrination campaign in Yan'an, but after some self-criticism he changed his views and became wholly devoted to Mao's way.

Here again, the parallels with religious faith and practice are striking. In the wake of his vision of Christ on the road to Damascus, the Apostle Paul had gone for a number of years into the wastes of Arabia to pray, to examine himself, and to gain a greater understanding of God and what God wanted from him. Throughout his subsequent ministry in the Roman world, he prayed and criticized himself constantly. In a particularly poignant passage in his letter to the Romans (7:16), Paul says: "I do not understand what I do. For what I want to do I do not, but what I hate I do. And if I do what I do not want to do . . . it is no longer I myself who do it, but it is sin living in me." It was this sin that Paul sought to absolve and halt by the intervention of faith in and obedience to the teachings of Jesus Christ. The Christian Church taught the need for constant introspection, confession, asking for pardon, renewal of faith, and dedication to the mission. As Paul says of himself, "Five times I received from the Jews the forty lashes minus one. Three times I was beaten with rods. Once I was stoned. Three times I was shipwrecked. I spent a night and a day in the open sea. In my frequent journeys, I have been in danger from rivers and from bandits, in danger from my countrymen and from the Gentiles, in danger in the city and in the country, in danger on the sea and among false brothers" (Second Corinthians 11:25).

Paul was attempting to create new men and women in the spirit of Christ. The CCP was attempting to create new men and women—and a new nation—in the spirit of Marxism-Leninism. In view of the hardships, self-abnegation, purges, betrayals, and constant danger in which they worked, the dedication of key CCP leaders like Zhou Enlai, Deng Xiaoping, and Liu Shaoqi suggests a deep faith, like that of historic religious figures, in the rightness of their mission and in the certainty of its eventual accomplishment. There are striking similarities between the Maoists' practices and objectives and those of the Christian Church. The Church calls for confession of sin; the Party called for self-criticism. The Church struggles against sin, the Party struggled against the old shibboleths and bankrupt wisdom. The Church calls for complete dedication, simple living, and service to the people, especially to the poor, weak, and downtrodden, all aimed at gaining salvation and eternal peace with justice. The Party called for simplicity, service, and dedication to the revolution that would create heaven on earth. The Church, at various times in its history, used torture and terror to expose and root out heresy. Likewise, the Party sought to sniff out even the least heresy and exterminate the heretics.

The Impossible Dream Comes True

With the end of World War II, on August 15, 1945, many observers understood that Chiang and his Nationalist Party would take back the parts of China that had been occupied by the Japanese and undertake the task of reconstructing the country. China had been a major ally of the Western powers, and Chiang had been recognized as one of the "Big Four" leaders alongside Franklin Roosevelt, Winston Churchill, and Josef Stalin. Moreover, under Chiang, China was to become a founding member of the United Nations and a permanent member of the UN Security Council along with the United States, the Soviet Union, France, and the United Kingdom.

What most observers didn't know was that Stalin's Soviet Union and the United States would move or fail to move in ways that severely undercut Chiang and his army. In February 1945, Roosevelt and Churchill requested, and Stalin agreed, that the Soviet Union would enter the war against Japan once Germany surrendered. On August 9, 1945, 1.5 million Soviet troops marched into northern China along a twenty-seven-hundred-mile front. Nor did they halt, as they were supposed to do, when Japan surrendered six days later. Instead they pressed on to within one hundred miles of Beijing and turned over the mineral-rich and highly industrialized province of Manchuria to Mao and the CCP.

Chiang's armies had been pushed by the Japanese into the south and west of China, and without American assistance he could not easily get to Manchuria to accept the Japanese surrender. The Americans seemed not to understand what Stalin and Mao were doing and delayed helping to ferry some of Chiang's crack troops to Manchuria. It wasn't until early November that the Nationalist army began occupying key regions of Manchuria. When it did, it found itself fighting the Red Army troops that were being supplied and transported by the Soviets and assisted by the two-hundred-thousand-man Manchurian army. Surprisingly to many observers, Chiang's troops won most of the early battles, and when the Soviet army finally left China in May 1946, the Nationalists rather easily retook all the main cities and rail lines, including Harbin, which had been a CCP stronghold. Despite massive assistance from the Soviets, Mao and the CCP were on the ropes.

But then the CCP began saying it was not communist at all, just a party of agrarian reform. President Harry Truman sent his top general, George Marshall, to mediate between Mao and Chiang in an effort to avoid civil war. Marshall is undoubtedly one of the great men of history, but this was not his shining moment. He wrote to Truman, "I had a long talk with Mao Tse-tung, and I was frank to an extreme. He showed no resentment and gave me every assurance of cooperation." The communist forces in Manchuria, Marshall continued, were "little more than loosely organized bands." Just when Chiang could taste victory, Marshall forced him to cease fire. On May 31, 1946, he wrote to Chiang: "Under the circumstances of the continued advance of the government troops in Manchuria, I must . . . repeat that . . . a point is being reached where the integrity of my position is open to serious question. Therefore, I request you again to immediately issue an order terminating advances, attacks, or pursuits by Government troops."[5]

With no real choice, Chiang agreed to a fifteen-day ceasefire that Marshall later extended to four months. Chiang desperately needed American financial aid and was thus not able to withstand Marshall's pressure. The result, however, was that the CCP gained control over an area larger than Germany, with long land borders and rail links to the Soviet Union. Moreover, while Washington was pressing Chiang to halt his armies and negotiate with Mao, Stalin was training Mao's forces and providing refuge at Port Arthur and Dalian, which the USSR had gained in the Big Three talks at Yalta. The Soviets also turned tens of thousands of Japanese POWs over to Mao to help with training and maintaining the communist armies. Mao himself compared this base to a comfortable chair, with Russia as a solid back and North Korea and Mongolia as armrests.[6]

This was essentially game, set, and match for the CCP. As Jung Chang notes: "Marshall's diktat was probably the single most important decision affecting the outcome of the civil war. Lin Biao concurred in private that this truce was a fatal mistake on Chiang's part."[7]

Who says Marxism is phony science? For the CCP veterans, the realization of their impossible dream could only have confirmed the truth of their faith and the soundness of their science.

Although Mao told his Party congress in 1949 that China had "stood up," his notion of standing up was wildly at odds both with the reality of China and with simple economics. He seemed to imagine that if he and the CCP just willed something strongly enough, it would come to pass. One of his first objectives was to make China into a major steel-producing country. To this end, everyone in China was directed to start making steel in backyard ovens. They were encouraged to melt their knives, forks, tools, and anything else made of metal to produce raw steel. The frenzy of steel production that ensued quickly backfired. Because farm tools were being melted they were no longer available for farming, and the lack of farming tools meant that little could be planted. The resulting famine eventually killed over 40 million people. All of this was accompanied by continuing purges, searches for traitors and foreign agents, loyalty tests, self-criticism, and the swearing of eternal loyalty to the Party line, whatever that happened to be at any particular moment. In short, it was a disaster of truly historic proportions, and very far from the promised land.

Some CCP leaders understood this and tried to bring reason to bear, but the problem with a true religion is that any hint of doubt can be seen as heresy and lead to being burned at the stake, or at least being sent to the farm for "reeducation."

Mao had long believed that only a complete remake of the Chinese person, the burning of the old books, and the reforging of civilization could make China great again. In 1966 he launched the Cultural Revolution, which tore the country apart for the next ten years. During the twenty-seven years from when China "stood up" in 1949 until Mao's death in 1976, Japan and the Asian Tigers—South Korea, Taiwan, Hong Kong, and Singapore—made a good start on getting rich, but China was as poor as it had been in 1949.

Socialism with Chinese Characteristics

Mao's death meant more than the passing of a major leader. It produced a crisis of faith. By the late 1970s it was becoming clear that Marxist ideology was bringing neither wealth nor freedom, and the communist states were falling farther and farther behind the West. The entire legitimacy of the CCP was at stake. Why should it be in charge? Why should anyone pay attention to it?

Deng Xiaoping, Mao's successor, was in many respects the opposite of the Great Helmsman. He did not read a lot, did not pretend to be an intellectual, and was certainly not an ideologue wedded to the notion of creating a new communist man. He was dedicated to one thing: the resurrection of China as a wealthy and powerful country, by whatever means that might be accomplished. He dispensed with class war and turned to market mechanisms, saying that "to get rich is glorious." (Actually, Deng never said exactly this. It is a simplified version of *rang yi bu fen ren xian fu qi lai,* which means "Let some people get rich first" —a phrase Deng used when he first started to marketize the Chinese economy. Orville

Schell's 1984 book *To Get Rich Is Glorious: China in the '80s* popularized the phrase, but Schell himself agrees that Deng didn't use those exact words.) He didn't care if some people got rich faster than others as long as China moved toward becoming a rich nation. The Party did an about-face and increasingly began to use market mechanisms while opening the country to trade and foreign investment.

This created two issues. One was how to deal with Mao's legacy. Had he been wrong? Had he led the Party and the nation astray? If so, hadn't Deng and all the top Party leaders gone along with him? How could they justify hanging on now? The solution was an official evaluation of the Mao era that concluded Mao had been 70 percent right and 30 percent wrong.

The second issue was what to call the new policy direction. If it was market capitalism, such a complete reversal from socialism would call the leadership's legitimacy into question. The Party found a semantic solution: the new direction was "socialism with Chinese characteristics." It was meant to convey continuity, but it was a clear step toward nationalism as the de facto CCP doctrine. This reflected Deng's own views. He wanted China to become again the great country and civilization it had once been and was quite ready to use market forces if they worked. Deng was not really a Marxist or a socialist, but he was a strong Leninist. He believed that only a highly dedicated, disciplined, well-trained, and well-organized political elite that dominated all elements of society could restore China to its former glory and its proper place among nations. In addition, the elite group responsible for carrying out this program had, above all other considerations, to hold complete power over not just the state but the entire society, and it had to hold it indefinitely. It must forever be wary of spies, of turncoats in its own ranks, and especially of enemies who presented themselves as friends. It would have to stifle all dissent and do so forever.

Nevertheless, by ending the Cultural Revolution and the class struggle, and introducing market and capitalist mechanisms, Deng began what MIT professor Yasheng Huang has told me was the greatest period of liberalization in China. Unexpectedly, he also unleashed political exploration and a great interest in free speech and democracy, especially among students and young people. Many China scholars agree that the 1980s were the period of greatest liberalization in China in the past hundred years. It was exhilarating but dangerous. Eventually, in May and June of 1989, students demonstrated in Tiananmen Square, calling for democracy and even creating a Statue of Liberty lookalike called the Goddess of Democracy. The student movement split the Party. Party Chairman Zhao Ziyang sympathized with the students, called on the Party to negotiate with them, and went to the square himself to discuss their demands. But democracy would erode the power of the Party, which Deng, as a Leninist, held to be essential to any decent future for China.

Deng had Zhao arrested and confined to his home, where he stayed until his death sixteen years later in 2005. He called in the People's Liberation Army (PLA) and had it concretely demonstrate a key element of Chinese communism: the army had nothing to do with the people. It was (and is) owned and operated by the Chinese Communist Party and pledged to defend it—against the people, if necessary. It did so on June 4, 1989, by firing into the crowds of hundreds of thousands of students. As noted above, the number killed remains uncertain, but it is widely agreed that it was at least five hundred, and possibly as high as twenty-six hundred.[8] In any case, that action ended any talk of democracy and freedom of speech in China. Deng packed the Party and the government with hard-liners who enforced censorship and the Party line.

At the same time, to avoid another experience like Mao's tyranny, Deng instituted a system of collective leadership, with the chairman of the Party and the president of the country (always the same person) holding a five-year term renewable for a second five years but no more. Deng was thus succeeded by Jiang Zemin for ten years and then by Hu Jintao for ten more. During this period, China experienced very rapid economic growth, boosted greatly by foreign investment in China and by China's accession as a member of the World Trade Organization.

In permitting China to join the WTO in 2001 even though it was not a fully free market economy, the United States and other economic powers were making a huge bet based on strong convictions about the power of free trade and democratic ideas. It had become an article of faith among Western leaders that free trade and globalization would inevitably liberalize and democratize China. And for the next eleven or twelve years, it seemed that that might be true. As Kerry Brown notes, during the 1990s and early 2000s, "those visiting China would have been hard pressed to distinguish entrepreneurs and business-people from government figures."[9] With the fading of the Party's ideological commitment and idealistic mission, barriers to temptation fell. Party members saw each day that they were awarding contracts and launching projects that were creating enormous wealth. As Wang Xiaofang notes in his novel *The Civil Servant's Notebook,* low wages, lack of a rule of law, and protection from whistleblowers combined with incredible economic growth to make the Party into a kind of "mega successful holding company atop countless subsidiaries all paying dues to it."[10] Countless Party officials became vastly wealthy. The best known of them is former prime minister Wen Jiabao. In 2012 the *New York Times* reported that his family had become multibillionaires.[11]

But this was at odds with both the moral ethic of the Party and its justification for a monopoly of power. The Party was coming to resemble the Roman Catholic Church in the Middle Ages, when priests sold indulgences and openly lived with women by whom they had children. The corruption of the Church undermined the faith and salvation it preached, and thus its moral and temporal power until the appearance of Martin Luther and the Protestant Reformation in 1517. Just so with the CCP of 2012.

In the case of the Church, Martin Luther famously nailed his ninety-five theses condemning its corruption to the door of the Castle Church in Wittenberg, Germany. The CCP's equivalent action was to select Xi Jinping as Party general secretary and president of China. Xi had always held fast to the notion of the Party cadre as someone dedicated to a political and cultural, even spiritual mission. He had not allowed himself or his family to become involved in the moneymaking race, and he had continually urged that cadres set examples. Between 2013 and 2018 he had more than eighty-eight thousand officials indicted and imprisoned for corruption. Under Jiang Zemin and Hu Jintao, the Party tended to base its legitimacy on the delivery of economic benefits. But Xi saw that such a justification could be fatal to the Party's demand for a monopoly on power. The CCP's imperium arises from more than its existence as an executive body. At its base, writes Wang Xiaofang, "it is a faith community."[12] As Brown notes: "Its power is based on the emotional and moral power of its beliefs. When challenges to its privileged status in Chinese political life arise, it can therefore appeal to a higher level of reasoning and vision to defend itself.

Economic growth is a means, not an end in this framework."[13] Party doctrine holds that history has a purpose and the end will be positive. Pragmatically using capitalism is fine, but that usage may be shifted or abandoned as the path of faith demands. Xi's vision of the Great Chinese Dream involves not only restoring golden ages of the past but creating a modern golden age toward which China is leading the way.

It is this view of itself and the future that leads the Party to take extraordinary measures to prevail over "evil" forces both within and outside the country. Domestically, the quasi-religious Falun Gong group has been hunted down and virtually exterminated. The Uighur Muslims of Xinjiang province are being corralled into concentration camps and "reeducated." Churches are being disbanded and attacked; the teaching of Western ideas has been forbidden; and Western universalism and democratic systems are under constant attack both in China and outside.

One may think of Xi as the pope of the Chinese anti-Church, and of the Party as a theocracy with the goal of creating a hegemonic China that will become a kind of heaven on earth.

Organization and Functions

A key thing to understand is that the CCP is the most important entity in China—far more important than the government. The most powerful person in the world today is not the president of the United States but the general secretary of the Communist Party—Xi Jinping—who is also the direct head of the Central Military Commission. It is very important to keep in mind that the Chinese armed forces, the PLA, is not run by the Chinese government but is an organization of the Party—and its mission is to protect the Party, not the nation. Beneath the general secretary is the Politburo Standing Committee of 7 members, and beneath that is the Politburo of 25 members, including those of the Standing Committee. The Central Discipline Inspection Commission reports to the Politburo, which is chosen from the 371 members of the Party's Central Committee. Reporting to the Central Committee are 31 provincial committees, 665 city committees, 2,487 county committees, 41,636 township committees, and 780,000 village committees. There are six major departments: the Organization Department, the Propaganda Department, the

United Front Department, the General Office, the Central Politics and Law Committee, and the International Liaison Department. Finally, there are a number of leading groups: Economics, Public Security, Rural Affairs, Party Building, Propaganda and Thought, Taiwan Affairs, Foreign Affairs, and National Security.

In his authoritative book *The Party*, Richard McGregor quotes the former Chinese foreign policy official Dai Bingguo saying that "China's number one core interest is to maintain its fundamental system and state security. . . . State sovereignty, territorial integrity and economic development, the priorities of any state, all are subordinate to the need to keep the Party in power." The government is merely a shadow of the Party, but the Party makes every effort to hide its power, and the fiction of a dominant government is convenient for world leaders who want to do business with China. It allows them "to pretend that it has an evolving governmental system with strengths, weaknesses, quirks and foibles, like any other, as if a Starbucks on every corner is a marker of political progress."[14] The reality is starkly different. The Party dominates all the key elements: personnel, propaganda, and the PLA.

Lenin, were he here today, would instantly recognize the CCP as a concrete manifestation of his idea of how a political system should be structured: the ruling party must penetrate and oversee the state at all levels. At the top, the system should be as centralized as possible. At the bottom, however, it should be decentralized, with all the information flowing quickly upward to the Central Committee. "For the center actually to direct the orchestra," MacGregor writes, "it needs to know who plays violin and where, who plays a false note and why, and how and where it is necessary to transfer someone to correct the dissonance." The Central Committee is like a board of directors that appoints the key executives of the Politburo, which in turn selects the top officers of the Standing Committee. The top priority of these leaders is to assure the Party's control of "the state, the economy, the civil service, the military, the police, education, social organizations, and the media. Indeed, the Politburo's remit includes controlling the very concept of China itself and the official narrative of its revival from a humiliated ancient empire to a powerful state and resurgent civilization."[15] The Central Committee does not, however, engage so much in day-to-day details. That is the work of government officials, who are mostly Party members. One way to envision how things work is to keep an eye on the license plates of official cars. For instance, the Shanghai Party secretary's plate number is 00001. The mayor's is 00002. The mayor handles day-to-day details. The Party secretary oversees the big picture.

The Party's secrecy puts it beyond the reach of the law and the citizenry. In today's China, ordinary citizens can sue the government. This was not always true, and even today the chances of success are quite small, but in principle, they can sue. But they can't sue the Party, because there is nothing to sue. The Party is not even registered anywhere as an organization. As He Weifang notes, "The Party sits outside and above the law."[16] It also controls the law firms that might be engaged to sue it. According to Richard McGregor, about one-third of all Chinese lawyers are Party members and 95 percent of law firms have Party committees. Moreover, one need not have studied law to become a judge, and judges are required by the Supreme People's Court to owe their loyalty first to the Party, then to the state, then to the masses, and finally to the law.[17] The Party is in no danger of being sued—or even identified.

Another example of how the Party hides itself is the central Party school. There are classrooms and campuses all over China, and Party members must attend training and indoctrination sessions regularly. The Party school in Shanghai, for instance, which is considered one of the top four, has a one-hundred-acre campus in the city's Pudong district. The school's official name in Chinese translates as China Pudong Cadre College. In English, however, it calls itself the China Executive Leadership Academy. As an outside observer, you might be forgiven for thinking that this is an MBA factory or some kind of a mid-level executive training center, rather than an elite finishing school for China's future rulers.

In a sense, the role, power, and ecclesiastical nature of the Party form an example of Jean-Baptiste Alphonse Karr's famous aphorism "The more things change, the more they remain the same." Despite war, revolution, and social experimentation, China today is not very different from the ancient China of the emperors. As the political scientist Fang Ning notes, "The secret of government in China is that all hats are controlled by the emperor. He can take them off and put them on. I don't think this part of the system has ever changed."[18]

The Chill

In the wake of the Tiananmen Square massacre of June 4, 1989, a vast chill settled over the Party and the Chinese government. Deng got rid of the more liberal Party leaders, and many Maoist hard-liners were raised to power. The moves Deng had made to liberalize markets were blamed by many of these conservative Party members for the rise of democratic ideas and the Party's loss of discipline and control. There was a huge crackdown. About 10 percent of the Party's 48 million members were investigated and either jailed, sacked, demoted, or forced to write long self-criticisms that were included in their personal employment files. Some potentially suspect members were even forced to reapply for Party membership to ensure that they would be communists in spirit as well as in word. Bear in mind that the Tiananmen Square incident happened shortly before the collapse of the Soviet Union and the retreat of communist/socialist regimes almost everywhere. The Party was scared to death.

Better Propaganda—Renewed State-Owned Companies

Economic policy and growth stalled as Party leaders debated whether to continue with market reforms or to return to the egalitarian socialism of the past. It was Deng who again outlined a new model. Appearing on television on June 9, 1989, only a day or so after the blood had been scrubbed from Tiananmen Square, he shook hands with the military commanders who had ordered the shooting of the students and thanked them for their loyalty to the Party. He also emphasized that the mistake of the 1980s had not been the freeing of the economy but a lack of ideological and political education efforts to accompany it. Political sections would be strengthened or established in government ministries, the courts, and the military to serve as an early-warning system for any rebellion in the future. Said law professor Jiang Ping, "They are there to ensure that the Party can have direct control over all important institutions."[19] The Central Propaganda Department was enlarged and given a much bigger budget as well as instructions on how better to sell economic reform to the public. The Central Organization Department was instructed to be absolutely sure of cadres' loyalty, not only in the government but everywhere, including educational bodies, the media, and any organization under state control.

But the question of exactly how to run the economy was still unanswered. At the peak, there were 76 million Chinese workers at state enterprises, all of them beneficiaries of the "three irons": the "iron chair" of a lifelong job, the "iron rice bowl" of guaranteed food, shelter, and medical care, and the "iron wage" of a guaranteed income and pension. These enterprises were villages or even cities unto themselves. Some had their own post offices, schools, and hospitals. Their purpose was not really to make a return on investment. In the past, there had been a central planning mechanism that at least established production and sales targets, but these had withered with Deng's economic liberalization, and the companies had essentially become huge sponges for soaking up government tax revenue.

One obvious option was simply to privatize them and let them sink or swim under the direction of their own management. But that route would have enabled the evolution of large, powerful organizations increasingly not under Party control—something that could eventually threaten the Party's rule and was therefore unthinkable. Debate eventually led to a secret meeting in late 1991 that resulted in a fourteen-thousand-character secret manifesto. Briefly, it said that "the Party must grasp not only the gun [armed forces and police], but also the asset economy as well."[20] The vast array of state- or government-owned corporations and properties would no longer be held in the name of the Chinese government but in that of the Party itself. But this had the downside of exposing the Party to blame and even possible legal action for any reverses or mistakes. Deng's solution was simplicity itself. The Party would not itself have full ownership of state assets, but henceforth it would have the right to hire and fire the management. In other words, the Party would quietly manage the state-owned enterprises, and it would manage them not with a view toward future privatization but so that they would become productive and profitable enterprises that would keep the Party in control of the economy and serve as a counterweight to any public influence from growing private enterprises.

The undertaking was enormous and widely misunderstood in the West. For example, Zhu Rongji, China's economic czar at the time, expressed surprise in 1998 after former president George H. W. Bush asked him how China's privatization program was proceeding. Zhu protested that China was not privatizing, only corporatizing its large state holdings, which was "just another way of realizing state ownership." Bush gave him a wink and said, "We know what is going on."[21] But neither Bush nor virtually the whole Western establishment—press, academic, political, or foreign policy— had any idea of what was "going on."

In fact it was the biggest turnaround operation in history. Over the ten years from 1991 to 2001, the Chinese government laid off 50 million workers from state-owned enterprises and reassigned 18 million to companies that no longer guaranteed employment or benefits. The banks had essentially been ATMs for officials and official businesspeople, so that by 1998, more than half the loans issued by China's biggest lender were unrecoverable. About 45 percent of the loans made before 2000 went into default. The investment in bank reform alone cost the Chinese taxpayer $620 billion, or about 28 percent of GDP in 2005. Compare that, for example, to the Bush administration's highly controversial financial rescue plan of 2008, TARP, which came to only about 5 percent of GDP. Or consider that from 1997 to 2007, as China's GDP grew to surpass that of Germany (it would surpass Japan's in 2010), workers' wages as a share of GDP fell from 53 percent to 40 percent.[22] The profits of China's economic boom thus benefited the state (and therefore the Party) significantly more than the average citizen. And with an eye to future raw materials and competitive demands, the Party began pushing its big, now cash-rich state companies to expand abroad.

There could be no doubt, then or now, that the CCP is in active control not only of the Chinese economy but of its key enterprises. The Xi Jinping era has only strengthened the Party's control of business. The role of the state-owned enterprises has been especially promoted by the Belt and Road initiative, by China's building of artificial islands in the South China Sea, and by the country's efforts to become a major maritime nation. It is mainly the state-owned enterprises that are buying or leasing ports like Piraeus in Greece and Trieste in Italy, building high-speed rail in Turkey, and doing infrastructure projects in Africa, South America, Asia, Europe, and Russia.

Moreover, the line between state-owned and private enterprise can be difficult to discern. The telecommunications giant Huawei is technically a private enterprise, but its founder and CEO is a former PLA officer, and

its ownership structure is simply indecipherable. It has been heavily subsidized by the state and has extremely close relations with the PLA and
the top tiers of the Party. These relationships reach deep into all private
Chinese enterprises. If there are at least three CCP members among a
company's employees, it must allow the establishment of a Party cell and
enable the cell to hold meetings and voice concerns to management. There
is no requirement for the Party to have a managerial role, but recent years
have seen a major emphasis on increased Party activity in private companies.
Because there is no rule of law, any private company can be informally
pressured to act according to the Party's wishes. For instance, Jack Ma,
the entrepreneurial founder and CEO of Alibaba, China's Amazon, has
said that if asked, he would gladly turn his Alibaba over to the state and
the Party. We can only imagine how Jeff Bezos or Bill Gates would view
such a request.

A good example of how China Inc. works is the 2007 takeover bid by
BHP-Billiton, the world's largest mining company, for its Anglo-Australian
competitor Rio Tinto. China saw the bid as a threat because it would create a near-monopoly in the iron ore trade on which China depends. The
Politburo immediately decided to oppose the bid, fearing that the deal
would result in higher iron ore prices for China's steel industry. It directed
state-owned Chinalco, China's major aluminum company, to intervene
with a competing bid. In doing so, Chinalco stoutly maintained that it was
run without interference from the state and insisted that all commercial
and management decisions were taken independently. Yet the Chinalco
bid was being financed by the China Development Bank. On top of this,
Chinalco was able to sustain its bid despite an international credit crunch
that drove BHP-Billiton eventually to drop its offer.

Yet the fiction of the Party's absence from China Inc. continues. American investment banks have all presented share offerings to international
investors that absolutely fail to identify the role of the state and the Party
in Chinese corporations.

The Party is in the background of any serious business undertaking by
foreign firms in China as well as by Chinese companies anywhere. Because
of the lack of rule of law, foreign companies in China can be harassed,
pressured, and threatened—and they have no recourse. The CEOs of these
companies are far more afraid of what Beijing can do to them than of what

Washington, London, Brussels, or Tokyo can do. They are effectively hostages to the Party, and even agents of the Party when they speak, write, or give testimony before their national legislatures.

Personnel

The main office of the Party's Central Organization Department is located only a little over half a mile from Tiananmen Square, but you would never find it unless you were guided by someone who knew where it is. There is no indication at all of what the building is and who occupies it. If you want to call the department on the telephone, you will find only a single listed number; calls are answered with a recorded message that instructs you to leave a message reporting any organizational problems above the county level. If you try to find it online, you discover a website with the same information as the recorded message.

This secrecy hides what is probably the most powerful office anywhere in the world. If a similar body existed in the United States, it would include all the cabinet secretaries, all the governors and their lieutenant governors, the mayors of all the major cities, the justices of the Supreme Court, the members of the Senate and House of Representatives, the heads of all the federal regulatory agencies, the CEOs of the fifty largest corporations, the editors of all significant news outlets, the heads of the TV networks and cable stations, the heads of the leading think tanks, the presidents of the major universities, and the leaders of all other even modestly significant bodies. The appointees to these posts would be vetted in secret, and when they were announced, there would be no explanation of why the appointments were made. The reverse also occurs. Important actors may be demoted, fired, or even imprisoned—or worse—also in secret.

When asked the reason for all this secrecy, even to the extent of having no name on the door, a top official says: "Government departments hang their plaque outside their buildings because they have to face the public. We are only here to service the cadres. The cadres all know where we are. It's a bit like knowing where your parents live."[23]

The organization maintains files on all top-level officials and constantly reviews their political reliability, job performance, and significant aspects of their personal life. Together with the Party's anti-corruption unit, the

Central Organization Department monitors behavior to identify any weaknesses that might disqualify a cadre for important positions. This system is copied at every level of government. The center oversees appointments in the provinces, the provincial department branches oversee the cities, and so forth down to the township level.

Of course, there is tension between the Organization Department and the desire of powerful leaders to have allies and supporters appointed to key positions. There is also huge potential for graft in the form of bribes for good reviews and appointment to key positions, particularly those that can be monetized. In the first decade of this century, this potential led to enormous corruption, and enormous internal battles. Just one example: a man "passing himself off as an Organization Department official . . . secured a payment of $63,000 from a local bureaucrat" to find him a senior government position.[24] It was graft like this that made Xi Jinping a national hero after he became Party secretary in 2012. One of his first promises was a vow to crack down on "tigers and flies." So far, more than one hundred thousand people have been indicted for corruption, including 120 high-ranking officials, military officers, and executives of state-owned companies.[25] Of particular significance has been the conviction and jailing of Zhou Yongkang, formerly a member of the Politburo Standing Committee.

Interestingly, this maximum central control is not an invention of the Party. It is quite similar to the structure and style of central control in China dating back to the Han Dynasty (AD 25–220).

More Propaganda

The Communist Party's Propaganda Department is not part of the government, but it is nevertheless an enormous bureaucracy dedicated to controlling what the Chinese public reads, sees, hears, and thinks. The English name was changed in 1998 to the Publicity Department of the Chinese Communist Party in response to English speakers' sensitivity about the truthfulness of propaganda. In Chinese, however, it remains the Propaganda Department. It extends into every medium that provides information, including newspapers, radio and television stations, publishing houses, magazines, universities, schools, cadre training, musical troupes, literature and art troupes, cultural amusement parks, and essentially anything that communicates anything at all to the Chinese people. The department also oversees hundreds of millions of Internet and cell phone accounts.

Its remit is licensing media outlets and giving instructions to the media on what may or may not be said. This is true particularly regarding so-called sensitive topics such as Taiwan, Tibet, and anything that affects state security or the power of the CCP. The editors in chief of all major media outlets are required to attend the department's weekly meeting, at which they receive instructions on which stories to play up and which to play down or not to report at all. These instructions are enforced by Party discipline. All media must be loyal to the Party.

Foreign journalists are carefully monitored and may be expelled from the country or not granted entry at all. This practice has now been extended to Hong Kong: in October 2018, veteran *Financial Times* reporter Victor Mallet's Hong Kong visa renewal was denied, the first time such a denial occurred in that city. In March 2020 reporters for the *New York Times,* the *Washington Post,* and the *Wall Street Journal* were all expelled from China. Presumably the Party didn't want them reporting to the outside world what was happening with the coronavirus epidemic in China. On the other hand, foreign writers who follow Propaganda Department guidance are welcome and well treated. For instance, Harvard professor Ezra Vogel is a hero in China for writing a biography of Deng Xiaoping that became a runaway best seller. Somehow, the Chinese version of the book failed to mention the massacre of students in Tiananmen Square, which Deng oversaw. Such an approach goes down very well with the Propaganda Department. On the other hand, longtime China watcher Michael Pillsbury was recently denied an entry visa to the country. Pillsbury wrote *The Hundred-Year Marathon,* which suggests that China has a comprehensive strategy intended to replace the United States as the top global power and to discredit and displace democracies wherever they may be. That message was not as popular with the Propaganda Department as Vogel's encomium to Deng.

Affairs Overseas

The CCP's United Front Work Department (UFWD) first arose in 1924, when the CCP sought to cooperate with potential allies, ranging from disaffected warlords to ethnic minorities to overseas Chinese, to defeat the "common enemy," Chiang Kaishek's Nationalists. The concept was very simple: "The enemy of my enemy is my friend—for now." This cooperation with outside groups made the CCP appear democratic and proved effective against the Nationalists when combined with military action, ideological work, and alliance building.

From 1936 through 1945, the Party formed an ostensible united front with the Nationalists against the invading Japanese. This extremely awkward quasi-alliance presented a façade of unity against the common enemy while each side continued to maneuver for long-term advantage. It was dropped after the Japanese surrender in 1945, and the CCP resumed cooperation with other groups in China that had reason to oppose the Nationalists. Once the civil war ended in the CCP's victory, the Party's emphasis shifted from the so-called mass line to class struggle. This greatly reduced the need for the United Front, and the department was used mostly to train young intellectuals to eliminate "bourgeois and idealistic political beliefs" and to instill faith in class struggle and revolutionary change.

After taking over leadership of the Party in 1979, Deng revitalized the UFWD to promote the common cause of economic reform and greater linkage with the international community. After the Tiananmen Square massacre, the UFWD was pressed into service internationally to help obscure the significance of the event and to justify it to foreign observers. It played a key role in promoting the "one country, two systems" slogan under which the Party engineered the return of Hong Kong and Macau to Beijing's control. Many in the West saw the collapse of the Soviet Union as the end of the Cold War, but for Deng it was just "a new cold war" in which the UFWD gained even more international significance. Deng spoke of the "unique opportunity" offered by the overseas Chinese community of some 60 million people. By drawing on their help, he said, China could break out of its international isolation and improve its international political standing by turning these people "into propaganda bases for China."[26] Overseas Chinese thus became an important initial target of the UFWD.

Since the turn of the century, the United Front has focused more and more heavily on the broader international scene. In their book *Nest of Spies*, Fabrice de Pierrebourg and Michel Juneau-Katsuya note that the UFWD "manages important dossiers concerning foreign countries and . . . these include propaganda, control of Chinese students abroad, and the recruiting of agents among both the Chinese diaspora and sympathetic foreigners." In 2007, the Party increased the UFWD's budget substantially in order to strengthen China's soft power overseas.[27] Then Xi Jinping made a speech in September 2014 that raised the significance of the UFWD, and of related bodies like the Overseas Chinese Affairs Office, to a whole new level. Echoing Mao Zedong, he called the UFWD "one of the CCP's magic weapons" to "unite all the forces that can be united to thwart enemy forces abroad."[28] Then in 2015, Xi made himself head of a United Front Small Leading Group, both to emphasize the importance of the broad United Front activity and to take full control of it. Under Xi, the UFWD budget is estimated to have risen to about $10 billion.[29]

It is precisely the purpose of the United Front to seek influence through connections that are difficult to prove publicly and to gain subtle influence over sensitive issues such as ethnic, political, and national identity, making those who seek to identify such influence vulnerable to accusations of prejudice. The United Front works to promote voices that are apparently unrelated to the CCP but are nevertheless sympathetic, as well as to smother and isolate any voices deemed unfriendly.

I recalled this recently when I collected my morning *Washington Post* from my driveway. Tucked inside the newspaper was a free copy of the *China Daily*. This is an English-language newspaper focused on China news that you can find in airports, hotels, and offices around the world. It is an organ of the Propaganda Department. Why was I getting it on my doorstep? I had never ordered it or subscribed to it. Was the *Post* giving me a gift? Surely it didn't support the editorial line of the *China Daily*. Could it be that the *Post* was paid to circulate this propaganda sheet? Well, yes. I was getting the *China Daily* courtesy of Xi's new beefed-up UFWD with the full blessing of the well-paid *Washington Post*, which espouses freedom of speech and democracy on its editorial pages.

In the wake of the coronavirus pandemic it has been interesting to note that many American friends have been receiving letters from old Chinese contacts from whom they have not heard for years. The letters offer to send protective masks from China. This is a measure of the reach and the thoroughness of the United Front Work Department.

Another way the United Front works is through Chinese student and scholar associations (CSSA), and through Confucius Centers located on college campuses. James Jiann Hua To notes that the associations receive critical support from Chinese embassies and consulates. In 2018, *Foreign Policy* reported that budget documents from the Georgetown University Chinese Student and Scholar Association showed that the CSSA received roughly half its annual budget from the Chinese government.[30] Of course, China is not the only country that supports student organizations abroad, but its political mobilization of students goes far beyond the cultural and educational activities typical of these groups. For example, in February 2017, the University of California at San Diego invited the Dalai Lama to give the commencement address. In response, the university's CSSA called for "tough measures to resolutely resist the school's unreasonable behavior." The association claimed it had coordinated with the Chinese consulate in San Diego and was "waiting for the advice of the Consulate General" on the issue.[31] The charter of the University of Tennessee CSSA requires members to "fervently love the motherland and protect the motherland's honor and image." In order to join, students from Taiwan, Hong Kong, and Macau were required to support Chinese national reunification and recognize the One China principle.[32]

In its 2018 book *Chinese Influence and American Interests*, Stanford University's Hoover Institution notes that Beijing is "seeking cultural and informational influence some of which could undermine our democratic processes" and quotes former Australian prime minister Malcolm Turnbull's observation that these efforts are "covert, coercive, or corrupting." The report notes that Confucius Institutes and Chinese Student and Scholar Associations sometimes report on and compromise the academic freedom of Chinese students and American faculty at U.S. universities with the direct support of the Chinese embassy and consulates. It further notes that American universities hosting events deemed politically offensive by the CCP have been subject to "increasing pressure, and sometimes even to retaliation, by diplomats in the Chinese embassy," and that Chinese diplomats and other entities have tried to influence the output of U.S. think tanks and punish American companies if they deviate in any way from the official Party line with regard to Taiwan, Tibet, and the South China Sea. Regarding technology, the report says that "China is engaged in a multi-faceted effort to misappropriate technologies it deems critical to its economic and military success. . . . Beyond economic espionage, theft by means of hacking into the files of U.S. high-tech companies and forced technology transfers required as part of joint venture deals in China, Beijing also captures much valuable new technology through its investments in U.S. high-tech companies and through its exploitation of the openness of American university labs. This goes well beyond influence-seeking to a deeper and more disabling form of penetration. The economic and strategic losses for the United States are increasingly unsustainable, threatening not only to help China gain global dominance of a number of the leading technologies of the future, but also to undermine America's commercial and military advantages."[33] Nor is this limited to the United States. Similar activities have been reported in Australia, Canada, France, Germany, Japan, New Zealand, Singapore, and the United Kingdom.

The report also deals with another interesting and important issue—censorship and self-censorship. Says one scholar: "I don't self-censor, but there is no need to launch a polemic every day of the week. Polemics get your visa cut off." Says another, "There is a conflict between protecting your institute and speaking truthfully. Whether it is over access or money. In public meetings, there is a tacit understanding that you will not be super critical of China." Another expert notes that "it is very hard not to subconsciously self-censor."[34]

Outside the United States, Australia, Canada, and New Zealand have also been prominent targets of United Front work. According to one key informant, at a conclave of Chinese ambassadors and foreign affairs officials in August 2004, Party secretary Hu Jintao told the gathering that from that moment, Australia should be included in what China defines as its "overall periphery." China has always paid special attention to countries in its "overall periphery" in order to neutralize them.[35]

In February 2005, China's vice minister of foreign affairs, Zhou Wenzhong, arrived in Canberra to explain the Central Committee's new strategy to senior officials of the Chinese embassy in Australia. He told them the short-term objective was to secure Australia as a reliable and stable supply base for China's continued economic growth over the next twenty years. The longer-term goal was to drive a wedge into the American-Australian alliance. The task, he told his team, was to attain "comprehensive influence over Australia economically, politically, culturally, in all ways."[36] Beijing hoped to turn Australia into a Western country that could say no to the United States.

These same attitudes and policies have been deployed in Canada, where China has become adept at influencing political leaders to enable it to acquire companies owning technologies banned from export because of their potential military uses. This became particularly apparent in 2017 when Canadian prime minister Justin Trudeau was persuaded to reverse a previous order to block the sale of Montreal's ITF Technologies to a Chinese company and to allow the sale of military communications products producer Norsat International to the Chinese company Hytera Communications.[37]

We know the situation in Australia without any doubt because Chen Yonglin, first secretary of the Chinese consulate in Sydney, was at the meeting with Hu and read the documents. In June 2005, he walked out of the consulate and sought political asylum in Australia, explaining to his hosts that "in accordance with their fixed strategic plans, the CCP had begun a structured effort to infiltrate Australia in a systematic way." He went on to say that "Australia and New Zealand were both seen as weak links in the western chain."[38]

Subsequently, a Fairfax Media investigation uncovered apparent United Front work targeting Australian politicians and Australia's overseas Chinese communities, cases subsequently alluded to in a major report by the Australian Security Intelligence Organization. In New Zealand, Anne-Marie Brady documented extensive Chinese political influence and United Front ties and also implicated member of Parliament Jian Yang as having connections to Chinese intelligence services. A report in the *Financial Times* quoting a UFWD handbook said it had claimed successes in getting favored candidates into elected positions in Canada.[39]

The Complete Team Game

The main thing to understand is that China is playing a complete team game. Everything is connected to everything else; there are no independent actors. When dealing with China, one is dealing with all of it, and all of China is relentless. Moreover, the team is owned, trained, coached, disciplined, and rewarded by a single entity—the CCP.

Chicken or Egg

The big challenge for the world's free market, rule-of-law democracies is to understand that this is the game China is playing, and that it is playing this game without reference to the actions or statements of the free world. In other words, the notion that the CCP will adjust its policies and actions depending on the attitudes and actions of the free world, often cited by free world establishment figures and China experts, is mostly nonsense. While there may be some truth to this in terms of tactics, there is no truth in terms of ultimate objectives. To say, for example, that a free world emphasis on maintaining leadership in key technology industries will only strengthen China's drive for autarky in these industries is completely meaningless. China is already striving for such autarky and always has and always will—because not to achieve such power would leave the CCP short of the all-controlling position it must have to achieve its ultimate religious objective of immortality for the Party.

3

The Strategy

Engineering souls is more important than producing tanks.
—*Josef Stalin*

In considering the CCP's national strategy for China, it is important to remind ourselves of the Party's roots, longtime objectives, and
religious-like dedication to achieving them. The Australian China expert
and journalist John Garnaut noted in a recent article that over the past ten
years he has had "to accept that economic openness does not inevitably
lead to political openness," especially "when you have a political regime
that is both capable and committed to ensuring it doesn't happen."[1]

Garnaut emphasizes that while "politics isn't everything, with the
exception of North Korea, there is no political system as tightly bound to
ideology as China's." This key fact tends to get lost in everyday discussion
of China because it is too alien a concept for the democratic world to
digest easily. It would have been easier in the nineteenth century, when
religion was taken more seriously in the West. For instance, President
William McKinley explained his decision to occupy the Philippines by
saying that "it was necessary to uplift and Christianize the Filipinos."
(He was apparently unaware that the largely Roman Catholic Philippines
was the only Christian nation in Asia.) But in today's democratic world,
where religion no longer dominates political discourse, it is easier for
writers to "normalize" events and concepts by describing them in secular
terms.

Trying to talk about China as something apart from the Communist Party has been a way of avoiding potentially painful debates about what China is, what it wants, and where it is going. But ultimately, this effort deprives us of full understanding.

An important key is that despite much rhetoric to the contrary, the founders of the CCP and People's Republic of China (PRC) did not do away with the past when they took control of the country. Rather, they grafted their understanding of communism (via Stalin) onto the ancient Chinese dynastic system. "Mao and his comrades," writes John Garnaut, "had grown up with tales of imperial China. They never stopped reading them. Indeed, Mao kept his bed full of them. The Dream of Red Mansions, The Three Kingdoms—the Chinese classics are all about the rise and decay of dynasties. This is the metanarrative of Chinese literature and historiography, even today."[2] The founding revolutionaries passed these tales down to their children. The descendants of the founding families, today's "princelings" (especially Xi), remain steeped in the dynastic system even as they preach new purification of communism.

In the princelings' view, China, although under the control of the Communist Party, is still in the dynastic cycle. When you lose political power in this system, you don't just lose your job, you lose everything: your life, your extended family's lives, and any mention of you in formal records and history. Winners take all and losers lose everything. In Chinese, the term "life-and-death struggle" is better translated as "You-die, I-live."[3] Xi and his dynasty believe that the moment they forget this reality, their future will become that of the Manchus or the Mings.

For a long time, the Western world took comfort in thinking that this ideological aspiration existed only on paper, while China's 1.4 billion citizens got on with the job of building families and communities and seeking knowledge and prosperity. But the ideology must be taken seriously. Since 1989 the Party has been rebuilding itself around what the draft National Security Law calls "ideological security," including defending itself against "negative cultural infiltration." Propaganda and security—*wen* and *wu*, the book and the sword, the pen and the gun—are inseparable. Party leaders, said Xi at his first National Propaganda Work Conference, on August 9, 2013, must "dare to show their swords" to ensure that "politicians run newspapers."[4]

Four months earlier, the General Office of the Central Committee, run by Xi's right-hand man Li Zhanshu, had already sent this now infamous political instruction to all high-level Party organizations. It was contained in Document 9, "Communiqué on the Current State of the Ideological Sphere," which set "disseminating thought on the cultural front as the most important political task." The document ordered cadres to arouse "mass fervor" and wage "intense struggle" against the following "false trends":

1. Western constitutional democracy—"an attempt to undermine the current leadership";
2. Universal values of human rights—an attempt to weaken the theoretical foundations of Party leadership;
3. Civil society—a "political tool" of the "Western anti-China forces" to dismantle the Party's social foundation;
4. Neoliberalism—U.S.-led efforts to "change China's basic economic system";
5. The West's idea of journalism—attacking the Marxist view of news, attempting to "gouge an opening through which to infiltrate our ideology";
6. Historical nihilism—trying to undermine Party history, "denying the inevitability" of Chinese socialism;
7. Questioning reform and opening—arguing about whether reform needs to go further.

Writes Garnaut, "There is no ambiguity in this document. The Western conspiracy to infiltrate, subvert and overthrow the People's Party is not contingent on what any particular Western country thinks or does. It is an equation, a mathematical identity: the CCP exists and therefore it is under attack. No amount of accommodation and reassurance can ever be enough—it can only ever be a tactic, a ruse."[5]

Without the conspiracy of Western liberalism, the CCP loses its reason to exist. There would be no need to maintain a vanguard party, and Xi might as well let it peacefully evolve. We know this document is authentic because the Chinese journalist who publicized it on the internet, Gao Yu, was arrested and her child was threatened. This led her, on February 8, 2016, to make the first Cultural Revolution–style confession of the internet era.[6]

In November 2013, Xi made himself head of a new Central State Security Commission, in part to counter "extremist forces and ideological challenges to culture posed by Western nations."[7] The key point about communist ideology—the unbroken thread that runs from Lenin through Stalin, Mao, and Xi—is that communist parties have always defined themselves as being in perpetual struggle with the hostile forces of Western liberalism.

Xi is talking and acting to further a project of total ideological control wherever possible. His vision, as he told "the broad masses of youth" in his Labor Day speech of May 2015, "requires all the Chinese people [including those of Chinese descent living outside China] to be unified with a single will like a strong city wall." They need to "temper their characters," he said, using a metaphor favored by both Stalin and Mao.[8] Stalin's original formulation in 1932 was "The production of souls is more important than the production of tanks."

There is no ambiguity in this project. It is in everything he does and says, and even in a system designed to be opaque to outsiders, we can see it in his words. He is pushing communist ideology at a time when the idea of communism is as unattractive as it has been at any time in the past century. But today's ideology bears little resemblance to Marxism. As one Communist Party leader, Chen Yun, has said, "We are the communist party and we will decide what communism is."[9] What remains is an ideology of power dressed up as patriotism in the service of long-term goals.

Xi has already shown that the subversive promise of the internet can be inverted. In the space of five years, with the assistance of big-data science and artificial intelligence, he has bent the internet from an instrument of democratization into a tool of control. The journey to Utopia is still in progress, but to defeat the forces of counterrevolution we must first pass through a cyber-enabled dystopia.

If the audacity of this project is breathtaking, so too are the implications. The challenge for us is that Xi's project of total ideological control does not stop at China's borders. It is packaged to travel with Chinese students, tourists, migrants, and especially money. It flows through the channels of the Chinese-language internet, pushes into the world's major media and cultural spaces, and keeps pace with and even anticipates China's increasingly global interests.

The Rise

In 1979, the significance of Xi Jinping and of China today could not have been imagined outside of China. My own first sight of China, in the fall of 1982, shocked me. I was an acting assistant secretary of commerce accompanying Secretary Malcolm Baldrige on the first-ever U.S. trade mission to China. Vice President George H. W. Bush had been U.S. ambassador to China and was committed to developing a closer U.S. relationship with Beijing. This trade mission was a step toward normalizing the two countries' trade and economic relations.

We flew on Air Force 2, entering Chinese airspace near Shanghai. From there our plane turned right and eventually landed at what passed for Beijing's international airport. To call it an airport, however, was to exaggerate its significance: it was more like the private airstrip near my boyhood home to which I would sometimes ride my bike to watch the Piper Cubs take off and land. Beijing International had one airstrip and an arrival hall that resembled a barn. The limos the Chinese had lined up to drive us into Beijing were copies of the Russian Zils, itself a copy of the 1955 Cadillac. The seats were literally made of wood.

There were no vehicles on the road we took into Beijing. At first I thought the Chinese government had cleared traffic for our motorcade. But as we came closer to Beijing and still saw no traffic aside from bicycles, it began to dawn on me that there simply were no cars or trucks in this country. There were no stoplights, and only one or two buildings higher than five stories. Everyone was riding bicycles and wearing black Mao suits. There was no economy to speak of.

Our discussions were at once highly symbolic and tediously elementary. We were talking real nuts and bolts regarding international trade—trying to determine, for example, how an American company might open an office in Beijing. It was certainly not rocket science, and I did not imagine that I was watching the audition of one of history's great economic miracles.

In fact, by the time I arrived, much of the start-up had already begun. Although China's economic growth in the Mao era had lagged far behind that of Japan and the Asian Tigers, there had been growth. Major investments in human capital had been made in the 1960s and '70s. There had also been substantial investment in manufacturing by state-owned enterprises (SOEs), which accounted for more than three-fourths of all production. But this production had been centrally planned, foreign companies were banned, and imports were limited to commodities that China could not produce itself.

The first step toward liberalization was to enable farmers on collective farms to sell some of their crops in a free market. The dramatic rise in agricultural output that this brought led to further liberalization of farming, and eventually to peasants' being able to determine their own production targets and working hours, and even to their being able to own the farms. Following on the success of the agricultural liberalization, Beijing established four special economic zones to boost exports and to import high-tech products. China had seen the Japanese economic miracle and the rise of the Asian Tigers and had studied these forerunners carefully. The leaders in Beijing fully grasped the significance of export-driven growth and, through the example of Singapore, they also understood the significance of introducing new technology through foreign investment. These special zones were able to offer tax and other incentives to attract foreign investors. For many industries, China's low wage level was also, of course, a major attraction.

While this was proceeding, economic control of various enterprises passed from the central government to provincial and local governments, which were enabled to adopt some free market practices. Citizens were encouraged to start up their own businesses and were granted incentives to do so. One major incentive was that millions of people at this time were losing their jobs, schooling, medical care, and retirement as the government closed or disposed of state-owned enterprises. Import barriers were also removed or reduced, creating more competition from foreign producers in Chinese markets. As the various reforms were analyzed, those that seemed to bring the best performance were gradually extended to the rest of the country. Deng Xiaoping described this process as "crossing the river by feeling the stones."[10]

Throughout the 1980s, the stones seemed to be evenly placed and very smooth—no toes or heels would be bruised. The economy doubled in size every seven years.

A Stumble and Then Recovery from Tiananmen Square

Then came the massacre at Tiananmen Square in June 1989, and the growth rate fell to 4.2 percent, and then to 3.9 percent in 1990.[11] While the intervention of the PLA had saved the Party, it definitely had not saved the economy. But as mourners began to gather to lament the failure of reform, the Party was rescued by a most unexpected troupe of actors—none other than the president of the United States, George H. W. Bush, and the CEOs of many of America's leading corporations. Bush lamented the use of deadly force by the PLA but urged America to "keep open relations with that very important country."[12] He said later that his major objective was to avoid alienating and isolating China. He refused suggestions to bring home the U.S. ambassador and persuaded the Congress not to withdraw its offer of most-favored nation status on trade with the United States. He also sent National Security advisor Brent Scowcroft secretly to Beijing to assure Deng that the United States would maintain diplomatic relations with the PRC even as other countries were reducing the status of their ties. This meant that the United States continued to grant to China the same treatment of its exports to the U.S. market that Washington offered to the United Kingdom, Japan, Germany, France, and other allies. Bush was encouraged in this by CEOs of the Business Roundtable and key members of the U.S. Chamber of Commerce, who feverishly hankered after the Chinese market.

Bush later explained that he had developed a feeling for the "real people of China" during his term as the U.S. ambassador in 1974 and 1975. (How he did this is a bit of a mystery. He neither spoke nor read Mandarin, and as the ambassador he was not in a position to interact with very many average Chinese.) He said he would have taken a much tougher line had it not been for that experience. He probably was more concerned to keep his spy posts on the Soviets. Had he done so, or had the CEOs felt moral qualms about profiting from dealing with a regime that unleashed its private army on the country's students, China's economy surely would have recovered only very slowly and would not today be the world's second largest.

In 1991, GDP growth bounced to 9.2 percent, and to 14.2 percent in 1992. The share of China's national production accounted for by foreign-owned companies grew rapidly, from about 2 percent in 1990 to nearly

30 percent by 1998. This was the result of a rush of foreign investment, largely American, following Bush's line. The share of China's total exports accounted for by foreign-owned companies rose from 10 percent in 1990 to nearly 50 percent in 1998, largely because so many American, European, and Japanese companies outsourced their production to China. Foreign direct investment in China rose from virtually zero in 1990 to $20 billion by 1992 and $40 billion by 1995. One big reason was that wages in China in 1990 averaged only about $50 a month, and they rose slowly, to only $100, by the end of the decade. Corporations also wanted to be early entrants into what they thought would eventually be a gigantic Chinese market. But they were equally interested in cutting their labor costs and circumventing labor unions, environmental restrictions, and liability for any factory mishaps by moving production to China and then, because of favorable U.S. trade treatment for China, exporting back to the United States and other developed-country markets.

Last Tiger and First Dragon

If China had ignored the economic miracles of Japan and the Asian Tigers during the Mao era, it did not neglect to study them after Deng rose to power—particularly Singapore and Japan. Although it was a small city-state rather than a country, Singapore was of special interest for two reasons. Its population was 75 percent of Chinese descent, and it was a one-party state rather than a democracy. It was a much more open and liberal one-party state than China, but it was nevertheless not fully democratic, and while speech was reasonably free, there were limits to what could freely be said in public.

The Japanese model, replicated by South Korea and to a large extent by Taiwan, was quite similar to the Singapore model, but there was a major difference in how Japan handled the entry of foreign direct investment, or FDI. Japan discouraged it. Having lived through a complete occupation by the United States after World War II, the last thing Japan wanted was for its market to be monopolized by giant U.S. corporations. It threw up a slew of barriers to FDI. The government sent word to Japanese companies that they were not to be sold to foreign investors, and corporations were encouraged to develop complex cross-shareholdings that would block foreign investors from gaining control. Little land was available for foreigners to purchase. In some cases, such as that of IBM, Japan badly needed the technology and products a company offered and so made exceptions. But even in those cases, the government required that certain technologies be developed in Japan.

The semiconductor industry was a good example. Texas Instruments wanted to establish a factory in Japan, and Japan at that time needed the technology TI was offering. But Japan's Ministry of International Trade and Industry (MITI) required that TI establish a joint venture with Sony and that Sony have access to TI's technology. Even that was an exception. Fundamentally, Japan did not want foreign companies, and foreign investment played only a minor role in the Japanese economic miracle. It must be remembered that before World War II, Japan had already become a formidable industrial and technological power. It had suffered great wartime destruction, but the human capital, experience, and know-how to recover were there.

Singapore, in contrast, was a truly underdeveloped country in 1965, without significant financial or human capital, indigenous technology capacity, or know-how. It couldn't hope to pull itself up by its own bootstraps. Nor did it have a significant domestic market that would tempt foreign investors, or the power to compel foreign corporations to transfer technologies and production to Singapore. Its strategy was not only to welcome foreign investment but actively to recruit it by offering incentives like long-term tax holidays, free land, government coverage of the cost of training the workforce, and reduced prices for utility services. Singapore sent its emissaries to the United States, Europe, and Japan, offering their corporations a deal they couldn't refuse.

The CCP adopted a hybrid of the two models, but one that was more weighted toward the Singapore model. Because its state of development was more like Singapore's than Japan's, it too decided to welcome and actively recruit foreign investment. Although South Korea had also been dirt poor and without human capital, it had chosen the Japanese path and succeeded. But China listened to Singapore and even had an agreement under which the city-state would operate a free trade zone in Suzhou, China. China also followed Singapore in offering tax holidays, investment incentives, free land, worker training, and reduced utility costs as inducements to attract FDI.

In 1999 I traveled in China with executives of Intel and met with high- and mid-level officials to discuss Intel's plans for China. It was striking that at every meeting, from the top to the bottom of the power pyramid, the Chinese side would inevitably ask, "When are you going to put a factory in China? Don't you realize that you need to maintain a high image in China?" (The phrase "high image" was sometimes code for "transfer technology." In a country without rule of law, it could also be a soft threat, meaning "Don't you realize that bad things could happen if you don't invest here?") That comment was inevitably followed by the question "How much does a semiconductor factory cost?" We would answer, "Around $4–5 billion." (Today it would be twice that or more.) The Chinese would then make their pitch: "Okay, we could give you the land free. No taxes for fifteen years. Utilities at half cost. We could pay for all the worker training and, oh, by the way, we might even be able to make a capital grant of around $1 billion. How does that sound?" In truth, it sounded pretty good. Although Intel's operating costs would be substantially lower in the United States than in China (keep in mind that labor is only 3 to 5 percent of the cost of producing a chip and that Intel's U.S. facilities had very high economies of scale), when you looked at the total financial return, including the cost of capital, and added in the financial incentives being offered, you could make the argument that it would be more profitable to produce in China than in the United States.

Aside from its treatment of foreign investment, the formula for the Chinese miracle resembled that of all the other Asian miracles. It began with the national rate of saving. To develop rapidly, a country must invest rapidly, and investment requires either a lot of domestic savings or a lot of foreign savings entering as FDI. China was trying to attract FDI, but it also aimed for a high domestic savings rate. It had started with a rate of about 32 percent of GDP in 1979, but that was mostly the income of SOEs that was used to fund the government.[13] To invest in infrastructure, it needed to raise the savings rate substantially. How does a country do that?

Simple. Like Germany, Japan, South Korea, Taiwan, and Singapore, China constrained consumption by providing zero consumer credit (forcing consumers to pay in cash), keeping prices of consumer goods relatively high and imposing taxes on those goods, prohibiting any flow of savings or capital out of the country, limiting domestic investment opportunities to a few government-controlled banks that paid virtually no interest on savings accounts, and providing only minimal health care, education, and retirement benefits. With these tools, China drove its national savings rate to about 52 percent of GDP. This is one of the highest rates of national savings ever achieved, roughly equivalent to what the United States did during World War II.[14] (Countries usually have their highest savings rates during wartime. One could call China's rate a wartime savings rate.) Today, the rate has dropped to about 45 percent, but that is still by far the highest of any significant country in the world. With these savings plus the rising flow in FDI, China invested at a higher rate than any country had done since Roman times.

Ports, high-speed rail, highways, airports, telecommunications networks, internet, scientific facilities, and anything else that could be called infrastructure became high-priority investment targets. The Central Government set investment quotas for provincial and local leaders and made life unhappy for any leader who failed to meet the assigned target for new infrastructure creation. As in the other miracle economies, manufacturing was the second major focus of investment. Steel, shipbuilding, textiles, light consumer products, consumer electronics, shoes, machinery, machine tools, forgings, castings, and other industries were high-priority investment targets, with quotas similar to those for infrastructure.

Why manufacturing? Any country, aside from major oil- or raw material–producing countries, that has become rich has done so through manufacturing. This includes the United Kingdom, which led the industrial revolution in the nineteenth century, the United States, all of the EU countries, and Japan. The reason is easy to understand. Manufacturing offers economies of scale. To understand that, let's compare it to agriculture and extractive industries like iron ore or silver.

Farmers plant their best ground first. Here they get high yields from their crops, but as they expand their operations, they inevitably are forced to use land that is not as good as the original land. Thus their yields per acre become less the more they expand. This situation is known as a diseconomy of scale. The bigger you get, the less productive you become. Mining suffers from a similar problem: the deeper one mines, the greater the cost. Of course, one might luck out and find a rich new vein, but one cannot count on that, and the profitability of that too will eventually be eroded by the rising costs involved in deeper mining of progressively less rich ore.

With manufacturing, scale works the opposite way. It takes a big investment to build a factory—say, an auto plant—and such a plant must be manned by a large group of workers. If the plant makes only one auto, that car must pay for the entire cost of building the plant as well as the workers' salaries. If it makes two autos, the burden is essentially cut in half: each car now has to cover half of the capital and labor cost. (Each one still requires its own materials, of course—steel, rubber and so on—so the burden is not quite cut in half.) And if it makes five hundred thousand autos, the cost per auto becomes very low. This is known as an economy of scale. The more of it you make, the less expensive the product becomes and the more people can afford to buy it. Manufacturing is particularly attractive for a poor, developing country because typically that country's wages are quite low. In 1990, when China was paying manufacturing workers approximately $1,000 a year, American factory workers averaged about $20,000 annually.[15] If the workforce in the developing country can be properly trained, the cost of production compared to that in a highly developed country can be much, much lower. And this solves another major problem.

Export-Led Growth

That problem is the lack of demand for the product in the developing country itself. Economies of scale require mass production, but all that production must be sold somewhere, and a poor, developing country doesn't have many buyers. The way around that issue, obviously, is exports. Like post–World War II Germany, Japan, and the Asian Tigers, China strove for what is known as export-led growth. In 1990 its exports totaled about $63 billion. By 2000, this had risen to $249 billion and was one of the three major drivers of China's economic miracle.[16]

One of the ways in which China assured the continuing growth of its exports was by making it a condition of investment in China that a foreign corporation had to export a stated percentage of its China-based production. Thus, if a company like Corning Glass produced $100 million worth of goods in China, it would be required to export perhaps half of that. (It might also be compelled to hire only people stipulated by the Chinese government or to form a partnership with a Chinese company, to which it would be obliged to transfer important technologies.)

A final and very important part of the "catch-up" strategy was education. China poured money into its school and university systems. But because these were initially inadequate (unlike those in postwar Germany and Japan), China also sent hundreds of thousands of students abroad, especially to the United States. Again, this owed much to President George H. W. Bush, who resisted pressure from the U.S. Congress to stop issuing visas to Chinese students. China was enabled to make a great educational leap forward to underpin its technological and economic development.

Joining the WTO

Although Chinese economic growth was strongly driven by American investment throughout the 1990s, by the end of the decade the United States had not given permanent most-favored nation status to China. Instead, each year the U.S. Congress would vote to extend MFN for another year. This was partly because China was not considered to have a true market economy, and partly because of the residue of anti-China feeling in Congress and the U.S. public as a result of the Korean and Cold Wars. Nor had China been admitted as a member of the WTO when the trade organization was founded in 1995. This also stemmed from the notion that China did not yet have a market economy.

But the annual congressional vote had become a hassle. The U.S. corporate commitment to China was so great that everyone knew MFN would be extended each year, and it had become only a convenient coat rack on which to hang other controversial congressional issues. Thus, as the Clinton administration neared its end, the White House entered negotiations with Beijing to grant China permanent MFN. Several other countries were also negotiating with Beijing about admitting China to the WTO, and the Clinton administration combined its MFN negotiation with a WTO negotiation.

The impetus was not only the world's rapidly growing trade with China. A wave of euphoria had washed over the West with the collapse of the

Soviet Union—fittingly enough, on Christmas Day 1991. It seemed that democracy, free market economics, and free trade were on a roll. Francis Fukuyama's best-selling book, *The End of History and the Last Man*, forecast that democracy and free markets would henceforth rule the world forever. President Clinton argued that globalization was Americanization, and it was the future. Moreover, the American and global foreign policy elite was convinced that China was rapidly dismantling its state-owned economy and moving to imitate the United States, the European Union, and Japan. Like Bush Sr., who had winked at Zhu Rongji and said knowingly, "We know what is going on" when Zhu insisted that China was not dismantling all of its SOEs, the entire Western intellectual world was sure it knew better than the CCP leaders what they were really up to. Many foresaw the end of CCP rule itself, possibly in the near future. No one paid attention to Deng's statement that the old Cold War might be over but a new Cold War was beginning. What did he know?

There developed an absolute conviction among the policy makers, pundits, intellectuals, and corporate leaders of the free market world that China could only become like themselves. Globalization would inexorably liberalize and democratize it, the Tiananmen Square incident notwithstanding. So Washington moved to grant China permanent MFN treatment and to back its entry into the WTO.

In retrospect, the WTO negotiation was either one of history's great misunderstandings or one of its great hoaxes. It was presented to the American public and the world as a trade negotiation. The U.S. trade representative, Charlene Barshefsky, talked a lot about tariffs and other trade barriers and made the case to the U.S. Congress and public that getting China into the WTO would do nothing but good for the United States, China, and the world. It was, she said, a win-win-win deal. Sophisticated econometric models proved that U.S. exports to China would soar while Chinese exports to the U.S. would continue growing exactly as they had done over the past ten years.

At the time, the U.S. trade deficit with China was about $83 billion, and a substantial number of U.S. manufacturing jobs had already gone to China as U.S. corporations increasingly took advantage of low Chinese wages.[17] Nevertheless, Barshefsky told the Congress and the American public, China's entry into the WTO would cut the U.S. trade deficit with

China in half. The reason was that China's high tariffs on U.S. imports would be reduced in half, while the already low U.S. tariffs on Chinese imports would stay the same. Thus all the concessions would be from the Chinese side, and the result would be a wave of new U.S. exports to China.[18] Barshefsky was not alone in saying this. She was fully backed by President Clinton, Treasury Secretary Lawrence Summers, and Secretary of State Madeleine Albright.

They do not seem to have discussed matters very deeply with American corporate leaders or with anyone who knew the nuts and bolts of trade with China—or else they conspired with these people to deceive the Congress and the public. For one thing, the Chinese domestic market at the time was not nearly big enough to absorb the wave of U.S. exports they envisioned. But putting that aside, the main fallacy was describing the negotiation as a trade negotiation when it was more of an investment negotiation. By putting China in the WTO and granting it permanent MFN treatment, Washington was giving a green light to American and other global corporations to increase investment in China. The U.S. government was indirectly guaranteeing the corporate world that any offshoring of production to China and consequent import of formerly American-made goods would be perfectly safe. It might as well have hung a sign on the White House saying, "Move to China."

For the evidence, we need look no further than the plain numbers. After a decade of rapid growth, FDI in China leveled off at about $25 billion annually as the WTO negotiation went forward. Then, immediately after China entered the WTO at the end of 2001, the number jumped to about $36 billion.

An important reason for this jump was the terms of China's entry into the WTO. The expectations of WTO membership were clearly set forth in the Marrakesh Declaration on April 15, 1994, in which WTO members declared their commitment to the market-oriented policies. None of the participating countries imagined that any member would adopt state-led economic and trade policies or pursue mercantilism instead of promoting a fairer and more open multilateral trading system. It was expected that each WTO member would work to open world markets on an equal basis to all comers. Regarding China, the other WTO members understood that Beijing was deeply committed to a fundamental shift from state-owned enterprises and central economic guidance to free market competition both domestically and internationally.

The Unexpected

But a funny thing happened along the way to economic Nirvana. Nothing turned out as forecast. Perhaps that should not have been surprising given that the only sure thing in life is the unexpected. In any case, that is what occurred both in international trade and in China's administration of its economy.

Rather than fall, as Barshefsky and the Clinton administration predicted, the U.S. trade deficit with China soared out of sight, rising from $83 billion in 2001 to $103 billion in 2002 and $274 billion in 2010. By 2018 it was over $400 billion. This was the result of both rising exports by Chinese companies and the rush of U.S. corporate investment as American companies moved production to China. U.S. companies cut 5 million jobs in the United States and exported much of their China-based production back to America. Consumers in the United States and elsewhere were pleased with the low prices of Chinese-made goods and the way this helped keep inflation and interest rates under control. But it was a mixed blessing. As the U.S. trade deficit rose, so did China's trade surplus and the displacement of American workers as China very quickly accumulated about $1 trillion of U.S. currency reserves. When Chinese exporters receive dollar-denominated payments, they are required to turn the dollars in to the central bank, which returns renminbi (RMB) to them at a set exchange rate. The central bank and government accumulate the dollars as national reserves, which in effect gives the CCP an enormous load of dollars at its disposal. This is unlike the situation in most other countries, where exporters who earn dollars may invest or exchange them as they please. China is still a developing country, but the CCP is by far the richest political party in the world.

It was China's investment of these dollar reserves in U.S. Treasury bills that kept U.S. interest rates down. But low interest rates over a significant time can distort markets and invite skullduggery. In the United States, housing prices soared as people who normally would not qualify for a mortgage were able to qualify because of the very low interest they would initially be required to pay. The resulting housing boom, along with relaxed U.S. regulation and corrupt Wall Street financial practices, led to the sub-prime mortgage crisis that triggered the Great Recession of 2007–9, in which many people lost not only their homes but their life savings. All in all, it is not clear that the trade deal with China was the win-win proposition that had been so confidently promised by U.S. political and corporate leaders. It may have been a net loss for the United States, as well as for much of the rest of the world.

But the really important point for our purposes is that China under the WTO did not proceed as economic and political leaders expected. George H. W. Bush had disbelieved and contradicted Zhu Rongji himself when Zhu tried to explain that China would not change to a fully private industry economy, but it turned out that Zhu knew what he was talking about. The CCP had never intended to privatize the SOEs—fully or even mostly. Rather, as Richard McGregor notes in *The Party*, "the top policy makers in Beijing were largely united over the need to consolidate and strengthen the power of the Party and the state, not let it wither away. The principle that the Party and the state should maintain control of the commanding heights of the economy lived on."[19] Zhu had developed a catchphrase to explain his and the Party's intent: "Grasp the big, let go the small." The less important, peripheral SOEs would be privatized, but not the important ones like big oil or telecommunications. The members of the Western establishment might have been able to kid themselves, but as the decade progressed, the reality increasingly conformed to Zhu's description of what would happen.

State-Owned Enterprises

In 2004, about 70 percent of listed nonfinancial firms in China were SOEs (defined as having 10 percent or more state ownership). By 2012, the share of SOEs had declined to about 50 percent, partly as a result of privatizing the smaller ones and partly because of the rapid growth of truly private shareholder-held companies. But defining what is and is not an SOE is a slippery undertaking. Many of them have some private ownership even though the government remains the biggest shareholder. Some SOEs have established offshore subsidiaries that then do business in China that often is not recorded as SOE business. So it requires a lot of detective work to track the trail of government influence in various markets. The key point, however, is that this influence is very significant, particularly in strategic or "commanding heights" sectors. Today, financial firms remain overwhelmingly SOEs. Among nonfinancial firms, SOEs have fallen to about 30 percent. But this figure obscures the state's overwhelming role in many key industries. For instance, in 2010, 96 percent of firms in the information transmission, computer services, and software sector were either state owned or had substantial state holdings. Electric-generation, gas, and water-supply sectors were 83 percent state owned. Scientific research, technical services, and geological-prospecting sectors were 68 percent state owned, mining 59 percent, construction 56 percent, leasing and business services 54 percent, and manufacturing 20 percent.[20]

In early 2006, the State-Owned Assets Supervision and Administration Commission (SASAC) of the State Council identified several industries as strategic, meaning the state would maintain a major presence. These included defense, electric power and grid, petroleum and petrochemical, telecommunications, coal, civil aviation, and shipping. Separately identified as pillar industries, in which the state would likewise maintain a strong presence, were equipment manufacturing, auto manufacturing, information technology, construction, iron and steel, non-ferrous metals, chemicals, and surveying and design industries.

Tracking the extent of state holdings and influence in the Chinese economy is difficult, tedious, and inexact. Any number can always be questioned. But one thing is very clear: the state has not disappeared and has no plans to do so.

A state-owned, state-held, or closely linked enterprise has many advantages. SOEs get preferred access to bank capital, below-market interest rates on loans from state-owned banks, favorable tax treatment, regulatory policies that create a favorable competitive environment relative to non-SOE firms, and large capital injections when needed. Importantly, they are the main suppliers to the government. SOEs are used to facilitate structural change, acquire technology from foreign firms, and secure raw materials from abroad. It is important to remember that the heads of these companies have dual incentives. They must aim to be profitable, but their futures are determined by the Central Organization Department of the

CCP, and they must therefore be careful to fulfill Party objectives. If they must choose between profits and Party and government objectives, they will focus on the goals of the state and Party. This is contrary to WTO expectations. In 2001, China promised WTO members that the government would not influence, directly or indirectly, the commercial decisions of SOEs. Not only is that not remotely a reality for SOEs, it is not even fully real for private corporations, since every significant corporation has a CCP cell that, under the law, management must listen to (if not necessarily obey). And given China's absence of the rule of law and the many informal ways in which the Party and government can apply pressure, there is no company that would not pay attention to them.

Going Out

Until the turn of the millennium, China's economy was driven by exports and FDI. Its large trade surpluses led to the accumulation of vast U.S. dollar reserves, which were mostly invested in low-paying U.S. Treasury notes. These surpluses caused two problems. First, they were becoming objectionable for several trading partners. Second, while U.S. Treasuries were safe, they paid a much lower return than might be achieved from alternative investments. Another important factor was a growing concern over China's access to food and critical raw materials. In addition, China was now at a point where its drive to reverse the past humiliations led it to wish for recognition as a rising nation of global significance. All these factors led Beijing in 1999 to adopt its "Go Out" policy, under which it encouraged Chinese corporations to invest abroad. The SOEs were designated to lead these efforts by establishing overseas offices and acquiring foreign properties and corporations. Here was a good example of the peculiar advantages of SOEs. On a purely financial basis, establishing overseas operations or making acquisitions abroad was not necessarily the investment opportunity that would yield the largest or quickest return to shareholders. A publicly traded company would not do this, or at least not much of this. But the SOEs could be counted upon to respond to Party and government guidance to make "strategic investments."

Starting in the 1999–2000 time period, over the next six years, China's outbound FDI grew from approximately $1 billion a year to about $18 billion a year in 2006. Interestingly, OECD recipient countries of FDI from China during those years reported that based on their own accounting, these numbers were actually—on average—about 40 percent higher than those reported by the Chinese.[21] This included investments in oil exploration, infrastructure construction, and agriculture in Nigeria; oil-related infrastructure in Sudan; textiles, tourism, electricity generation, and construction in Laos; biotechnology in Denmark; aeronautics in France; raw materials in Australia and much of Africa; and significantly more. In its eleventh Five-Year Plan (2006–10), the government encouraged companies to "go further outwards." This was partly an attempt to guide surplus capital away from speculative domestic investment and partly to ease upward pressure on the exchange rate of the RMB. The National Development and Reform Commission developed a list of overseas natural resources and technology that it wanted Chinese companies to target. The result was that China's outbound overseas direct investment to non-financial sectors totaled $216.6 billion in the 2006–10 period.[22] Lenovo acquired IBM's PC business, Beijing Automotive Industry Company (an SOE) acquired Sweden's Saab Motors, and Geely acquired Volvo from Ford. That was just a beginning.

By the end of 2010, China's Ministry of Commerce announced that more than thirteen thousand Chinese investors had created sixteen thousand enterprises in 178 countries or regions. Their total assets topped $1.5 trillion and employed 1.1 million workers.[23] By 2015, China's outbound investment of about $130–140 billion topped the roughly $125 billion of foreign investment into China.[24] In 2016 alone, China invested over $45 billion just in the United States.[25]

One Belt One Road

I have already remarked that Xi Jinping is a princeling whose father worked closely with Mao and who, despite his father's demotion to living in a cave in a very primitive part of China, grew up to be a true believer in the CCP faith. His ambition, for both himself and China, is immense. Soon after his election as general secretary of the CCP in November 2012, during a high-profile tour of the National Museum of China, he began speaking of the Chinese Dream and the Great Rejuvenation of the Chinese

People. He even set a target date of 2049—the one hundredth anniversary of the establishment of the People's Republic of China—for realizing that dream. His message evokes the reemergence of China as the new Middle Kingdom and perhaps his own elevation to a status rivaling or surpassing that of Mao.

In speeches in Kazakhstan in September 2013 and to the Parliament of Indonesia a month later, Xi announced a huge step toward realization of the dream. He initially called it the One Belt One Road project, explaining it in terms that suggested a kind of reverse Marco Polo expedition. His Belt would be a reconstruction of the old overland Silk Road that Polo followed, and his Road would be a reinstitution of the ancient Maritime Silk Road used by Middle Eastern traders. In ancient times and into Polo's fourteenth century, traders had come via both routes to acquire China's tea, silk, porcelain, and other riches, and carry them home. Now Xi was proposing to rebuild these routes to carry the modern riches of China to Europe and the Middle East. By 2017, the original vision had been expanded to include Latin America, Africa, and most of the rest of the world.

This was grandiose and audacious enough, but it got even better. China, said Xi, would finance the whole thing, or at least most of it. It would do so without insisting that partner countries have any particular kind of government, without embarrassing questions about corruption or treatment of minorities, and without niggling over the details of financing arrangements, as would be the case for projects financed by the World Bank, the Asian Development Bank, or other entities established by the United States and the Western countries. It was like a new Marshall Plan, but rather than being aimed at rebuilding Europe after the Second World War, it was aimed at rebuilding—or building—most of the world, and for many participants it looked as if it might be close to free. For Hungary and Serbia, for instance, China agreed to build a high-speed rail line from Budapest to Belgrade and to provide a loan to finance the project. Of course, Serbia and Hungary eventually would have to pay China back, but once operating the project would produce the revenue necessary to repay the loan, and all sides would be happy.

One has to admire Xi for the brilliance of this concept. (Actually, the author was Wang Jisi, dean of the School of International Studies at Peking University and also a professor at the Central Party School.) It broke no international rules, attacked no one, and alienated no one while attracting bevies of supporters and partners. At a stroke it made China into a major world power whose influence in some ways surpassed that of the United States. Rather than becoming a "responsible stakeholder in the global order" (essentially the Western global order promulgated by the United States), as proposed by former World Bank president Robert Zoellick, China was stepping out to establish its own Middle Kingdom order. Moreover, it was doing so by finding a potentially more profitable way, and certainly a more strategic way, to invest its vast dollar reserves than putting them in U.S. Treasury notes. In theory, at least, the project would not only cost China nothing at the end of the day, it would earn interest and profits for China greater than that on Treasury bills. And here is where the SOEs came to the fore.

Buying the essentially bankrupt Greek port of Piraeus is not something a purely privately held corporation might find attractive unless it had a huge taste for risk. But for a state-owned or state-held enterprise that will always have state resources available to bail it out if needed, such a deal could be attractive. On one hand, it could perhaps be made profitable by a company that really knew how to run a port and would bring lots of Chinese state-owned shipping companies to provide new business. On the other hand, being state-owned meant that management didn't have to top the league in earnings if the government considered the investment strategically positive.

Strategically, of course, this deal took advantage of Greece's financial weakness and its difficult relationship with the European Union, especially with Germany. By buying the port, China could sow division within the EU and draw Greece toward its side as an ally. It could weaken the Western alliance while also making some money. Greece might also win by having the port upgraded and patronized by Chinese shipping and by earning some of the money it needed to pay back the usurious German banks. This example illustrates another important point: as China's own infrastructure has become built out and its economic growth has slowed, it has many industries with excess production capacity. OBOR is a way to soak that up.

To date, China has put about $300 billion into OBOR. (This is a bit less than China's annual trade surplus with the United States. Perhaps we should say that the United States has put up $300 billion.) The list of projects and participants is much too large to review in detail here. While it is difficult to know for sure, it appears that more than 140 countries are part of OBOR in one way or another. The following are some examples of the reach and significance of the program.

At least twenty-four African countries have contracted to have Chinese companies (primarily SOEs) build them new projects, mostly hydroelectric power plants. Zambia is the largest participant, followed by Nigeria, Angola, Uganda, Côte d'Ivoire, and others. China is building a trans-Africa highway from Dakar to Djibouti as well as rehabilitating the Dakar-Bamako rail line. A China-funded special economic zone (SEZ) outside Dakar enables Chinese industry to manufacture in the SEZ and export to the United States and Europe through Senegal, which is a member of the African Growth and Opportunity Act (AGOA).

Doraleh, a multipurpose port in Djibouti, is partially owned by a Hong Kong–based subsidiary of the Chinese state-owned conglomerate China Merchants Group. In 2017, when the Chinese-built Djibouti-Ethiopia railway was inaugurated, the *South China Morning Post* called it "an important step toward increasing China's influence in the region."[26] Shortly thereafter, the Chinese Defense Ministry opened a naval logistics center in Djibouti, a few miles from U.S. Camp Lemonnier. Ethiopia, meanwhile, was "gifted" a headquarters building for the African Union. It was outfitted with Huawei servers. In 2018, local engineers said these servers had transferred huge batches of sensitive data to China every night for years, supplementing the listening devices found in the walls of the facility. The African Union was compelled to replace its servers and install new security equipment. It turned down an offer from Huawei to help it reconfigure.[27]

In Europe, Chinese companies (mostly SOEs) own 9.5 percent of London's Heathrow Airport, 49.99 percent of Toulouse Airport, 82.5 percent of Frankfurt's Hahn Airport, and 100 percent of some airports in Albania and Slovenia. In addition, China's Bankers Petroleum has full rights to develop Europe's largest and second-largest onshore oil fields, in Albania.[28] Every week, thirty Chinese trains arrive in Duisburg, Germany's inland port, where the train tracks run to the edge of the Rhine River and goods are loaded directly onto boats for further distribution around Europe. This is becoming Europe's central logistics hub, aided by billions of dollars in

Chinese subsidies.[29] Chinese SOEs have also invested billions in Portugal, where they own the previously state-owned power grid operator REN, the largest insurance company, and several hospitals and banks. Portugal was in economic difficulty, with huge national debt, and China found the opportunity to help it by making strategic investments that European states and companies (especially Germany and German companies) wouldn't.[30] This again is where an SOE has enormous strategic advantages.

Between 2008 and 2019, Chinese state-owned and private companies made about 678 deals, valued at about $255 billion, in thirteen European countries. About 360 companies have been completely taken over, including the Italian tire maker Pirelli, the Irish aircraft-leasing company Avolon, and thirteen professional soccer teams. London has been a focal point of the buying spree: Chinese companies have bought a dozen office towers in the City of London and Canary Wharf financial districts.[31]

Ports are a favorite target of Chinese SOEs. They own some share of the following ports in Europe: Piraeus, Zeebrugge (Belgium), Valencia (Spain), Dunkirk (France), Genoa (Italy), Bilbao (Spain), Rotterdam (Netherlands), Le Havre (France), Marseilles (France), Nantes (France), and Antwerp (Belgium).

After having started as a rejuvenation of the old Silk Road, OBOR became so popular that it has now gone global. Latin America is a good example. With the recent addition of Peru, there are now nineteen Latin American and Caribbean countries involved in the project, a level of economic involvement not seen since the days of the old Manila galleons, which sailed from China to Manila to Acapulco from the sixteenth to nineteenth centuries. Chinese investment in Latin America in 2017 alone hit $115 billion, and Xi is predicting it will reach $250 billion by 2025. Brazil and Argentina have been the biggest investment targets, but let's look at Panama, a country in which the United States has a very substantial interest. In 2017, a Chinese-Dutch consortium won the contract to build a new cruise port on Perico Island, at the Pacific entrance to the Panama Canal. In 2018, a Chinese consortium won the contract to build a fourth bridge over the canal, with two rail lanes and six for autos. China Landbridge (not an SOE) is developing a new container port at Colon, near the canal's Atlantic entrance, and there are reports that the Chinese government is considering constructing a high-speed rail line to connect

Panama's two major west coast hubs, Panama City and Chiriqui province. If it is completed, riders will be able to travel between Panama City and David in just two and a half hours.[32]

Brics Bank–Asian Infrastructure Investment Bank

While pursuing these and many other overseas projects, China has also busily promoted the development of new institutions for infrastructure investment.

At the turn of the twenty-first century, economic growth was particularly robust in Brazil, Russia, India, China, and South Africa. As a marketing scheme, Jim O'Neil, asset management chairman of Goldman Sachs, coined the acronym BRICS, pronounced "bricks," by taking the first letter of each country's name. The acronym caught on. It caught on so well, in fact, that it led to a new financial architecture, complete with annual summit meetings, global policy recommendations and warnings, and a new bank. At the 2009 Bric Summit (without an "s" because South Africa had not yet joined) at Yekaterinburg, Russia, the Bric countries called for a new global reserve currency to replace the U.S. dollar.

In June 2012, the BRICS (South Africa joined in 2010) jointly pledged $75 billion to boost the lending power of the International Monetary Fund (IMF), conditional on IMF voting reforms. When these did not materialize right away, in 2013 the BRICS agreed to create a new financial institution to rival the IMF and World Bank by 2014. But discussions proved difficult. China, the holder of the world's largest foreign currency reserves, was asked to provide the bulk of the funds—$41 billion out of $100 billion. In return, it wanted to have the biggest managing role, and it wanted the bank to be in China. No deal was reached until mid-2014. Over the weekend of July 13, when the final game of the FIFA World Cup was held in Brazil, the new Brics bank was announced with capital of $50 billion, along with a Brics Monetary Fund with $100 billion at its disposal. The bank was headquartered in Shanghai.

For China, however, this was small beer, hardly an appropriate vehicle for a rising superpower. Beijing had been working on a more ambitious project since the 2009 Boao Forum (China's answer to the World Economic Forum's annual meeting in Davos, Switzerland). The initial stimulus was to find a better use for China's foreign currency reserves in the wake of the global economic crisis of 2007–9. Then, during a state visit to Indonesia in October 2013, Xi told his hosts that China was frustrated by the slow pace of reforms at the IMF, World Bank, and Asian Development Bank, which China felt was too dominated by American, European, and Japanese interests. The next spring, Chinese premier Li Keqiang told the Boao Forum that China was ready to move ahead with discussions with relevant parties to establish an Asian Infrastructure and Investment Bank (AIIB).

The Asian Development Bank itself had forecast how much funding would be necessary for infrastructure development in the region between 2010 and 2020. China had initially proposed capitalization of $50 billion, but it doubled that in October 2014, when it invited twenty-one countries (itself, Bangladesh, Brunei, Cambodia, India, Kazakhstan, Kuwait, Laos, Malaysia, Mongolia, Myanmar, Nepal, Oman, Pakistan, Philippines, Qatar, Singapore, Sri Lanka, Thailand, Uzbekistan, and Vietnam) to sign a memorandum of understanding to create the bank. Indonesia signed up a month later. Then, in a surprise, the UK's chancellor of the exchequer announced in March 2015 that Britain would also join. The United States was more than hesitant: it had urged other Western countries not to join because, it said, it had reservations about the lending standards the AIIB would adopt. But the British said they were joining to influence those standards. Their decision opened the floodgates. Germany, France, Italy, South Korea. and others quickly followed, and by the time the articles of agreement went into force, on Christmas Day 2015, there were fifty-seven founding members. Santa was being very generous with Xi.

Although the United States has never joined, the bank today has seventy members. Why would China want to be a "responsible stakeholder in the global [Western-dominated] order" when it can so easily establish its own order?

Made in China 2025

At a dinner of the Asia Pacific Economic Cooperation group in Shanghai in 1998, I sat next to a high-ranking Chinese official from the Ministry of Commerce. He explained to me that in the future, China would need to import only raw materials and perhaps some agricultural goods. I was skeptical. Even highly industrialized countries like Japan, the United States, and Germany import large amounts of manufactured goods. When I mentioned this to my tablemate, he replied that "China is a large country with a lot of talent and resources. We will make everything." That forecast turned out to be truer than I could have imagined.

From the beginning of its economic reform, the Party and the Chinese government have pursued industrial policies like those of Japan and South Korea, under which key industries like steel, aluminum, machinery, and solar cells were protected from foreign imports and also received low-interest loans, direct subsidies, and the benefits of an undervalued currency. One result, which has caused huge problems for non-Chinese producers, is excess investment leading to enormous excess production capacity. For instance, China now has enough steel-producing capacity to supply the entire world. If Japan, Europe, and the United States shut their steel industries, China could easily satisfy their domestic demand. This results in Chinese steel being sold below cost on international markets, which creates friction and legal cases with trading partners whose steel industries suffer and may even close.

When this occurs in new, high-tech industries, it can mean that production in countries other than China never gets off the ground. A good example is the solar panel industry. Germany was an early adopter of photovoltaic solar power and one of the first two countries (along with Japan) to install one gigawatt of solar power capacity, in 2004. Making solar panels became a sizeable new German industry, and in the mid-2000s the country was the global leader in solar panel technology and production. Its last producer, Solar World, filed for bankruptcy and halted production in 2017. China had targeted solar panel production, created enormous production capacity through subsidized investment, and dumped its excess production on the world market. The American experience was initially similar to that of Germany, but in 2012 the Obama administration placed a 31 percent tariff on imports of Chinese solar panels, and in 2018 the Trump administration put a 30 percent tariff on all imported equipment.[33] As a result, the U.S. solar panel industry has enjoyed a bit of a rebound, but it remains far smaller than the Chinese industry.

Despite having joined the WTO and having apparently committed itself to open markets and global competition, China continues to put a lot of effort into economic and industrial planning and to promote what it considers key industries. The 2006–20 National Medium- and Long-Term Plan, developed after a Central Committee decision to elevate "indigenous innovation" to a strategic level equal to that of Deng's "reform and opening up" policy, led to laws, policies, and actions aimed at creating Chinese indigenous intellectual property and technology.[34] This only encouraged the constant pressure on foreign corporations investing in China to transfer technology as a condition of approval for their investments, or to take on a Chinese partner as a condition for approval of production in China.

General Electric is a good example. In early 2011, it announced it was moving its entire avionics business into a joint venture in Shanghai with China's state-owned company AVIC. At the time, GE chairman Jeff Immelt was also chairman of President Obama's Commission on Jobs and Competitiveness. Nevertheless, Immelt did not hesitate to move the business from the United States to China even though China had virtually no capability in that industry. Why? Surely the fact that China is a large and growing market for aircraft has something to do with it. So do the government's focus on indigenous technology development, the ample financial support it gives to its SOEs like GE's new partner, and its tendency to buy national.

As a follow-up to the Medium- and Long-Term Plan, the State Council on Accelerating the Cultivation and Development of Strategic Emerging Industries announced in 2010 a plan to accelerate development of seven strategic emerging industries: environmental technologies, next-generation information technology, biotechnology, high-end equipment manufacturing, new energy, new materials, and electric vehicles.[35] Shortly thereafter, the twelfth national Five-Year-Plan for Development of Strategic Emerging Industries set priorities and recommended fiscal and tax policy support. This eventually led to a government listing of companies that would receive aid from the government at various levels. There were no foreign capital companies on the list. Even more notably, the 2014 Integrated Circuit Industry Plan also did not foresee much participation by foreign companies, even though U.S., Korean, Japanese, and European companies are the world leaders in this sphere.

This all led up to the announcement by the State Council in May 2015 of the Made in China 2025 plan, which targeted ten strategic industries for indigenous development and would be led by the Ministry of Industry and Information Technology (MIIT). The industries the plan identified included advanced information technology, automated machine tools and robotics, aviation and spaceflight equipment, maritime engineering equipment and high-tech vessels, advanced rail transit equipment, neighborhood electric vehicles, power equipment, farm machinery, new materials, bio-pharmaceuticals, and advanced medical products.

The Chinese telecommunications giant Huawei, much in the news now because of Washington's opposition to the wide adoption of its 5G technology, provides a good example of what this targeting means. Founded by former PLA officer Ren Zhengfei, Huawei is nominally a private, employee-owned company, although no one has been able to identify all the owners. Its first customer was the PLA, which still accounts for a very large part of its business. It received an enormous $30 billion line of credit from the China Development Bank and gets preferred treatment from Chinese government procurement agencies. It is closely tied to government R&D efforts, receives government support for its research, and has also benefited from the fact that China has walled off its entire internet from outside influence and suppliers. The likes of Amazon, Google, and Facebook having been barred from the Chinese market, their places are taken by Chinese clones such as Baidu, Alibaba, and WeChat—all of which know who is the government's favored supplier of telecommunications gear. Huawei has been involved in placing listening devices and spying equipment in sensitive places and has a reputation for being extremely close to the intelligence agencies of Beijing.[36] It would certainly be a main element and beneficiary of the Made in China 2025 program, to the detriment of foreign competitors.

Thus the plan has sparked an international uproar. The United States, the European Union, Japan, and other free trading countries note that it seems to be anti-globalization and anti–free trade despite China's nominal commitments to global openness. It is partly in response to this plan that the Trump administration has launched an unfair trade action against China and that the European Union has formally named China a "Strategic Competitor." China's actions clearly contradict its words on trade, openness, and globalization. But they are completely consonant with the thinking of leaders who have little interest in being a "responsible stakeholder" in a global system designed by another power and who might entertain a desire for a different system.

The Gun

Sir Walter Raleigh said, "Whosoever commands the sea commands the trade; whosoever commands the trade of the world commands the riches of the world, and consequently the world itself."

Mao made it an iron rule that the Party must firmly command the gun rather than the reverse. But for most of the PRC's history, the country, and hence the Party, could not afford much of a gun. That, of course, is no longer true. China can afford a very large and powerful gun, and its growing investment abroad, shipping, and imports of essential raw materials give it much to protect. It has been rapidly building formidable military capabilities. In 2007, it shot down its own orbiting satellite, demonstrating that, if it wishes, it can wreak havoc on orbiting communications and spy satellites. Through PLA Unit 61398 it has hacked the computer systems of many of the world's top technology and defense companies and stolen designs, blueprints, and specifications for a wide variety of advanced weapons and defense systems. Says forensic investigations and cyber-crime expert Steve Mancini: "Theft of intellectual property has been going on for at least fifteen years. Strategically, China is a country absolutely hellbent on regaining what it thinks is its rightful place as the center of the universe."[37] One interesting example is that of Portland, Oregon–based Elemental Technologies, which became a candidate for possible acquisition by Amazon.com in 2015. It used computer servers designed by Super Micro Computer, Inc., based in San Jose, California. One of the largest server suppliers, it sourced many of its components from China (China makes 75 percent of the world's cell phones and 90 percent of its personal computers.). At one point in the acquisition negotiations, Amazon grew suspicious and hired a third party to take apart some motherboards used by Super Micro. Sure enough, they contained tiny "spy" semiconductor chips the PLA had directed subcontractors to install on the motherboards. *Business Week* magazine eventually found that the computing systems of at least thirty U.S. companies and some parts of the U.S. government, including the U.S. Navy, had these chips. The chips were capable of telling the computer to communicate with some anonymous servers elsewhere on the internet, and could prepare the device's operating system to accept code from the anonymous computers, which could be controlled by the PLA. "China is more than capable of pulling off such a penetration," says Andrew Grotto, who served on the National Security Council in both the Obama and Trump administrations.[38] Similarly, the blueprints of the US C-17, MQ-9 Reaper, F-22 Raptor, and F-35 were hijacked and used by the PLA to develop its own versions of those aircraft.[39] Not only are China's hacking skills first rate, its intelligence gathering is without question the most extensive and best coordinated of any nation. On top of that, Beijing is rapidly building a blue-water navy that has already significantly affected the balance of power in Asia and the Indo-Pacific region without a shot fired.

The conclusion must be that China does not intend to find a niche for itself in the so-called liberal global order; rather, it is bent on setting its own course to great-power status. Indeed, the call from America for China to become a responsible stakeholder in the liberal global order might sound condescending to ears in Beijing. This does not mean that it seeks direct conflict with the free world, but it does mean that it will not easily be deterred by the free world from reaching its goals. It will not seek to establish its own order by war but, following Sun Tzu's advice, it will do so by achieving superior power in key areas such as investment, technology, and dominance of particular areas—in short, through constant pressure and by seeking weak points to be exploited by the Party/state.

It is a formidable strategy.

4

The Threat

Emperor Xi's China is done biding its time.
—*Kevin Rudd, former Australian prime minster*

The overriding question before the world is whether the Chinese Party/state's strategy and vision of the future poses a threat of any kind to other nations that might deserve a cautious or defensive response.

Perhaps the best way to begin answering that question is to ask what the Party/state's fundamental guiding principles are and how it applies them to its own citizens who, after all, make up about 20 percent of the global population. Because the CCP is a communist party of the Leninist-Stalinist tradition, we know that it abhors what much of the world calls "human rights," that it insists on holding in its own hands all levers of power, that it insists on dedication to the Party line of the moment, that it does not brook dissent or freedom of speech, and that it rejects the concept of a rule of law, insisting that, like God, the Party is above any law. Thus, we know that it would be more accurate to call what is presented in China as news and editorial commentary, propaganda. We know that the Chinese internet lies behind its own formidable Great Fire Wall and is heavily censored in order to keep information available to the public in close accord with the prevailing Party line. We know that government surveillance of citizens by means of facial-recognition technology and tracking technology is pervasive. So much so that each individual citizen will soon receive a monthly "social credit" score regarding his or her public behavior.

What is less known but of enormous significance is the fact that the Chinese public is among the most policed and guarded against in the world. Indeed, looking in from outside one could be forgiven the conclusion that the Party sees its own public as its most dangerous enemy. The country spends even more money on internal security than it does on the very rapid military buildup we looked at in the last chapter. In 2017, the budget for Internal Security was about RMB 1.3 trillion (about $197 billion), while that for national defense was just a bit over RMB 1 trillion (about $170 billion). To compare China's internal security spending to what the United States spends on policing and similar activity, we translate China's budget into U.S. dollars at what is known as "purchasing power parity" (what all the things China is doing would cost if they were done in the United States). By this method, China is spending the equivalent of $349 billion, compared to actual U.S. expenditures of $165 billion—more than twice as much.[1]

The reason for this enormous spending on internal security was explained in 2009 by the defector Li Fengzhi, a former Ministry of State Security (MSS) officer, who noted that the MSS's most important mission is "to control the Chinese people to maintain the rule of the Communist Party."[2] At the time, the ministry strove to repress religious groups like Christian churches and Falun Gong (an exercise/spiritual group with millions of members in China), block cultural meetings of all kinds, and censor the internet to prevent the Chinese people from knowing what is happening outside China—or even about events in China that might reflect badly on the CCP.

Since 2009, China's internal security measures have grown exponentially. Enough words and phrases are banned from the internet to fill a dictionary, including: *immortality, go against the tide, unlimited refills, blue-clothed female reporter, great men sent from heaven, slavery, 1984, Winnie the Pooh, shameless, Nobel Prize,* and hundreds of thousands—perhaps even millions—of others. It takes a major effort just to be sure they never appear.

Imagine how hard the censors have to work, and how many are needed, to prevent more than a handful of Chinese in China from knowing anything at all about the nearly 2 million people who demonstrated against the government in Hong Kong beginning in the spring of 2019. Inevitably, some people in Guangzhou or Shenzhen with relatives in Hong Kong may obtain some knowledge. But of the roughly 43 million people living in Shanghai and Beijing, the number who would be aware of the events in Hong Kong (and certainly the number who would be clearly aware) would be amazingly small. It seems to be a security matter of the highest priority for Beijing to keep ordinary Chinese people unaware of any stories but those Zhongnanhai wants them to hear. (Zhongnanhai contains the central offices and residences of all the top CCP leaders. It is equivalent to the White House as the center of authority.)

Moreover, technology like artificial intelligence (AI) is strengthening the authoritarian hand. Many of the nearly 2 million Hong Kong citizens who marched in protest of a proposed government extradition measure had relatives and friends who regularly travel between Hong Kong and Mainland China. There was a well-founded fear that facial-recognition technology was being used to identify them. As noted above, cameras and AI analysis are becoming ubiquitous in China. If citizens are found jay walking, arriving late to work, paying bills late, leaving work a bit early, or committing dozens of other infractions, they will find their social credit score marked down. This could mean anything from a loss of vacation time to loss of job to loss of access to certain schools, hospitals, and other institutions. Even those who have committed no infractions know that they are constantly monitored.

A new development, known as Operation Dove, is the use of flying drones disguised as birds to surveil large areas. So authentic are the drones that they fool real birds, which sometimes join up with the flocks of drones. Another new development is requiring workers to wear helmets that scan their brainwaves for rage, depression, anxiety, and other strong emotions in order to alert bosses to potential problems.

The Party's most intense oversight is inflicted on the Muslim Uighur people in Xinjiang province and on Buddhists in Tibet. These people, especially in Xinjiang, are being herded by the millions into what might best be described as brainwashing camps, where they are not permitted to pray or wear Muslim attire. Men cannot have beards, and women cannot wear headscarves. Nor may they eat their customary food or sing their traditional songs. They are kept under constant observation and are drilled on how to think and act "properly." Officials monitor citizens of Xinjiang to identify other persons to be sent to the camps or investigated, and to keep tabs on those who have been released. The objective is to "transform them into secular citizens who will never challenge the ruling Communist Party."[3] The police in Xinjiang, equipped with smartphones running Android, have a mobile app that lets them monitor "suspicious" behavior such as extended travel abroad or use of unusual amounts of electric power. The app allows police to identify people who have stopped using their smartphones, have started to avoid using the front door when returning to their homes, or have refueled someone else's car.

Not surprisingly, in the face of these enormous efforts to control public debate and even thought, what we in the West call journalism is virtually nonexistent in China.

Zhang Wenmin was once one of China's most powerful journalists. She revealed police brutality, wrongful convictions, and environmental disasters. Now she struggles to be heard. The police intimidate her sources, the authorities close off her social media accounts, and she is living mostly on her savings. "The space for free speech has become so limited," she says. "It's now dangerous to say you are an independent journalist."[4]

Journalists like her once preserved official accountability, exposing scandals like babies sickened by baby formula full of melamine or blood-selling schemes backed by the government. Now the Chinese press has lost all questioning voices. Critics call it the "total censorship era." Xi says the mission of the news media is to spread "positive energy" and "to love the party, protect the party, and serve the party." Says Liu Hu, a reporter from Sichuan who was detained by the police for more than a year after he investigated corrupt politicians, "The government has made its citizens ignorant, the public's eyes are blind, their ears are deaf and their mouths have no words."[5]

National Security

It is from this perception of an everlasting potential threat from its own people that the Party/state addresses the issue of its external national security. More colloquially, one can say that if it is that afraid of its own people, imagine how scared it must be of foreigners whom it can't control.

General Secretary and President Xi Jinping has responded to that question by launching a movement to achieve the Chinese Dream and the Great Rejuvenation of the Chinese People to make the country strong, "for without a strong military, a country can neither be safe nor strong."[6] A fundamental precept of the Chinese state ideology, Marxism-Leninism-Stalinism-Maoism—socialism with Chinese characteristics, is the conviction that socialism is in eternal struggle and conflict with the forces of bourgeois capitalism. We must keep in mind again that the PLA is the army not of China but of the CCP, and its task is to protect the CCP before anything else. Thus, any threat to the Party or the PLA is automatically defined as a threat to the country. That was demonstrated most dramatically at Tiananmen Square on June 4, 1989, and it continues to inform the PLA's organization and strategy. Thus the PLA is responsible, through the People's Armed Police, for maintaining domestic order and tranquility as well as for China's external defense. At the same time, the PLA has grown into a major force as China's rapid economic growth has created both greater interests for the military to protect and much more money to pay for that protection.

Xi Jinping's views of the world situation and of how China must respond were well conveyed in a May 2015 article in *China's Military Strategy:* "There are . . . new threats from hegemonism, power politics, and neo-interventionism. International competition for the redistribution of power, rights, and interests is tending to intensify. Terrorist activities are growing increasingly worrisome. Hotspot issues, such as ethnic, religious, border, and territorial disputes, are complex and volatile. Small-scale wars, conflicts, and crises are recurrent in some regions. Therefore, the world still faces both immediate and potential threats of local wars."[7]

Ever since the U.S. invasion of Iraq in the spring of 2003, the PLA had been urgently seeking to upgrade its war doctrine, equipment, and organization. In late 2015, Xi responded to this situation with far-reaching reforms aimed at making the PLA a leaner, meaner fighting machine that could compete with the U.S. military. Today, with 2.2 million active soldiers and five hundred thousand in reserve, the PLA is already substantially larger than the U.S. military, which has about 1.2 million active-duty personnel and about eight hundred thousand reserves. But what Xi really wanted to do was to modernize the PLA, especially its naval, air force, and other strategic commands.

To this end, the PLA Command units have been changed and shifted, and all but the army are new and rapidly growing. They now include the army; PLAN (naval force), PLAAF (air force), PLA Rocket Force (strategic missiles and space), and PLA Strategic Support Force (cyber intelligence, hacking, and technology acquisition). China's first aircraft carrier, the *Liaoning,* has formally been added to the PLAN fleet; another is afloat but not yet named, while a third is under construction. It is speculated that China will eventually build as many as six aircraft carriers. This would be about half the eventual total number of U.S. carriers, but the PLAN (which also includes the Chinese Coast Guard and Maritime Militia) already has 496 ships plus 232 auxiliary vessels—and more are probably coming—compared to 282 active ships and another 200 in reserve for the U.S. Navy.

On top of this, the PLAAF is building the world's biggest transport airplane and, as noted earlier, it has benefited by hacking and lifting U.S. fighter plane blueprints to turn out state-of-the-art jet fighters closely resembling the U.S. F-16, F-22 Raptor, and the F-35. China also has a full complement of intercontinental ballistic missiles and intermediate-range missiles, and is working on super-fast underwater drones and hypersonic missiles. As I write this, in May 2020 the media are reporting live tests of Chinese anti-ship missiles in the South China Sea. This is clearly a warning to all who transit the South China Sea that they ignore China at their peril. Last but not least, China is in the forefront in developing space warfare weapons, and of course has formidable cyber-warfare tools and skills.

For a long time, China maintained to the world that it would never establish military bases outside its own territories. In early 2015, however, Xi abandoned that policy. His emissaries began negotiating with Somalia to establish a naval base in Djibouti, which was opened and occupied by the PLAN in July 2017. As the *South China Morning Post* reported, "China has taken a decisive step towards establishing a maritime force that can reach across the Indian Ocean." The paper might have added that this force would sit astride the Gulf of Aden near the southern entrance to the Suez Canal. Ostensibly its purpose is to run anti-piracy operations, but, of course, it also observes the shipping of Japan, India, Vietnam, South Korea, and others, some of which expressed concerns, especially given that China is also reported to be increasing its marine corps by 400 percent. The paper further reported that "additional facilities throughout the Indian

Ocean are possible as China seeks to create 'a string of pearls' running from Hong Kong past Sri Lanka and Pakistan to Africa where it has been funneling investment and building infra-structure as part of the maritime component of its belt and road strategy." According to the *South China Morning Post*, further reports put the size of the deployment at ten thousand troops.[8]

In March 1996, then President Clinton ordered two U.S. aircraft carriers to patrol the Taiwan Strait at a moment when Beijing was threatening Taiwan. The PLA at the time had difficulty even finding the carriers, let alone daring to attack them. The danger passed and peace has prevailed. But the situation today is quite different. In various so-called war games or scenario-planning exercises for the region, U.S. forces don't always "win" in the face of the new carrier- and aircraft-killing missiles China has deployed, along with its own carriers, missile-armed surface ships, silent submarines, and submarine-killer torpedoes.

It is important to understand that to "win" in a war in the South China Sea, China does not have to defeat U.S. forces outright. It only needs to be able to make the war so costly that the United States will hesitate to become engaged at all. Some analysts believe China has already achieved that capability. According to the *New York Times*, U.S. admiral Philip S. Davidson, commander of the United States Indo-Pacific Command, testified to the U.S. Senate in March 2018 that "China is now capable of controlling the South China Sea in all scenarios short of war with the United States." Indeed, he described China as a "peer competitor" that is gaining on the United States not by matching it weapon for weapon but by using geography strategically, developing relatively inexpensive anti-ship and anti-aircraft missiles, and using a policy of "fusion" whereby so-called private sector consumer goods makers double as weapons makers by adapting their consumer technology to strategic purposes. In effect, all Chinese corporations might be considered producers of strategic weapons. According to Admiral Davidson, "There is no guarantee that the United States would win a future conflict with China."[9]

In the same vein, Australian global policy analyst Hugh White wrote in the *Guardian* of July 14, 2019, "Australia must prepare itself for the establishment of a Chinese military base in the South Pacific."[10] China has formidable armed forces that will soon be of a world-class order and that may have certain advantages over U.S. forces. White continued, "This requires us to ask what China is likely to do with its military."

Once Claimed, Always Chinese

Of course, China intends its forces to deter any thought of an attack or infringement on Chinese territory, or on anything it defines as a significant interest, such as its global shipping and sources of food, oil, and other essential materials. In addition, however, China has two other priorities. The first is to reunite the pieces of the old Qing Dynasty and resurrect China as a hegemonic power in Asia and perhaps in the world. The second is to displace the liberal world order established by the United States and its allies in the wake of World War II in favor of a global governance more favorable to authoritarian regimes and based on power relationships rather than law and peaceful adjudication.

Beijing began reconstructing the Qing map in 1950 with its invasion of Tibet. That Tibet had not been part of China for most of its history meant nothing to Mao. It had been an independent country from ancient times. It had not been conquered by Genghis Khan or incorporated into the Yuan Dynasty under Kublai Khan. It had become a loose vassal state to the Qing Empire, but whether it was ever fully incorporated into China proper and administered by the Qing government is still debated by some, such as the Dalai Lama. After the fall of the Qing Dynasty, Tibet reverted to complete independence. But the previous existence of a loose tie to the Qing Dynasty and its weak army was all the basis the CCP needed to claim Tibet as an inalienable territory. A revolt in 1959, which caused the Dalai Lama to escape to India, led to a brief war with India in 1962 over conflicting claims for territory joining Tibet and China's Xinjiang province. A truce was declared, but the underlying conflict has not been resolved. There remains significant potential for armed conflict between India and the new PLA.

Xinjiang province was governed by various conquerors over the centuries. It did not become a formal part of China until about 1755, during the Qing Dynasty. After the fall of the Qing Empire, it remained loosely attached to the new Republic of China, but much of it was occupied by the Soviet Union during World War II. With Moscow's backing, it became the East Turkestan Republic in 1944. This lasted until October 1949, when

Mao's armies took Xinjiang's former attachment to the Qing Empire to mean that it was part of China. As a supporter of Mao, Stalin declined to defend the republic against the PLA invasion.

The example of Xinjiang raises interesting questions about Mongolia. It too was part of the Qing Empire, but it declared independence upon the fall of the Qing Dynasty in 1911 and, with help from the Soviet Union, achieved full independence in 1921. It remained essentially part of the Soviet Empire until 1989, when it conducted its own peaceful revolution and established a multiparty system based on a market economy. Beijing was not prepared to go to war with the Soviets in order to integrate Mongolia into the PRC, but Mongolia today is highly dependent economically on China and is significantly penetrated by the CCP. It would not be a total surprise if Beijing one day decided to send in the PLA to fill in the blank spot on the Qing Dynasty map, and if so, it's an open question whether the Russians would dare to intervene. Perhaps Beijing already controls Mongolia to an extent that makes further force unnecessary, but its formal incorporation into China would certainly make the map look better from Zhongnanhai.

The fates of two other territories remain unsettled. Hong Kong was ceded in perpetuity to Britain by the Qing government in 1842, after the First Opium War. Kowloon was ceded, also in perpetuity, in 1860 after the Second Opium War. Then, in 1898, London negotiated a ninety-nine-year lease on the New Territories. Having decided that it would be impossible to maintain Hong Kong and Kowloon independent of the New Territories once the lease ran out in 1997, Britain agreed then to turn Hong Kong completely back to China. However, London negotiated an arrangement first proposed by Deng Xiaoping: a "one country, two systems" model under which Hong Kong would be granted a "high degree" of independence for fifty years. Thus, the Hong Kong Special Administrative Region was created to be an integral part of China but ruled under its own mini-constitution guaranteeing free speech, human rights, and the rule of law (essentially British law in this case) for fifty years until 2047.

It became apparent in 2019 that the people of Hong Kong were increasingly concerned that their system was in danger of being obliterated by Beijing before the fifty years ended. Demonstrations by up to 2 million of Hong Kong's 7 million citizens forced Carrie Lam, Hong Kong's chief executive, to shelve a proposed extradition agreement with Beijing. The demonstrators called for her to step down and for citizens to be able to vote directly for the members of the Hong Kong legislature. It was similar demonstrations that led to Tiananmen Square in 1989. It would have been extremely embarrassing and costly for Xi Jinping and the CCP to unleash the PLA on Hong Kong then, as it once had done on its own students in Beijing, but it was also embarrassing to have 2 million people in Hong Kong demonstrating specifically against the CCP. Indeed, it was more than embarrassing: it undermined the tale of the inevitability of China's rise and thus undercut Beijing's ability to project a positive image internationally.

Indeed, so troubling was Hong Kong's democratic opposition to Beijing that it violated its own fifty-year one country, two systems deal by passing national security legislation that effectively nullified one country, two systems and made Hong Kong into just another Chinese city. This triggered a U.S. response erasing special trade terms that had long been extended to what had been considered a free Hong Kong. As I write at the end of July 2020, the situation is extremely tense as China has also removed the word *peaceful* from its normal formulistic demand for reintegration of Taiwan with Mainland China.

By far the most important territory on the map is Taiwan. For many years there was broad international agreement on the concept of one China, of which Taiwan is a part, but not subject to Beijing authority. This formula emerged from the meetings between President Nixon and Chairman Mao in 1972. It was then not clear whether the United States would defend Taiwan against a military invasion by the CCP. Many observers felt that Nixon and Kissinger might not care so long as there was a "decent interval" before Beijing launched the invasion. But Nixon did not establish formal diplomatic relations with China. That was done by President Jimmy Carter on January 1, 1979. In the wake of this, the U.S. Congress passed the Taiwan Relations Act on April 10, 1979, requiring the United States to ensure Taiwan's ability to defend itself by providing arms and even military support in the event of an attack on the island. The hope was that cross-border trade and investment would gradually lead to peaceful political integration of the two parts of the country. But it has not done so to date.

Instead, Taiwan has developed a robust democracy as well as a prosperous free market economy. While it has deep economic ties with Mainland China, it is drawing further away politically. Even more significantly, an increasing proportion of the population no longer identifies as Chinese but as Taiwanese, with no interest in integrating politically, socially, and culturally with the CCP's China.

This evolution has always been anathema to the Party and is especially contrary to Xi's dream of the "Great Rejuvenation of the Chinese People." Beijing emphatically objects to any action or policy that appears to normalize the effective independence of Taiwan. In the spring of 1996, after Taiwan president Lee Teng-hui visited the United States, Beijing expressed its anger and disagreement by shelling Taiwan from shore-based batteries on the mainland. So large were the barrages that President Clinton sent two aircraft carrier battle groups to the area of the Taiwan Strait. One carrier group sailed through the strait while the other watched at its far end. Yet a third group approached, indicating that it could also help if necessary. The PLA backed off and halted the firing.

But it did not halt installation of new and better missiles, which are now so formidable that it's questionable whether a president today would send a carrier group through the strait. The danger to the U.S. Navy is supplemented by a real blue-water Chinese navy that could engage U.S. warships or perhaps even prevent them from reaching Taiwan.

If he returns Taiwan to full Chinese control, Xi would undoubtedly go down in history as a leader equivalent to or perhaps even more significant than Mao. For a while it looked as if he might succeed. Taiwan's economy has become tightly integrated with the mainland's, with perhaps 750,000 to 1 million Taiwanese living in Mainland China, approximately $150 billion of Taiwanese investment in the mainland, and approximately 40 percent of Taiwan's exports going to the mainland.[11] Moreover, the United Front and the Propaganda Department work overtime to interfere in Taiwanese elections to promote the rise of politicians friendly to Beijing. Ironically, the Kuomintang (the Nationalist Party of Chiang Kaishek that long ruled Taiwan) has evolved into a pro-China party.

But the protests in Hong Kong have deeply affected Taiwan, and Tsai Ing Wen, the pro-independence president of the Republic of China (Taiwan), overwhelmingly won reelection in early 2020 despite strong support from Beijing for her opponent. This is, of course, comforting to most Taiwanese as well as to supporters of democracy everywhere. But it also raises the danger of attack and invasion by the PLA. As I write, PLA Air Force planes are flying over the median line between Taiwan and Mainland China virtually every day. China's navy and naval auxiliaries are also grabbing more reefs and sinking more Philippine, Malaysian, and Indonesian fishing boats. Recognizing that he may not be able to reclaim Taiwan peacefully, Xi might decide to solve the problem once and for all by invading and occupying the island. The probability is not high, but as these recent moves indicate, it cannot be blithely discounted. If there is one place in the world toward which Beijing might aim a major military attack, it is Taiwan which, of course, is highly dependent on the shipping that traverses the South China Sea.

South China Sea

That sea, of course, is precisely what China is now making strenuous efforts to control. For China, it has always been a source of vulnerability to attack, invasion, and blockade. Today, the shipping that goes through the Strait of Malacca near Singapore and then crosses the sea is China's lifeline at least as much as it is Taiwan's. It would be much easier for China to pressure Taiwan if the sea were under strong Chinese control, and it would be virtually impossible for China to emerge as a challenger to U.S. global hegemony as long as the U.S. Navy has free run there. It is thus not surprising to see Beijing making extensive claims and enormous efforts not only to establish control of the key island groups but also to militarize them so as ultimately to be able to force the U.S. Seventh Fleet and other navies out.

The South China Sea carries about a third of the world's shipping and is a major artery for oil and other critical raw materials as well as for the export of manufactured goods from Japan, South Korea, Philippines, Taiwan, Vietnam, Thailand, Malaysia, Cambodia, Indonesia, and of course China itself.[12] Nearly 2 billion people depend on this vital sea-lane, which is shallow and full of islands, islets, and reefs that rise above the waves only at low tide.

In 1959, a briefing note to Australia's Joint Intelligence Committee read, "If, in the longer term, the Communist Chinese were to develop the Spratly islands [reefs and islets in the middle of the South China Sea] militarily, they could make a nuisance out of themselves on the international shipping and air routes on the pretext of infringements of territorial waters and air space and might even shoot down an aircraft occasionally. . . . There is little the West is likely to do, except protest."[13] This barely registered as a worry at the time. For the next half century, the South China Sea was an

American lake, fully under the protection of the U.S. Seventh Fleet and of the Commander in Chief Pacific (CINCPAC) at Pearl Harbor in Hawaii.

But beginning with the rise of Xi Jinping to the positions of Party secretary and president of the nation in 2012, China began casting its eyes on those islands. Never mind that they were nearly two thousand miles from China and much closer to the Philippines, Vietnam, and Malaysia. Beijing justified its attention by pointing to a nine-dash line initially drawn not by the PRC but by the Republic of China in 1946, after it had accepted the Japanese surrender of some of these islands in 1945. The line showed virtually the entire South China Sea as being owned by China. Today, this is one of the few issues on which the government of Taiwan agrees with Beijing.

The line went unnoticed until 2009 when, for economic reasons, Malaysia and Vietnam applied to the United Nations to extend the boundaries of their continental shelves. This induced China to point to the long-ignored dashed line, which encompassed some of the areas Malaysia and Vietnam were requesting. These countries appealed for international support and got a response from U.S. secretary of state Hillary Clinton. She had already been planning the foreign policy shift that later became known as "the Pivot to Asia," and at the ASEAN Summit meeting in Hanoi in July 2010, she declared the South China Sea an area of American national interest, adding that "the US supports a collaborative diplomatic process by all claimants for resolving the various territorial disputes without coercion. We oppose the use or threat of force by any claimant." That was too much for China's foreign minister Yang Jiechi, who responded: "China is a big country and other countries are small countries, and that's just a fact."[14] In the October 2011 issue of *Foreign Policy*, Clinton wrote: "In the next ten years we need to be smart and systematic about where we invest time and energy. One of the most important tasks over the next decade will be to lock in a substantially increased investment—diplomatic, economic, strategic, and otherwise—in the Asia-Pacific region.[15]

A month later, President Barack Obama said to the Australian Parliament: "As we end today's wars, I have directed my national security team to make our presence and missions in the Asia-Pacific a top priority." He added that he was sending approximately fifteen hundred U.S. Marines to be stationed permanently at the northern Australian port of Darwin.[16]

China noticed. It had begun to assert sovereignty in the sea as early as 1988, when it seized Subi Reef, which lies within the continental shelf of the Philippines, and built a radar station there. In 1995 it seized Mischief Reef, which is a low-tide elevation (LTE) within the Philippines Exclusive Economic Zone (EEZ). Although the United States has a mutual security treaty with the Philippines that commits it to defend the island nation, neither President Bush nor President Clinton made any moves or even noises in response.[17] But matters didn't begin to heat up until February 2011, when the Chinese frigate *Dongguan* fired three shots at Philippine fishing boats near Jackson Atoll and ordered them to leave the area. That May, Vietnam claimed that Chinese maritime patrol boats cut the cables of a Vietnamese oil and gas survey ship near the Vietnamese coast (China denied it). In June, another survey ship under contract to Vietnam had its cables cut. Vietnam complained, "China's action is turning the area into disputed territory in order to materialize China's nine-dotted line claim. This is unacceptable."[18]

In April 2012, Philippine navy surveillance aircraft identified Chinese fishing boats around Scarborough Shoal, an island long used for temporary shelter by Philippine fishermen and well within the Philippines' Exclusive Economic Zone. The dispute over who owned the shoal continued until July 18, when Chinese ships placed barriers across the shoal's lagoon, blocking entry by Philippine vessels. Ironically, on July 13, the PLA Navy's notorious missile frigate ran aground on Hasa Hasa Shoal, just sixty nautical miles from the Philippine island of Palawan. In November, China informed the Philippine government that Chinese coast guard vessels would permanently guard Scarborough Shoal. At the suggestion of the United States, in January 2013, Manila filed an arbitration case against China in the UN's Permanent Court of Arbitration, requesting that it settle the dispute. But China refused to recognize the court's jurisdiction. The court proceeded with the case without Chinese cooperation.

While all this maneuvering was occurring, China subjected imports of Philippine bananas and other fruit to long waits for inspection. The fruit rotted on the docks, leading Chinese importers to refuse to pay for it.

At the same time, China was making a major move. As soon as the Scarborough Shoal was closed off, the China State Shipbuilding Industry Corporation published draft blueprints on its website for man-made islands on top of reefs, including drawings of structures that would later appear on some of the Spratly Islands. This website was visible for all to see, yet Washington either missed it or kept quiet.

In May 2013, thirty Chinese fishing vessels along with three Chinese government ships were spotted at Ayungin Shoal, just off the large Philippine island of Palawan. A few days later, a Chinese warship circled a nearby reef occupied by Filipino marines. Manila issued a statement saying it would "defend what is ours."[19]

In September, China launched another subtle trial. It dispatched the dredger *Tianjin* to Cuarteron Reef, where it was plainly visible to U.S. spy satellites and other surveillance. For three weeks, the dredger did nothing—it just floated there enjoying the weather. Satellite images from a bit later showed it at Fiery Cross Reef, again doing nothing. Again, no one in Washington or any other significant capital seemed to notice.

A dredger fragments sediment on the seabed and dumps it on a reef until it creates a low-lying man-made island that rises above the water even at high tide. The *Tianjin* can fragment at a rate of 4,530 cubic meters per hour. This, of course, destroys all sea life within reach and creates a zone that will be completely dead for many years. But China was not really in it for the fish. In December, it sent the *Tianjin* to dredge at Johnson South Reef in the Spratly Islands, near the Philippines, Brunei, and Malaysia and at a critical choke point in the South China Sea. Within four months the *Tianjin* had created eleven hectares of land, along with a harbor while a Chinese warship stood guard. By the summer of 2015, Johnson South had a four-thousand-yard airstrip, two helipads, a radar tower, and ten satellite communications antennas. Xi claimed he had no intention of "militarizing" the islands China had created and occupied in the South China Sea. But it was not entirely clear what he meant by the term *militarize*. What is clear is that despite the UN's finding in favor of the Philippines regarding Scarborough Shoal, China has equipped several other islands the same way as Johnson South. These include Fiery Cross, Mischief Reef, Scarborough Shoal, Woody Island, Triton, Tree Island, Taiping Island, and Amboyna Cay. China's government has suggested that there may be others in the future. American unwillingness or inability to do anything about this has been cited as an important reason why new Philippine president Rodrigo Duterte is developing a closer relationship with China.

Following the White House meeting between Xi and Obama, Ambassador Yang Jiechi said that "navigation in the South China Sea is guaranteed."[20] But a careful listener could be forgiven for thinking he had said: "Hillary, didn't I tell you that China is a big country and these others are small?"

Wholly without firing a shot, China has established an iron grip on the South China Sea that cannot be loosened short of a major military conflict between China and the United States—in which these reefs would be instantly blown away. But neither China nor the United States wants such a conflict, so for all practical purposes the South China Sea has become a Chinese lake. Indeed, China's new embassy in Kiribiti may be a harbinger for the South Pacific, Indian Ocean, and other places that become important for Beijing.

In the South China Sea itself, what had been tiny outposts with little combat power were now giant bases with air stations capable of handling both fighters and bombers. Missiles able to sink warships and shoot down aircraft hundreds of miles away had been installed. Since this was far more firepower than was needed to fend off the Philippines, Indonesia, Vietnam, or Malaysia, it could only be aimed at altering the balance of power with the United States. If that was not completely obvious in 2017, it became undeniable in 2019, when China tested its medium-range and anti-ship missiles over the South China Sea, warning all ships to avoid the areas of the test. Admiral Davidson told the U.S. Congress on February 12, 2019, "China is now capable of controlling the South China Sea in all scenarios short of war with the United States."[21]

This evolution has enormous implications. It takes China a long, long step toward cementing a position of hegemony in East and Southeast Asia. It tells all the region's nations that they can best get along by going along with China. It tells the world that the more than $5 trillion of shipping that annually crosses the South China Sea is essentially under Chinese control.[22] It makes U.S. allies wonder if the United States can defend the first island chain (consisting of Japan, the Senkaku Islands, Taiwan, and the Philippines) it has long defined as its forward position of defense in the Pacific. Perhaps most significant are the implications for Japan.

Japan and the Senkaku Islands

Stretching northeast from Taiwan and just below the Ryukyu island chain that runs south from Okinawa, the uninhabited Senkaku (Diaoyu in Mandarin) Islands are administered by Japan but have long been a point of dispute between Tokyo and Beijing. They had been considered Chinese in the eighteenth century, but Japan took them in 1895 along with Taiwan as a result of the Sino-Japan war at that time. During the U.S. post–World War II occupation of Japan, the islands were administered by the United States as part of Okinawa. After the United States returned Okinawa to Japan in 1972, the islands automatically came under Japanese administration along with Okinawa. But China asserted a claim over the uninhabited territory (really just a few rocks in the ocean) that was left in abeyance in 1978 negotiations between Chinese premier Zhou Enlai and Japanese prime minister Tanaka Kakuei over normalizing relations between the two countries. Zhou apparently didn't want to deal with this issue at the time and suggested it be tabled. During his 1978 visit to Tokyo, Deng said that "at the time of diplomatic normalization both sides agreed not to touch this issue," and he suggested that perhaps the next generation of the countries' leaders would be "wise enough to find a mutually satisfactory solution."[23] But neither Japanese leaders nor Chinese have proven wise to date.

Reports of the potential presence of oil and gas under the waters around the islands began circulating around the time Okinawa reverted to Japan. But the issue remained quiet until 2012, when the flamboyant right-wing mayor of Tokyo, Ishihara Shintaro, threatened to buy the islands from their Japanese owner and develop them. To head this off, the Japanese government itself bought the islands, but that looked to Beijing like a conspiracy by Tokyo to gain control of whatever oil and gas were there. Soon, Chinese fishing boats and coast guard cutters were swarming around these islands as they were around the Paracels and Spratlys. Approaching Chinese aircraft caused repeated scrambles by the Japanese Air Self-Defense forces to defend the Senkakus' air space. The arrest by the Japanese of a Chinese ship captain whose boat was cornered in Japan's territorial waters only exacerbated the issue. Both Tokyo and Washington saw a Chinese invasion and seizure of the islands as a real threat, the more so because the U.S. position was fuzzy. Washington said it took no side regarding ultimate ownership and wished only for a peacefully negotiated settlement between the two countries. This left it unclear whether Washington considered the islands to fall under the coverage of the U.S.-Japan Mutual Security Treaty. Some thought American ambiguity spurred the Chinese harassment of the islands. Thus, during his 2014 visit to Japan, President Obama stated explicitly and loudly that the islands do fall under the treaty's jurisdiction and are under the U.S. nuclear umbrella.

Since then, Chinese activity around the islands has declined, but there has been no formal agreement between China and either Washington or Tokyo regarding the disposition of the territory. Armed conflict between China and Japan and the United States over these rocks remains a real possibility. The rapidly increasing power of the PLAN only adds to the danger. Despite Obama's statement, a lurking question remains: will the United States really go to war with China over a few rocks that might have a bit of oil and gas around them?

Behind all this is a much more vital issue. Japan imposed enormous humiliation on China when it seized Taiwan and other territories in the late nineteenth century, in the wake of World War I, and when it invaded and occupied large parts of China in the 1930s. Beijing has not forgotten. In 2012, when the Senkakus issue was hot, mass riots against Japan were organized in China, and Japanese-owned businesses and factories were attacked. Whenever a high-ranking Japanese official visits Tokyo's Yasukuni Shrine (this Shinto religious shrine for the souls of all Japanese soldiers who died in battle has come to symbolize extreme Japanese nationalism), there are dark words from Beijing and danger of a new outbreak of anti-Japanese riots.

Virtually all of Japan's vital materials—oil, iron ore, coal, and other goods—pass through the Straits of Malacca at Singapore and then through the South China Sea before reaching Japan. With its increasing chokehold on the South China Sea and its enormous economic leverage on many of the countries bordering the sea, China might be able to blockade Japan and ultimately to starve it. Given that the United States is committed to defend Japan, a full blockade is not going to occur just yet. But with President Trump asking why America is responsible for Japan's defense seventy-five years after the end of World War II, Japan spending only 1 percent of GDP on its own defense, and China's naval power expanding exponentially, the situation looks increasingly unstable. The potential for Chinese harassment of Japanese shipping is significant, and such action could lead to military conflict between China and Japan, which almost inevitably would involve the United States.

South Korea and Vietnam

What holds for Japan holds also for South Korea and Vietnam. Along with Tibet and India, they hold the distinction of being countries China has invaded since World War II. Beijing intervened in the Korean

War in 1950, seized control of the Paracel Islands from Vietnam in 1974, and invaded Vietnam itself in 1979. Given continuing tensions between these parties, further military action cannot be ruled out. And since the United States also guarantees South Korea's defense, there is always potential for open hostilities between China and the United States over Korean issues. While the likelihood of open warfare in any of these places in the near future is low, we need to keep in mind that it has happened before.

Russia

China and Russia are joint members of the Shanghai Cooperation Organization and recently have been quite friendly. During a June 2019 meeting in Moscow, Xi said that "in the past six years, we have met nearly 30 times. Russia is the country I have visited the most times, and President Putin is my best friend and colleague." Putin responded in kind, saying that ties between Russia and China stood at "an unprecedented level."[24]

Historically, however, these countries are ancient opponents. They may be somewhat united now against American pressure on both of their systems. But while China has the world's largest population, 1.4 billion people, Russia has only a rapidly aging 143 million. China has few natural resources while Russia is full of them. Russian Siberia lies on China's northern border and is populated by only 36 million people—and much of it was ruled by China at one time. As China's power grows and as global warming makes Siberia more hospitable, it would not be surprising to see Beijing taking an interest in the area. Indeed, why is it even now building new icebreaker ships?

India

China and India have two long-running border disputes that are intensifying as I write now in July 2020. Aksai Chin lies between Jammu-Kashmir and Xinjiang. Both countries claim it, and they fought over it in 1962 and are now doing so again. The Indian province of Arunachal Pradesh near Sikkim was also fought over in 1962. The dispute was resolved in 1996 on the basis of an agreed Line of Actual Control. But in 2006 the Chinese ambassador to India claimed all of it as Chinese territory, and China engaged in a military buildup in the area, leading to incursions by both countries' armies.

In 2009 India deployed additional forces, and in 2014 it called on China to adopt a "One India" policy to resolve the issue. Not only has it not done so, but on May 5, 2020, fighting again broke out at Pangong So Lake at about fourteen thousand feet in the Himalayas. As I write, India and China are both saying the conflict can be resolved through negotiation. But, for the moment, it remains unresolved and could easily lead to a much larger military conflict.

The United States and Europe

At present, China is extremely unlikely to take military action against any territory or holding of the United States. Nor is it likely to attack any country in Europe, where it is striving to build a new Silk Road. But the United States could become involved in hostilities with China through its military alliances with Japan, South Korea, Taiwan, and the Philippines. This may at some point raise the issue of whether Washington wants to revise or even cancel those commitments or whether some of the allies might want a change. Manila has already indicated that it will withdraw from the Visiting Forces Agreement it has with the United States. There is also a question as to what extent the United States wants to be obliged to send American young people in harm's way to defend countries that do little to protect themselves or, like Japan, even have constitutional obstacles to defending themselves.

Australia

As China's major supplier of iron ore, coal, and other raw materials as well as a major destination for Chinese tourists and students, Australia might not appear to be in danger of military conflict with China. But it is.

Australia is doubling the size of its naval fleet and buying 72 F-35A strike fighters from the United States. It has also been participating in the so-called freedom of navigation voyages that the U.S., British, and French navies carry out in the South China Sea. Australian officials have spent the past year beefing up ties with such countries as the Solomon Islands (the scene of intense Allied battles with Japan in World War II), Papua New Guinea, Vanuatu, Fiji, and Tonga. Australia has even promised the Solomons a $175 million infrastructure investment program.

Why?

Because Australia senses and fears that China is beginning to do in the South Pacific what it has already done in the South China Sea. Indeed, it is more than a fear. China is already building ports in Papua New Guinea and increasing surveillance of Manus Island, where the United States and Australia are attempting to develop a naval base.[25] As Australia's Strategic Policy Institute (ASPI) notes, there are "four key similarities between the South Pacific and the South China Sea: both contain significant resources; both are dotted by uninhabited atolls that are close to undersea cables; both contain a number of critical maritime chokepoints (for example, those through Melanesia's Bismarck Archipelago); and both regions count China as their largest trading partner." These similarities clearly present a temptation to Beijing. Its Institute of Marine Geology has already found polymetallic and cobalt nodules around Kiribati, the Cook Islands, and New Caledonia, as well as sulfide deposits in the Bismarck Sea. ASPI notes that "China's history of using resource-extraction platforms as 'mobile national territory' mean similar seafloor mining projects warrant close attention from a dual use point of view."[26]

The ASPI report goes on to note that "other dual-use assets are also at work in the South Pacific. Reports seen by the ABC [Australian Broadcasting Corporation] show that two ships from China's 'Distant Ocean Research Fleet' have been collecting bathymetric data in waters between Manus Island and Guam, which 'helps determine the acoustic conditions for submarine operations.' At least one of these ships, *Haice 3301*, was formerly known as *China Marine Surveillance 83* and played a leading role in China's expansion into the South China Sea. China's fishing fleet, which doubles as a maritime militia, is also moving further into the Pacific. The PLA is known to disguise surveillance ships as fishing vessels."[27]

Thus Australia faces the real possibility of conflict with China—and so, as Australia's treaty ally, does the United States.

Devastation

Beyond direct conflict, there is an imminent threat of the devastation of many of China's neighbors, such as Laos, Thailand, Cambodia, Myanmar, and Vietnam, by its infrastructure-building projects along the Mekong River. As the *New York Times* reported on April 14,

2020, February 2020 saw the Mekong at its lowest ever levels in Laos, threatening farmers, fishermen, and drinking water supplies. At the same time, U.S. climatologists showed that in China near the Tibetan plateau from which the Mekong springs there was no such shortage. Rather, Beijing's engineers directly caused the record low water levels in Laos by artificially limiting the river's flow. "The satellite data don't lie, and there was plenty of water in the Tibetan plateau, even as countries like Cambodia and Thailand were under extreme duress," said Alan Basist, cowriter of a report for Eyes on Earth, a water resources–monitoring organization. "There was just a huge volume of water that was being held back in China."[28]

In the dry season, the Mekong provides 70 percent of the downstream water. If its flow is blocked or even slightly reduced, the impact on the hundreds of millions of people who live along the river is deadly. According to Brian Eyler, director of the Stimson Center's Southeast Asia program and author of the book *Last Days of the Mighty Mekong,* "The problem is that the Chinese elite see water as something for their use, not as a shared commodity." Adds Chainarong Setthachua, a lecturer at Mahasarakham University, "This is part of China's business development. The lay people who depend on the resources of the Mekong for their livelihoods and income are automatically excluded."[29]

Nor is it only the Mekong that is being affected. Other rivers like the Brahma-putra, which is holy to Indians, Indus, and Salween, are also increasingly being affected.

Coercion

Although not alien to China, straight-out armed conflict is not the country's favorite tool. Beijing recalls Sun Tzu's advice: the optimal policy is to conquer the opponent without fighting. China therefore prefers coercion to war. Its history and the ultimate coordination of virtually every aspect of Chinese life by the CCP make it far and away the world champion in using this technique, and many leaders around the world know it.

They certainly know it in Manila, as we saw with the bananas left to rot on the docks of Shanghai in retaliation against Philippine complaints over Chinese occupation of what Filipinos (and the rest of the world) had long considered Philippine territory. They also know it in Singapore, where I recently met with several high-ranking leaders who told me they are in a difficult position. They don't like that China has grabbed control of the South China Sea. They know their country is small, and they know how Minister Yang and other Chinese feel about small countries. They want the U.S. Seventh Fleet to keep patrolling the area and for America to stay engaged in the region. But they emphasized that they must be careful of what they say and how they act. Singapore's economy is fundamentally built on exports, and its biggest export is tourism: visitors pay airfares, hotel bills, and local restaurant tabs with dollars or foreign exchange that is easily turned into dollars. Most tourists coming to Singapore these days (before the coronavirus) are from China. Now here is the key element. Unlike most other countries, the Chinese government and the CCP can control where their citizens go. If the CCP Party/state is unhappy with Singapore, Chinese tourists can be directed to go to Australia, Thailand, or anywhere except Singapore. To use the language of my Singaporean friends, China can "weaponize" tourism.

Another of Singapore's major exports is education. Thousands of Chinese students come to Singapore for university study each year. That too can be weaponized. If they don't come, the universities lose tuition fees and might even have to reduce the number of their faculty. In other words, what my Singaporean interlocutors were saying was that virtually any economic tie with China can be turned by Beijing into a tool for gaining policy influence—without an open declaration or directive.

I heard the same story in Australia. There I met with the head of one of Australia's major banks who didn't even trouble himself to explain weaponization to me. He assumed I already understood the dynamic. I asked myself, what if the shoe were on the other foot? What if it were the U.S. or Japan or Germany that was the importer of the coal and iron ore and the source of the students and tourists? Would I be hearing the same story? Of course not. Those countries are all democracies operating under a rule of law. They would not be able to weaponize their students, imports, and tourists. Only China can do that, because of the pervasive power and influence of the CCP.

In 2019, as if to prove my banking friend correct, changes in Australian law aimed at restricting foreign interference in Australian politics and public life were followed by a sudden reduction in Chinese imports of Australian coal.[30] China-bound coal exports fell 19 percent that January, as China suddenly delayed customs clearance procedures by up to forty days. The China Coal Transport & Distribution Association said that traders and power plants in China had been avoiding purchases of Australian coal. China claimed the longer inspection time was due to increased enforcement of environmental standards, but it declined to say if coal imports from countries other than Australia were subject to the same scrutiny. The message was heard loud and clear.

In the small Pacific island nation of Palau, the hotel rooms and tour boats normally full of Chinese were suddenly empty in the summer of 2018. Palau diplomatically recognizes the Republic of China on Taiwan rather than the People's Republic of China in Beijing. This had never before been a problem for tourists. In 2017, half of Palau's roughly 120,000 tourists had come from Mainland China, and Mainland Chinese companies had avidly bought hotels, beachfronts, and other property there. But now Beijing really wanted Palau to switch its diplomatic recognition to itself and away from Taiwan. Some in Palau think a carefully orchestrated strategy was at work. Says one hotel owner: "Some believe that the dollars were allowed to flow in and now they are pulling it back to try and get Palau to establish diplomatic ties."[31]

Nor is it just small countries that feel Beijing's lash. In late 2016 and early 2017, the United States and South Korea began deploying a terminal high-altitude area missile defense system (THAAD) in south-central South Korea. Beijing strongly objected, saying the system could be used against China, and Chinese tour groups were banned from visiting South Korea. The state and social media in China also called for boycotts of Korean products sold in China. Regulators citing "fire-code violations" shuttered Korean businesses in China, including 80 percent of the supermarkets operated by the Korean company Lotte, upon whose old golf course the new THAAD batteries were to be constructed.

Nor are such actions confined to China's close neighbors. In late 2013, a Spanish court ordered an arrest warrant for Chinese president Jiang Zemin, former prime minister Le Peng, and three other retired top CCP officials. Spanish law at the time allowed Spanish judges to pursue crimes against humanity even if committed outside the country, and the case against Jiang was filed by a Tibetan exile who had Spanish citizenship. Two days after the filing, Beijing expressed "strong dissatisfaction and firm opposition" to Spain's action and suspended all high-level meetings between the two countries, including a planned state visit by Prime Minister Mariano Rajoy.[32] Madrid hurried to calm the troubled waters.

Spain had lost 10 percent of its entire GDP as a result of the financial crisis of 2007–9, and four years after the crash it was still struggling to pay the interest on its enormous government debt. Even a small increase in interest rates could have had a devastating effect on the Spanish economy. China had been strategically buying Spanish government bonds when no other market players would, and while no one knew for sure, it was thought to own about 20 percent of the total amount in circulation. Madrid now feared that Beijing might dump these bonds on the market, pushing up interest rates and stopping what little there was in the Spanish economy.

Within seventeen days, Rajoy had passed legislation through Parliament to rescind the extraterritorial reach of Spanish courts and halt any suits by Tibetan or other exiles.

Mongolia had a similar experience. A heavily Buddhist country, Mongolia had in centuries past played a decisive role in establishing the institution of the Dalai Lama, Tibet's spiritual leader. Now, however, he is no longer welcome, even for a short visit.

In November 2016, the Dalai Lama visited Ulan Bator, Mongolia's capital, not at the invitation of the Mongolian government but strictly for religious purposes. Beijing strenuously objected to the visit. At the time, Ulan Bator was suffering from a crash of an economic boom driven by raw materials extraction, and it was looking for a loan from China, its main customer for raw materials. Beijing canceled all meetings, and all mention of economic dealings with Mongolia vanished from Chinese media. Beijing also added fees on imports of Mongolian commodities, along with new transaction taxes. Very quickly the Mongolian foreign minister, Tsend Munkh-Orgil, stated publicly that the government "feels sorry" for allowing the Dalai Lama to visit Mongolia and that "he probably won't be visiting again during this administration."[33]

My final and perhaps most significant example is that of Norway and the Nobel Peace Prize. In 2010, Liu Xiaobo, a leading figure in the Chinese democracy movement for almost thirty years, was awarded the prize for his efforts to implement the fundamental human rights protections set forth in international treaties China had signed, as well as in the constitution of the People's Republic of China. For many years, Norway had been the largest supplier of salmon to China. After the award to Liu, Chinese imports of salmon from Norway virtually halted. A new bilateral seafood agreement between the two countries came only after a high-level meeting and a subsequent Chinese statement: "Norway has deeply reflected upon the reason why mutual trust had been harmed."[34]

Nor does China overlook "transgressions" by Americans and American companies. In January 2019, hotel giant Marriott fell afoul of proper manners by listing Taiwan, Tibet, Hong Kong, and Macau as "countries" on an emailed questionnaire. It came to Beijing's attention after a Marriott Rewards worker "liked" a tweet by the "Friends of Tibet" praising the questionnaire. The Chinese government rounded up Marriott officials for questioning, closed Marriott's Chinese website and mobile apps, and demanded an apology. In perfect CCP speak, Marriott CEO Arne Sorenson announced: "We don't support anyone who subverts the sovereignty and territorial integrity of China and we do not intend in any way to encourage or incite any such people or groups."[35]

Beijing also carefully watches movies. Have you seen a film with a Chinese villain recently? Do you remember the Cold War movie *Red Dawn*? It showed the Chinese army invading an American town. Or rather, it did until the script was leaked and somehow got to Beijing, where it was intensely disliked. The studio that produced it, MGM, spent $1 million to digitally erase any evidence of Chinese and substitute North Koreans instead. China's economic growth has been a lifeline for Hollywood studios desperate to offset falling ticket sales in the United States and competition from Amazon and Netflix. But, of course, nothing is free. Since about 2013, Chinese investors have bankrolled lots of Hollywood productions. A decade or two ago, films critical of China, like *Seven Years in Tibet* (showing Chinese brutalization of Tibetans) or *Kundun* (on the Dalai Lama's early life), could still be produced in Hollywood. Now, says Asian studies professor Larry Shinagawa of Hawaii Tokai International College, "you're not going to see something like that anymore." Any studio that made such a movie would likely be banned from China. According to Orville Schell of the Asia Society, "There is a notion [in China] that its propaganda has not worked well enough." So Xi is emphasizing the need to "tell China's story well."[36]

The Case of Australia

We have already noted the February 2005 arrival of Zhou Wen-zhong, vice minister of foreign affairs in Canberra, Australia, to explain the CCP Central Committee's new strategy for Australia to key members of the Chinese embassy staff. He told them that Australia was now being included in China's overall periphery (countries and areas considered strategic for Chinese control) and that the new objectives were first to secure the country as a reliable and secure supply base for China's economic growth, and second to drive a wedge into the U.S.-Australia alliance. Recall that we know this because Chen Yonglin, then first secretary for political affairs at the Chinese consulate in Sydney, attended the meeting a few months before seeking political asylum in Australia, explaining that "in accordance with their fixed strategic plans," the meeting marked the start of "a structured effort to infiltrate Australia [and New Zealand] in a systemic way." He emphasized that Australia was seen in Beijing as a weak link in the Western camp and had been chosen as the test site for infiltration and subversion. Its large number of immigrants of Chinese origin, commitment to multiculturalism, and relatively small population were seen to weaken the country's ability to recognize and defend against the Chinese effort. Thus did an amazing project unfold.

It began with the Qiaowu, the diaspora of Chinese living in Australia, which numbers around 1 million persons out of Australia's 25 million population but makes up a much larger share of the population in some key areas. Historically, Beijing had distanced itself from the overseas Chinese, but after 2011 it reversed course and began embracing the diaspora. As He Yafei, a deputy chief of the CCP's Overseas Chinese Affairs Office, explained: "As the standing of overseas Chinese rises abroad, and as their ethnic consciousness awakens, they will have the desire as well as the ability to collect their power in order to push forward the development and advancement of China."[37]

The plans for how to do this and the history of how it has been done are laid out in great detail by New Zealand scholar James Jiann Hua To, who gained access to a large cache of secret documents on the topic in Beijing. These became the basis of his book *Qiaowu: Extra-territorial Politics for the Overseas Chinese*.[38] The strategy was not only to smother dissent toward Beijing among the Australian and New Zealand Chinese but to make them into a pro-Beijing lobby under the direction of the Chinese embassy and consulate staffs in Australia and New Zealand. Responsibility for this program is shared by the CCP United Front Work Department (what Xi calls his "secret weapon"), the Overseas Chinese Affairs Office, and the Propaganda Department of the CCP.

The China Council for the Promotion of Peaceful National Reunification (CCPPNR) is a key organ of the UFWD. As a vehicle for the effort in Australia, a local arm of the group was created: the Australian Council for Promotion of Peaceful National Reunification (ACPPRC). This became the key body for directing and coordinating the Qiaowu program. It is staffed by people the Chinese embassy trusts, and billionaire political donors such as Chau Chak Wang and Huang Xiangmo (of whom more later) have held senior positions. It is prominent in promoting cultural events such as the new Chinese New Year event (which in the last century was called Lunar New Year since it is shared by other Asians as well as Chinese) and advancing ties between businesses and Chinese immigrants and businesspeople. But it has also become a tool for hushing any dissent from Beijing's line by local Chinese, and a pathway into Australian politics. Prime Ministers Gough Whitlam, Malcolm Fraser, and Bob Hawke were all patrons of the ACPPRC, and its list of prominent advisors reads like a Who's Who of Australian politics. A frequent visitor to council events was New South Wales prime minister Mike Baird, who was persuaded in 2015 to allow the world-famous Sydney Opera House to be lit up in the red of the PRC flag for the Chinese New Year. The Chinese consul-general's comment that "Sydney Opera House was draped in red with Chinese Characteristics" made front-page headlines in the *People's Daily* in Beijing.[39]

In April 2016, a new group called the Australian Action Committee for Protecting Peace and Justice appeared from the circles affiliated with the Chinese embassy and the ACPPRC under its new chairman, Huang Xiangmo. This group gathered some sixty community leaders to call for support of Beijing's claims to islands in the South China Sea. When then Prime Minister Turnbull made his first trip to China in 2016, these leaders urged him "to firmly safeguard the rights of China in the South China Sea."[40]

The Australian-Chinese John Hu emphasizes another important element at work.[41] Many Australian Chinese do not at all agree with Beijing or with its plans for Australia. But, he says, the Australian Chinese community is always operating with a persistent, low-level fear that powerful people can do nasty things to them if they are seen to disagree with Beijing in any way. They know they can be photographed, have their names sent to the embassy, or be denied a visa to return to China to see a sick relative. Or their brother's business in China can be raided.

On the other side of the ledger, the CCP has made a steady and successful effort to have all Chinese-language media in Australia brought under pro-Beijing control. According to Clive Hamilton, Chinese-language radio and almost all newspapers have their news and editorial commentary literally written in Beijing. Patriotic media owners are rewarded for their loyalty with special access to new business opportunities.[42] Media outlets that don't toe the Party line come under intense pressure. The Sofitel hotel in Sydney was even told by the Chinese consulate to stop putting copies of the *Epoch Times* (a Falun Gong publication) in its lobby for guests. As we already saw with the *Washington Post*, the *China Daily* is also distributed as an insert in some mainline Australian newspapers.

This was all accompanied by the development of a huge pipeline for political money from China to Australia. The best illustration of that is Huang Xiangmo, who attended the banquet given for President Xi during his 2014 visit to Australia and who gave the keynote speech at the farewell dinner for the Chinese ambassador to Australia in 2016. You don't get asked to do that unless you are trusted by the highest levels of the CCP. How do you earn that trust?

Huang started in the real estate development business around 2001, in the prefecture of Jieyang, China, when an enormous real estate development boom was just getting off the ground. He cultivated the local business leaders and particularly the local Party secretary, who was responsible for overseeing permits, inspections, and other regulation. Sometimes Huang give these people gifts or signed on to help with projects they cared about, such as a new, monumental city entrance built for Jieyang in 2009, to which he donated $20 million—no strings attached, of course. When the anti-corruption campaign got going in Jieyang and his business associate and the Party secretary found themselves being investigated and then in jail, Huang went to Australia, where he bought a $12.8 million mansion on top of a hill in the Sydney harborside suburb of Mosman.[43] Then he invited many of his associates from China to buy adjoining estates, at slightly lower elevations than his.

Once nicely settled, Huang incorporated his business, Yuhu, Inc., in Australia and began making friends and looking for opportunities. He schmoozed the Chinese embassy and the consulate in Sydney, and in 2014 he was made chairman of the ACPPRC, the key United Front operation in Australia. He used this post as a base from which to spread money and influence. Over a four-year period, he donated $1.78 million to the New South Wales branch of the Labor Party. He began to hobnob with the great and good. He met with former and possible future prime minister Kevin Rudd and with Prime Minister Julia Gillard, as well as with former New South Wales prime minister and minister of foreign affairs Bob Carr. He liked Carr so much that he donated $1.8 million to the University of Technology in Sydney (UTS) to create an Australia-China Relations Institute (ACRI) and appointed Carr to run it, despite his having zero experience in the academic or think tank worlds. But Carr quickly showed that he was up to the job. Whereas on June 6, 1989, two days after the Tiananmen Square incident, he had denounced the Marxist-Leninist Party as a "ludicrously outdated notion" and in 2012 criticized Australia's pro-China lobby, Carr now declared that "we take an unabashedly positive and optimistic view of the Australia-China relationship" as he pushed for a China-Australia Free Trade Agreement and criticized opponents as having "Cold War instincts."[44]

Huang himself has also become accepted as a commentator in both Beijing and Australia. In July 2016, he was granted space in the *People's Daily* to write: "Communist Party culture is a common gene that enables over 60 million overseas Chinese to breathe together and to share in a common fortune." A month later, he wrote a piece for the *Australian Financial Review* in which he described Australian support for the U.S. Freedom of Navigation exercises in the South China Sea as a "folly that Australia may end up regretting."[45] He urged that Australia adopt the "pragmatic" approach of Philippine president Rodrigo Duterte.

Unlike Huang, Chau Chak Wing is publicity shy. But it was inevitable that his $20 million donation to the University of Technology in Sydney would get attention. Indeed, it is surprising that his philanthropy did not draw attention sooner. Between 2007 and 2016, he gave about $4.6 million to the main Australian political parties, including to future prime minister Julie Bishop's West Australian branch of the Liberal Party. This prompted some wags to say that if money talks, in Australia it now speaks in Mandarin.[46] In any case, although he paid $70 million to buy gambling king James Packer's Vaucluse mansion La Mer—then a record for a private residence in Australia—he stays mostly at his estate in Guangzhou, where he entertains the great and beautiful from around the world. In 2004 and 2005, he partially funded trips to his estate for future prime minister Kevin Rudd, future treasurer Wayne Swan, future foreign affairs minister Stephen Smith, and future agriculture minister Tony Burke.

In June 2017, Australia's Fairfax Media ran a program describing Chau's association with the United Front. He strongly denied this and launched a lawsuit against Fairfax, saying, "I have no idea what the United Front Work Department is."[47] Fairfax immediately demolished this claim with Chinese government documents naming him as a member of various UFWD-aligned organizations. In addition, Fairfax found a report by a U.S. diplomat in which Chau had described himself as a member of a business association, the Guangdong Overseas Chinese Businessmen's Association, that is known to be a United Front operation.

By 2017, Australia's domestic intelligence agency, the ASIO, was reporting to the Parliament that it believed foreign payments into Australian society were creating "a threat to our sovereignty, the integrity of our national institutions, and the exercise of our citizens' rights."[48] Two years earlier, the agency had warned the Parliament about Chinese interference via massive cash donations. Nevertheless, major political figures had continued to receive foreign payments, of which 80 percent came from China.[49]

In its new report, the ASIO explained that the Chinese influence campaign extended beyond political donations to the monitoring of Chinese nationals in Australia, including many students who were warned not to criticize Beijing in any way if they wanted their relatives in China to remain in good health. In addition, the ASIO reported, official Chinese observation of teaching on China in Australian classrooms was beginning to censor debate within Australian higher education. Said ASIO head Duncan Lewis: "We have to be very conscious of the possibilities of foreign influence in our universities."[50]

On top of that, the ASIO noted that Australian media are increasingly compromised, with Chinese state media controlling virtually all Chinese-language news outlets in Australia, ensuring that they publish only Beijing-approved stories. In addition, the Confucius Institutes (ostensibly Chinese-language teaching and cultural offices, they also act as propaganda and enforcement organs) are suspected of censoring criticism of Beijing. One has even been established within an Australian state government.

The reality of the China-Australia relationship began to become clearer in late 2017 as a result of several incidents, not big deals in themselves, that pointed to larger problems. In April 2015, Labor Party senator Sam Dastyari received a bill from the Department of Finance for a travel overspend of $1,670.82. Instead of paying it himself, he passed it on to Zhu Minshen's Top Education Institute. Zhu was a representative of Fudan University in Shanghai and a member of the board of the Confucius Institute at Sydney University. His Top Education Institute seemed to consist almost entirely of students who showed up regularly at pro-China demonstrations in Australia. The institute quickly settled the account, but somehow word of this transaction seeped out. It seemed obvious that Dastyari thought of Top as a convenient slush fund. And it turned out this wasn't the first time he had done this. A year earlier, he had gotten Huang's Yuhu Group to pay a $5,000 legal bill for him. This caused a huge fuss, but it was just a prelude. As his Chinese supporters wished, Dastyari kept spreading the notion that "the South China Sea is China's own affair. On this issue, Australia should remain neutral and respect China's own decision."[51] But he was unable to persuade the Labor Party to adopt a more pro-China stance on the South China Sea before the 2016 elections. This led Huang to withdraw a promised donation to Labor of $400,000, and when this was discovered by Fairfax Media investigators, it made big headlines. Then, in late November 2017, Fairfax revealed that a few weeks after the donation story hit, Dastyari drove to Huang's estate to warn him that ASIO might be tapping his phones. They were. ASIO heard his treason, and then so did all of Australia. In Parliament, Prime Minister Turnbull asked: "Whose side is Sam on? Not Australia's, it would seem."[52]

Since that scandal, there have been significant changes in Australia. A new law bans foreign political donations. Huang won't be spending much time at his Mosman estate. His application for citizenship was denied, and he was stripped of his permanent resident visa. He is still permitted short visits, but these are probably not enough for the United Front Work Department's purposes.

Australia has also put tighter regulations on inward direct foreign investment, particularly in electricity infrastructure and agricultural land, both of which received enormous amounts of Chinese money. This reform was to some extent triggered by the 2015 sale of the Port of Darwin, home to a detachment of U.S. Marines, to the Chinese state-owned corporation Landbridge. In the wake of these activities, in April 2018 Australia undertook its first freedom-of-navigation voyage in the South China Sea.

Gaining further power in Australia, however, and driving a wedge between it and the United States remain major objectives for Beijing, and despite the increased resistance, Australia has already been penetrated more deeply than most of its citizens are aware. Since 2007, the United States has received $100 billion of new, nonfinancial investment from China. Australia, with a population one-thirteenth that of the U.S., has received $90 billion. It is swimming in Chinese investment. Wherever you look, you see something with Chinese ownership. In the single year of 2016–17, Chinese investment in agricultural land rose tenfold. China now owns a fourth of all foreign-owned land in Australia. One reason for this is that Australia makes no distinction between investment from SOEs and that of private Chinese companies. A joint report by Australian National University economist Peter Drysdale and a CCP think tank concluded, "There is no logical basis for treating the vast bulk of SOEs differently from other potential investors in Australia."[53] China's State Grid Corporation, an SOE, owns enormous chunks of Australia's energy network, including part ownership of three of Victoria's five electricity distributors and the transmitting network of South Australia. Cheung Kong Infrastructure (Li Kashing's giant company in Hong Kong, which is not an SOE but is very close to Beijing) owns other parts. Energy Australia, one of the country's big three electricity retailers, is wholly owned by the Hong Kong company China Light and Power, which is also close to Beijing. Alina Energy, one of Australia's largest energy infrastructure companies, was acquired by the

Hong Kong jewelry retailer Chow Tai Fook Enterprises—also close to Beijing. Because electricity distribution is now combining with telecommunications services, ownership yields access to internet and telephone messaging as well. Cheung Kong also acquired the big energy utility operator DUET, which controls the strategically important gas pipeline from Banbury to Dampier as well as a large portion of Victoria's electricity-distribution infrastructure. The same consortium already owned the gas distribution network in Victoria.

We have already noted the sale of the Port of Darwin to Landbridge. The SOE China Merchants bought the Port of Newcastle, the world's biggest coal export port, which is located close to an air force base. When the Port of Melbourne was sold to investors, the Chinese sovereign wealth fund CIC snapped up a 20 percent share. Chinese firms have also expressed interest in building the new international airport to the west of Sydney. It will become *the* major airport in Australia and will have all sorts of potential for monitoring and tracking people. I could go on, but you get the idea. China owns a lot of Australia.

The now well-known Chinese company Huawei has long been an issue in Australia. In 2012, the government banned it from supplying equipment to the National Broadband Network. ASIO had warned that it had credible evidence that Huawei was linked to the Third Department of the PLA, known as 3PLA, China's cyber espionage arm. Huawei founder Ren Zhengfei, ASIO noted, had been a director of the PLA's Information Engineering Academy, responsible for telecom research for the PLA and especially for 3PLA. Although Huawei does not supply the National Broadband Network, it does supply the Vodafone, Optus, and Telstra networks in Australia and is very close commercially to State Grid, which may be using Huawei equipment to suck up enormous amounts of data about Australian power usage. The effective operation of Australia's electricity network could well come to depend on software installed on Huawei hardware.[54]

A final important point concerns Australian academia and the influence of the students. In his book *Silent Invasion*, Clive Hamilton notes that in every discussion he had with Australian China scholars, the issue of how China could punish them if they crossed "the line" inevitably came up. Says Hamilton, "They all know where the line is." They know that they must speak and write carefully lest they be refused a visa to visit China, are not invited to key meetings, or are quietly disciplined in any of a hundred invisible ways. According to Rowan Callick, an old China hand, "Our universities have substantially withdrawn their capacity for sustained, genuinely independent analysis of contemporary China or Chinese history." But the issue is not limited to scholars. It is also to do with students. In May 2017, a lecturer at Monash University gave students a quiz taken from a widely used textbook. They were requested to complete the following statement: "There is a common saying in China that government officials only speak truth when . . ." The right answer is: when they are drunk or careless. This is not an unknown concept in China. Nevertheless, a Chinese student in the class complained on WeChat (roughly China's WhatsApp), and soon a Chinese consulate official phoned Monash's dean to demand that the university investigate, warning that the consulate would monitor the situation. With forty-four hundred Chinese students in his university paying full tuition, the dean knew exactly what to do. He suspended the lecturer, had the quiz withdrawn, and banned the textbook.[55]

Nor has the COVID-19 pandemic at all reduced tensions between Australia and China. In March 2020 Australia's prime minister called for an international inquiry into the origins of the pandemic.[56] He did not even mention the word *China*. But his request was met with an arbitrary reduction of Chinese imports of Australian beef and barley.[57]

Canada

Canada may be thought of as kind of a Northern Hemisphere Australia. As Canadian journalist Jonathan Manthorpe notes in his best-selling book *Claws of the Panda*, Canadian prime minister Justin Trudeau was greatly surprised in the fall of 2017 when Chinese officials rejected his proposals for a bilateral free trade agreement that would have required the Party/state to follow Canadian standards on such things as labor laws, gender equality, and environmental standards. In a "What was the prime minister smoking?" tone, Manthorpe notes that that was never going to happen. "Canada is never going to change China," he emphasizes, adding that "far more pertinent is the question of whether China is going to change Canada."[58]

As with Australia, Manthorpe notes that a major effort has been made by the Party and its United Front Work Department as well as by its Overseas Chinese Affairs Office to penetrate Canadian corporations, government ministries, universities, publication and broadcasting media, and political parties. Often, victims have been Canadians of Chinese origin whose human rights as Canadian citizens were ignored and violated in order to keep them quiet, to force them to pass along secret information, or to kidnap them for forcible return to China. As in Australia, the local Chinese-language newspapers of Canada have largely been bought out and placed under editors and newscasters who adhere to the Party line. As in Australia, Canadians of Tibetan, Uighur, or Taiwanese origin, along with those who follow the Falun Gong faith, have been intimidated, harassed, and told to keep quiet or else. In extreme cases, dissidents have been tortured. Indeed, Amnesty International Canada has issued a report saying it "considers the scale and consistency of many reports of rights violations to be consistent with a coordinated, Chinese state-sponsored campaign to target certain political, ethnic, and spiritual groups considered to be opposed to Chinese government interests."[59]

As in Australia, Chinese state-owned and state-guided enterprises have made extensive acquisitions of high-tech Canadian corporations such as ITF Technologies, the British Columbia–based military communications company Norsat International, and Semi-Tech Corporation of Markham. Indeed, Operation Sidewinder, a secret government report leaked to the press in the fall of 1999, showed that Chinese intelligence had managed to infiltrate large areas of Canadian corporate and public life. It noted that since 1980 more than two hundred Canadian companies had come under the influence or ownership of the CCP, and that Macau tycoon Stanley Ho was the principal shareholder in the above-mentioned Semi-Tech Corporation, which is a specialist in secure information systems designed for governments, national defense departments, and police forces. The report also described Beijing's placement of agents in influential universities such as the University of Toronto and the University of Western Ontario. It further detailed accounts of how Chinese intelligence agencies had used business ties between China and Canada as a cover for the theft of nuclear technology from Ontario Hydro to China's State Science and Technology Commission.[60] At the time, the report was extremely controversial, but it has aged well as many of its allegations have turned out to be true.

As in Australia, Chinese Student and Scholar Associations and Confucius Institutes have proliferated, maintaining both observation of Chinese students and close ties to the Chinese embassy in Ottawa and to the Chinese consulates in the rest of the country. The Confucius Institutes are overseen by a Chinese body known as the Hanban, which establishes highly secret agreements between the Hanban and host institutions. One leaked secrecy clause stipulates: "The two parties to the agreement will regard this agreement as a secret document and without written approval from the other party, no party shall ever publicize, reveal, or make public, or allow other persons to publicize, reveal, or make public materials or information obtained or learned concerning the other party, except if publicizing, revealing, or making public is necessary for one party to the agreement to carry out its duties under the agreement."[61] Extremely unusual is article 5 of the standard agreement, which requires the Confucius Institutes to follow the customs, laws, and regulations of China as well as of the host country, in this case Canada.

In Canada as in Australia, investment by state-owned Chinese corporations soared after 2003 as $60 billion was poured into acquiring Canadian mining, chemical, and energy companies. For example, in 2012, China National Offshore Oil Corporation (CNOOC) acquired Canada's Nexen (oil and gas) for $15.1 billion. It was a controversial deal because it effectively gave the CCP ownership not only of assets in Canada but also of assets in the North Sea, the Gulf of Mexico, West Africa, and the Middle East. After allowing the deal, the Canadian government began to get more cautious and announced that it would no longer allow state-owned companies to acquire majority stakes in Canadian oil sands.

As in Australia and much else of the world, the Chinese telecommunications company Huawei has been extremely active. In warning about it, former Canadian Security Intelligence Service (CSIS) head Ward Elcock says: "It's hard for me to believe that Huawei would not do the bidding of the Chinese government. I would not want to see Huawei equipment incorporated into a 5G network in Canada." If Huawei loses out, however, it will not be for lack of effort. It has spent about $150 billion on research and development in Canada, and has also obtained grants from the National

Sciences and Research Council of Canada. Interestingly, none of this taxpayer-funded work is for the benefit of Canada, since the Canadian researchers doing the work agreed that the patents and intellectual property generated will be assigned to the company.[62]

In considering the case of Canada, it must be kept in mind that together with the United States, Australia, New Zealand, and the United Kingdom, in which the CCP has also taken a great interest, Canada is a member of the Five Eyes intelligence network. From China's perspective, spying on the United States might well be done in the other four nations.

So, let us now turn to what in Hawaii would be called the big kahuna.

United States

Australia and Canada represent some of the most advanced cases of Beijing's penetration of the free world, but they are by no means alone. The United States is experiencing the same phenomenon. Stanford University's Hoover Institution senior fellow Larry Diamond and the Asia Society's Orville Schell led a working group that published a report, *Chinese Influence & American Interests,* in 2018. It makes for an enlightening read.

In its opening summary, the report notes that the Party's United Front Work Department, the Central Propaganda Department, the International Liaison Department, the State Council Information Office, the All-China Federation of Overseas Chinese, the Chinese People's Association for Friendship with Foreign Countries, the Ministry of Foreign Affairs, and the Overseas Chinese Affairs Office of the State Council are all charged with penetrating and influencing all aspects of American life—university study, journalism, business, government policy—that may impinge on China in any way. It notes that the Confucius Institutes recently established on many American university campuses must be subjected to high standards of academic freedom and that they require "more rigorous university oversight." "With the direct support of the Chinese embassy and consulates," the authors write, "Chinese Students and Scholars Associations (CSSAs) sometimes report on and compromise the academic freedom of other Chinese students and American faculty on American campuses. American universities that host events deemed politically offensive by the Chinese Communist Party and government have been subject to increasing pressure and sometimes even to retaliation by diplomats in the Chinese embassy and its six consulates as well as by CSSA branches."[63]

The report further notes that "although the United States is open to Chinese scholars and researchers studying American politics or history, China restricts access to American scholars and researchers seeking to study politically sensitive areas of China's political system, society, and history. . . . China often uses its companies to advance strategic objectives (Belt and Road) abroad, gaining political influence and access to critical infrastructure and technology. China has made foreign companies' continued access to its domestic market conditional on their compliance with Beijing's stance on Taiwan and Tibet. This report documents how China has supported the formation of dozens of local Chinese chambers of commerce in the United States that appear to have ties to the Chinese government."[64]

The study notes that China has all but eliminated what was once a multitude of independent Chinese-language media serving Chinese American communities. It has bought and co-opted the existing outlets and established new ones while also creating a strong foothold in the English-language market. All the while, the Chinese government has severely limited the ability of U.S. and other free world media to conduct normal newsgathering in China.

In its summary, the report emphasizes:

> In the technology sector, China is engaged in a multifaceted effort to misappropriate technologies it deems critical to its economic and military success. Beyond economic espionage, theft, and the forced technology transfers that are required of many joint venture partnerships, China also captures much valuable new technology through its investments in American high-tech companies and by exploiting the openness of American university labs—[including] . . . the arrest of the Chairman of Harvard's Chemistry and Biological Chemistry Department for unreported payments from Chinese sources. These activities go well beyond influence-seeking to a deeper and more disabling penetration. For example, in 2018 Chinese funding of U.S. high tech start-up companies hit $3 billion and included investment in such sensitive technology firms as data center networking firm Barefoot

Networks, autonomous driving start-up Zoox, and speech recognition start-up AISense.[65]

The economic and strategic losses for the United States are increasingly unsustainable. They threaten not only to help China gain global dominance of the future's leading technologies but to undermine America's commercial and military advantages."[66]

A final and very important aspect noted by the report is self-censorship. U.S. scholars and journalists who write about China must, of course, have visas to be able to go there for study and inquiry. They know they are monitored by a wide variety of Chinese organizations and that any statements or articles at odds with Chinese policy might assure that they won't get a visa in the future. Thus there is a strong incentive to keep any criticism of China unvoiced. An example of this is well-known Harvard professor Ezra Vogel, who has written the definitive biography of Deng Xiaoping. Vogel had to have access to records and people in China in order to write the book, which is a masterwork. Interestingly, however, the Chinese edition makes no mention of the Tiananmen Square massacre.

Dilemmas

The term *threat* typically implies military action and war. The PRC does pose this kind of threat in some areas. As noted above, it has invaded Tibet, India, South Korea, and Vietnam. It has also used what are known as "gray-area" forces and tactics (not regular military but police forces and "militias" backed by a few regular PLAN ships) to seize control of the South China Sea. It has also used irregular forces disguised as fishing boats to harass the Senkaku Islands, currently under Japanese administration.

Now that the PRC effectively controls the South China Sea, Japan may find itself under subtle but increasing pressure. In July 2019, China reserved a substantial area of the South China Sea for missile tests. This, of course, affected shipping lanes. More of these actions could impede delivery of oil and vital materials to Japan, all done more or less informally with no direct declaration of hostile intent. These tactics could be combined with a sudden order forbidding Chinese tourists to go to Japan or Chinese students to enroll at Japanese universities, or with a boycott of Japanese goods in

China. Meanwhile, Japanese high-tech companies will face barrages of highly professional electronic hacking and the theft of the formulae and designs for their most advanced products. Japan is also, of course, targeted by Chinese medium-range nuclear missiles. These are unlikely ever to be launched, but it is not their purpose to be launched. It is to condition behavior so that they need never be used.

Japan must also understand that China's main aim is to get U.S. forces out of the First Island Chain (Japan, Okinawa, Senkaku islands, Taiwan, Philippines, Malaysia, Singapore) and that for the United States, patrolling that chain is a choice, not a necessity. Tokyo must ask itself how long the Americans will choose to defend the chain without substantially increased assistance from the main beneficiary, namely, Japan. In that calculation, it must carefully consider what its national life might be like as a full-fledged vassal state of China.

Australia has already been subjected to a major campaign to steer it away from the free world into Beijing's orbit. This will not stop. China's embassy and consulates in Australia, the United Front Work Department, and all other propaganda and quasi-official organizations will continue their efforts to penetrate and guide Australia in a "right-thinking way." Indeed, on August 16, 2019, the *Straits Times* reported on attacks by Mainland Chinese students in Australia upon demonstrating students in Melbourne from Hong Kong: "After China's Consul General in Brisbane, Mr. Xu Jie, stated his support of 'the spontaneous patriotic behavior of mainland Chinese students,' Australian Foreign Minister Marise Payne warned that overseas diplomats shouldn't encourage 'disruptive or potentially violent behavior.' " In the midst of similar scenes in New Zealand, the Chinese consulate in Auckland complained that the Hong Kong demonstrators were "demonizing the image of China" and "inciting anti-China sentiment."

In view of this, Australia and New Zealand are correct to understand that the PRC will do all in its power to turn the South Pacific into an extension of the South China Sea. They will have to decide whether, as analysts like Australian National University (ANU) professor Hugh White suggest, Canberra and Wellington should appease and accommodate China while loosening their ties to the West and especially to the United States, or strengthen those ties and extend them to other nations in the region, particularly India.

Beyond the question of a substantial increase in Australian defense spending, this decision will raise issues of values. China could pressure Australia by reducing its imports of coal and iron ore or halting the flow of students and tourists to Australia. How much is the average Australian willing to sacrifice to preserve the rule of law? How much is the right to a trial by an independent jury of one's peers worth? Will Australia fudge on these issues of fundamental human rights in order to sell more coal to the PRC? Some elite Australians have already told me how they would vote: they're for selling the coal. I still doubt that most Australians feel that way, but in any case, that will be the question.

Interestingly, the coronavirus pandemic has already showed Australia that China is not necessarily a reliable customer, as it has cut imports in retaliation for Australian requests for an open inquiry into the origins and spread of the virus. One positive aspect of the advent of the virus is that it has driven a reduction in greenhouse gas emissions that may somewhat mitigate the continued bleaching of the Great Barrier Coral Reef.

Looking into the future, Australians will also have to decide how many Chinese students it is safe, over the long term, to educate in their country, and how these students should be screened and monitored—not because they themselves are undesirable people but because they are subject to pressure and manipulation from Beijing.

What is true of Australia is even more true of New Zealand, where Chinese penetration of the political system, universities, and society at large is even greater than in Australia.

India will face a substantially increased Chinese presence in the Indian Ocean as China uses port building and Belt and Road projects to create strongholds in Sri Lanka and Pakistan. Beijing is also building a "string of pearls" of islands, ports, and bases along the maritime Silk Road from China to the Suez Canal and on into Europe. India will probably respond by increasing the size and professionalism of its navy, and perhaps by installing missiles along its coast.

As I have noted, Europe and the European Union have long been targets of Chinese investment, diplomacy, the United Front, and the Belt and Road. The poorer countries of Europe have especially been targeted for Chinese investment and loans. China's acquisitions in Portugal, Spain, Greece, Serbia, Hungary, and elsewhere have given it unexpected influence over the EU's economic and foreign policy, partly because it operates in international affairs on the basis of unanimity. Thus, when the question of China's mistreatment of the Uighurs in Xinjiang province arises, the European Union cannot take a stand or issue a statement because China, through its investments Serbia and Hungary, effectively controls their position on this issue. Those countries care more about the economic pain from a withdrawal of Chinese largess than they do about human rights in faraway Xinjiang. And because their vote is required under the unanimity rule, the European Union makes no criticism of China.

In Africa, China is heavily invested all over the continent and has developed close relations with a wide variety of authoritarian or quasi-authoritarian regimes..One might even say that China's biggest export is authoritarianism.

I could go on, but the key thing to understand is that China poses a variety of economic, political, and military challenges to the liberal world order that has prevailed since World War II. A world dominated by China would be authoritarian, without rule of law, pursuing state-guided economic policies, with complete surveillance of individuals at virtually all times, and without freedom of speech or a free press. The struggle for freedom in Hong Kong today is a harbinger of what could easily come on a larger scale.

The fundamental threat, to be clear, is not the people of China. Taiwan and Hong Kong demonstrate not only that Chinese people can operate democratic governments but that when able to speak freely, they prefer them. The threat is the Communist Party of China and its ambition and ability to create a global authoritarian order.

We must recognize that China is dedicated to achieving this order and that it is using every tool at its disposal to obtain it. Most of China's 1.4 billion people understand that their country is essentially at war with America and liberal democracy. Every member of the 90-million-member Communist Party is constantly and insistently being indoctrinated with the need of the CCP to displace the United States and any system of rule of law with the authoritarian hegemony of a resurrected Chinese Empire of Tianxia.

This is not such a highly unlikely event as it is widely considered to be. Suppose we were to create a world map (see map on pages viii and ix) in which the United States and its allies were solid dark gray, less solid allies were solid medium gray, in-between countries were solid pale gray, China and solid Chinese allies were hatch lines, China's less solid allies were diagonal lines, and countries equally affiliated with the United States and China were dots. Such a map might look something like this:

Solid dark gray—United States, Canada, Mexico, Japan, Australia, UK, France, Belgium, Netherlands, Denmark, Sweden, Finland, Norway, Ireland

Solid medium gray—South Korea, Vietnam, Saudi Arabia, Turkey, Niger, Ivory Coast, Ghana, Cameroon, Egypt, Germany, Austria, Papua New Guinea, Ukraine, Israel, Cameroon, Singapore

Solid pale gray—Indonesia, India, Bangladesh, Guyana, Suriname, French Guiana, Colombia

Hatch marks—China, Laos, Cambodia, Myanmar, Iran, Venezuela, Ecuador

Diagonal lines—Pakistan, Russia, Kazakhstan, Kyrgyzstan, Turkmenistan, Uzbekistan, Belarus, Poland, Hungary, Serbia, Czech Republic, Slovakia, Greece, Italy, Sudan, Ethiopia, Somalia, Eritrea, Kenya, Chad, Uganda, Zaire, Tanzania, Mozambique, Central African Republic, Angola, Zambia, Gabon, Nigeria, Syria

Dots—Thailand, Turkey, Iraq, Spain, Portugal, Morocco, Algeria, Tunisia, Libya, Namibia, Botswana, South Africa, Brazil, Peru, Bolivia, Argentina, Chile, Uruguay, Paraguay

Furthermore, within the solid dark gray, solid medium gray, and hatch line countries, Beijing has many fellow travelers of one stripe or another. For example, prominent think tank analysts who focus on China have learned to be careful about what they say and write to preserve their access to Chinese officials and their ability to get visas for China. Larry Diamond and Orville Schell wrote in their Hoover Institution report, "As one scholar who also does a lot of consulting noted, 'Access to China is my livelihood.' At the same time, he argues, 'I never say anything contrary to my views, but I write it in a way that is less shrill.' Another scholar noted, 'I don't self-censor, but there is no need to launch a polemic every day of the week . . . polemics get your visa cut off. China's greatest power is the power of visa control."[67]

Perhaps the most telling indication of the quiet reach of Chinese power is the *Washington Post* editorial board commentary of July 20, 2019. It called a UN Human Rights Council letter expressing concern about China's mass detentions of Muslim citizens in Xinjiang province "another tepid gesture in what has been a weak international effort to respond to Beijing's campaign of cultural genocide against the Uighur ethnic group and other Muslim minorities." It went on to note that even more remarkable was the fact that four days later, countries recruited by Beijing delivered their own letter to the council, signed by thirty-seven ambassadors, which endorsed what it whitewashed as a "counter-terrorism and de-radicalization" operation, claiming that "the fundamental human rights of people of all ethnic groups there are safeguarded." The signatories included the usual global rogues' gallery—Cuba, Russia, North Korea, and Venezuela. But a dozen Muslim governments also joined in—thereby sanctioning one of the largest assaults on Islam in modern times.

The *Post* went on to note that this statement represented a shameful capitulation by Pakistan, Saudi Arabia, Egypt, the United Arab Emirates, Algeria, and other majority-Muslim states that frequently pose as defenders of the faith—especially when it involves condemning Israel. And it offers an augur of what international affairs will look like if the Chinese regime of Xi Jinping realizes its global ambitions: a world where most states meekly submit to Beijing's dictates and endorse its crimes.

China will affect many countries and peoples in a wide variety of ways. Some may find themselves in military conflict with China. Others (one thinks of Laos and Cambodia today) may essentially become provinces of China or some form of vassal states. Yet others may be able to maintain their full independence from China and even develop mutually beneficial relations.

Moreover, many "useful idiots" (or, more politely, fellow travelers) in fully democratic, rule-of-law countries will argue that China cannot be contained and that we must therefore make all efforts to avoid conflict with it in order to avoid the "Thucydides trap" of war between a rising power and a reigning power.[68] These experts, upon inspection, usually turn out to be China scholars or businesspeople who need visas to visit China or contacts there to maintain their credibility as "experts." We must beware of people who write things like "I have just returned from China where I met all the top people." One does not meet all the top people in China unless one is singing their song.

There will always be one set of constants. The CCP will constantly seek to gain leverage and control of any relationship. It will not accept limits on its own power and will not abide any rule of law. It will insist on the Party line and will attempt to beat down and destroy any attempt to find the real facts of history or to stand for open debate, free speech and inquiry, and human rights. Those are antithetical to the CCP, and it will do whatever it can to destroy those values and the people who embrace them.

There will always be a risk of war between the United States and communist China. But the greater risk is the dissolution of the free world in the face of gradually advancing coercion by authoritarian forces.

PART

II

Know Yourself

—Sun Tzu

5

How America Got Rich

> I use no porter or cheese but such as is made in America.
> —*George Washington*

To properly understand ourselves, we must clearly know how America became the richest and most powerful country the world has ever seen. The tale is encrusted in the myths of rugged individualism, free markets, entrepreneurs, small government, immigrants fleeing tyranny to seek opportunity in the New World, and plain hard work done with a "can-do" spirit.

It's a nice story, but the truth is otherwise. The United States got rich by imitating Great Britain and thereby marking a trail followed by Germany, France, Japan, South Korea, Singapore, the Netherlands, Switzerland, Sweden, Taiwan, and South Korea—all of which eventually became rich. The model was not one of free trade, open markets, and global investment. Rather, it was one of mercantilism and protectionism.

The story begins in the late fifteenth century when Henry VII became king of England. Having spent his childhood in Burgundy, he had observed how affluent that region had become from the production of woolen textiles, and also how, ironically, the wool for that industry came from England. He decided that England was in the wrong end of the business: rather than exporting inexpensive raw wool with little value added, it should, he thought, become the leading maker of wool-based products by adding the processing value itself rather than watching the Burgundians do that and make all the money. His solution was to impose duties on the export of wool, recruit skilled craftsmen from the Netherlands and Italy to ply their trade in England (one might call this theft of technology), provide tax relief to manufacturers of woolens, and grant monopolies for production to certain cities and provinces (we call this "infant industry support" in modern language). The description for this kind of approach to economic development today is "mercantilism" or "export-led economy" or "catch-up strategy." It worked: England became the dominant maker and exporter of the world's woolens.

Indeed, it worked so well that it was extended to virtually all other industries in England; every effort was made to ensure that the world's manufactured goods came from there. The spirit of this was well captured in King George I's Address to Parliament in 1721, in which he emphasized that "it is evident that nothing so much contributes to promote the public well-being as the exportation of manufactured goods and the importation of foreign raw material."[1]

Fast-forward to about 1760 and the beginning of the industrial revolution. The key trigger of that revolutionary event was the dramatic increase of British exports. Between 1700 and 1750, Britain's home industries increased their output by 7 percent, while export industries expanded by 76 percent. As E. J. Hobsbawm notes: "The country which succeeded in monopolizing the export markets of a large part of the world in a brief period of time, could expand its export industries at a rate that made industrial revolution not only possible but virtually compulsory."[2] It also tended to make such industries global monopolists.

At the moment of the adoption of the U.S. Declaration of Independence, a man destined to become the world's most famous economist, one Adam Smith, appeared on the scene. Smith was concerned that British mercantilism was turning into government-controlled monopolization that might strangle British innovation and efficiency. He emphasized the role of the "unseen hand" of the market and the need for market forces to be free of government or monopolistic control and argued that subsidies, grants of monopoly, and protection be lifted to enable free competition to drive growth and productivity.

Regarding international trade, Smith's thinking was a bit simplistic and was conditioned by the fact and the expectation that Britain was and would be for the foreseeable future the leading and most efficient industrial producer. Thus, he was not much worried about competition from foreign rivals. His New World trading order called for countries to specialize in production so that each nation would concentrate on doing what it did best at a particular moment in time. So, for example, America would produce timber, cotton, and other raw materials, while Britain would do the manufacturing and engineering. His focus was on the immediate maximization of welfare rather than long-term planning, and a fundamental premise of his argument was that the sole purpose of production should be consumption, not the building of national industrial strength. Here, however, he added an important proviso that is often overlooked by his laissez-faire followers. He emphasized that "defense is more important than opulence" and noted that only a manufacturing country could win a war. This suggested that he did favor some government promotion of manufacturing, but generally his focus was on how to increase consumption and meet the needs of the consumer. His most famous book, *The Wealth of Nations,* was thus a powerful argument for a new kind of individualistic, consumer-oriented market economics that also seemed to fit nicely with the concept of an open, democratic, free society.

It did not seem to occur to Smith that because the finishing and manufacturing steps in the process added more value and were thus more profitable, they could support higher wages. Nor did it seem to occur to him that the British manufacturers' techniques and machinery could be copied, and that after an initial period of high start-up costs (perhaps offset by government subsidies or tariffs on imports of British goods), producers in America and elsewhere could match or even improve the efficiency and costs of British manufacturers. Indeed, he argued that America should not enter manufacturing because at that moment British manufacturing was less costly. In his mind, the role of America was to supply raw materials. He thus supported British policies under which the American colonies were actively prevented from pursuing industrial and commercial development and limited to supplying agricultural products, timber, and raw materials. Once they gained their independence, however, they hotly debated whether they should imitate Britain and attempt to participate in the industrial revolution, or remain primarily agricultural producers as Smith suggested.

The Debate

Central to their discussion was the issue of trade, which was also being discussed again in London. With the ratification of the U.S. Constitution in 1788, all tariffs on trade between the states were abolished, and the value of the removal of those state barriers to trade was widely accepted. Whether the country should also open itself to free trade with foreign competitors was quite another matter.

Thomas Jefferson and his fellow planters embraced Smith's free trade views, but others, led by Alexander Hamilton, favored imitating Britain's protectionist approach to industrialization. The Jefferson faction argued that property and wealth had always been the cornerstone of political power. Therefore, if the U.S. government wanted to establish a new politics more reflective of the will of the people, it must create a relative equality of economic circumstances. To do so, it must enhance the economic power of the class of yeoman farmers. This, Jefferson argued, would result in a political majority that would block the rise of any tyrannical elite. This check on tyranny would be reinforced by powerful state legislatures that could hold their own against a power-grasping Congress.

In Jefferson's formulation, the new American economy would be based on agriculture and the country would prosper by trading freely for manufactured goods with outside producers. Jefferson and others, such as James Madison, Thomas Paine, and Benjamin Franklin, were largely in accord with Smith's notions of specialization and free trade. Paine described free trade as an engine of peace, a view that echoes frequently in both British and American history. "Our plan," he wrote, "is for commerce, and that, well attended to, will secure us peace and the friendship of Europe." Franklin was not as wedded to Jefferson's agrarian republican vision, but he did strongly embrace Smith's concept of open trade, arguing that "free trade never ruined any nation."[3] It's important to point out, though, that Franklin's understanding of free trade was what we would today call reciprocity or "fair trade," with all players doing away with protectionism.

On the other side of the debate was Alexander Hamilton. With important support from George Washington, he argued that the new nation needed a strong central government based on a firm financial foundation that would foster the growth of manufacturing industries. He seemed to intuit the value of economies of scale (the more you make of something, the less it costs to produce) and firmly believed that this would be the superior route not only to economic growth but to effective national defense. Asserting that "a nation cannot long exist without revenue" (Federalist Papers no. 12), he called for a tariff on imports that would both finance the state and provide incentives for local manufactures.

One of Hamilton's first acts after Washington appointed him secretary of the treasury in 1789 was to propose a 9 percent general tariff, which was passed and signed into law on July 4, 1789. Although Washington was a plantation owner like Jefferson, he felt strongly that the new America needed a manufacturing base, a conviction that undoubtedly reflected his bitter experience during the Revolutionary War, when the American army lacked cannon, clothing, and shoes. In his first annual message to Congress, on January 8, 1790, he emphasized that a "free people ought not only to be armed but disciplined; and their safety and interest require that they should promote such manufactories as tend to render them independent of others for essential, particularly military, supplies." He promised the Delaware Society for Promoting Domestic Manufactures "to demonstrate the sincerity of my opinion by the uniformity of my practice, in giving preference to the produce and fabrics of America."[4]

Vital in the support of American industry was Article I, section 8, of the U.S. Constitution, which gives Congress the power "to promote the progress of science and useful arts, by securing for limited times to authors and inventors the exclusive right to their respective writings and discoveries." This was put into practice by the Patent Act of 1790 and was followed by Hamilton's Report on Manufactures in December 1791, which called for high tariffs to protect nascent American industry. A highlight of the report was the recommendation to establish patents to encourage and protect inventions. The Patent Act also instituted "Buy American" policies to ensure a favorable balance of trade until domestically manufactured goods achieved the quality demanded by overseas markets. And it allocated substantial federal funds for the building of roads, bridges, canals, and harbors to facilitate both internal and external commerce. Hamilton was closely following the English mercantilist model (which later became the German, Japanese, South Korean, Taiwanese, French, and now Chinese model).

Free trade, Hamilton argued, would be devastating to the young country's economy. "If the system of perfect liberty to industry and commerce were the prevailing system of nations," he wrote, "the arguments against a program of manufactures would have great force." But in the absence of equal treatment and reciprocity, the United States could become a "victim of the system" and be led into "a state of impoverishment."[5] Hamilton also believed that a diversified economy was more likely to grow rapidly and productively than a narrowly specialized agricultural economy.

To counter the free traders' argument that tariffs would increase costs to consumers, Hamilton noted that "the fact does not universally correspond with the theory. A reduction of prices has in several instances immediately succeeded the establishment of a domestic manufacture." And once established, a domestic manufacture "invariably becomes cheaper, being free from the heavy charges which attend the importation of foreign commodities." Thus, he argued, "a temporary enhancement of price must always be well compensated by a permanent reduction of it." This has since come to be known as the infant industry theory.

The debate over these issues continued over the next twenty years, but several key developments brought the American economy around to the British-like mercantilist system that it maintained all the way through World War II.

One important event was Eli Whitney's invention of the cotton gin in 1793, for which he duly received a patent under the strong new patent laws passed in 1794. While the cotton gin was revolutionizing the U.S. economy, Whitney became bogged down in endless legal challenges to his patent and nearly went bankrupt. Eventually, however, he managed to finance his legal bills with a government contract for production of ten thousand muskets and won his case. In fulfilling the contract he also developed the concept of interchangeable parts that, in combination with power machinery and specialized labor, revolutionized production and became known worldwide as the "American System of manufacturing." This system revolutionized the U.S. economy and is perhaps the earliest example of how government contracting can combine with private enterprise to spur innovation and productivity growth.

Another key factor was that British manufacturers began dumping their products on the U.S. market at far below cost in order to prevent U.S.

manufactures from gaining ground. The British navy had also started boarding U.S. merchant ships and impressing their sailors into service. Objections to these practices precipitated the War of 1812, a war that glaringly demonstrated the U.S. economy's limitations in defending against major powers with strong manufacturing industries. Former president Jefferson did an about-face, noting that the war had taught him "that manufactures are now as necessary to our independence as to our comfort." He began to promote Buy American thinking and challenged free traders to "keep pace with me in purchasing nothing foreign where an equivalent of domestic fabric can be obtained without regard to difference of price."[6] Others, including James Madison, James Monroe, John Adams, and his son John Quincy Adams, echoed Jefferson, and in 1816 the first true protective tariffs were imposed by Congress, with a 30 percent duty on iron imports and 25 percent on cotton and woolens.

As president in 1822, Monroe called for more tariff increases, noting that "whatever may be the abstract doctrine in favor of unrestricted commerce, that doctrine rests on two conditions—international peace and general reciprocity—which have never occurred and cannot be expected." Leaders of the more populist and agrarian faction of the Democratic Party, who might have been expected to take a different view, agreed. John C. Calhoun, despite his representing the cotton-exporting state of South Carolina, called in 1816 for a tariff on cotton manufactures. Andrew Jackson commented, in the wake of the war he contributed so much to winning, "We have been too long subject to the policy of the British merchants. It is time we should become a little more Americanized, and instead of feeding the paupers and laborers of Europe, feed our own, or else in a short time, by continuing our present [laissez-faire] policy we shall all be paupers ourselves."[7]

Smith Reexamined

At the same time, journalists and political economists took a more critical look at Adam Smith's teachings in *The Wealth of Nations*. Among the most influential of these was Daniel Raymond, who is recognized as the "first systemic American economist." Raymond opposed Smith's preoccupation with individual wealth, arguing that political and economic leaders should focus on the welfare of the nation and the overall society. Smith's notion that consumers should buy imports when they are cheaper than domestic products, he wrote, risked "destroying the unity of the nation by dividing it into classes and looking to the interests of individuals, instead of looking to the interests of the whole." Raymond argued that an individual "ought not to be allowed to afford patronage and support to the industry of foreigners, when his own fellow-citizens are in want."[8] Unlike later economists, he did not assume that the winners from trade would compensate the losers or that a society was better off overall as long as trade produced net gains, even if the gains were monopolized by a very few at the top of the society.

A new consensus emerged on the need for the development of the American System, a concept best articulated and promoted by Kentucky congressman Henry Clay.[9] He called for free trade only in cases of "perfect reciprocity"; protection and subsidization of America's infant manufacturing industries; extensive government-led development of national roads, waterways, railroads, and other infrastructure; expansion of the country's borders; removal of the Indians; and settlement and development of the land. Tariffs were not seen as a device for taxing consumers for the benefit of manufacturers but as a way to stimulate investment in the United States and eventually allow Americans to produce articles much more inexpensively than they could be procured abroad.

In response to Monroe's request, Congress raised tariffs in 1824 and again in 1828 with the so called Tariff of Abominations, under which rates on dutiable goods rose to 61.7 percent—higher even than those later imposed under the notorious Smoot-Hawley Tariff of 1930, which is often blamed for worsening the Great Depression. Over the next few decades, tariffs declined from these punitive rates but were then raised sharply during the Civil War at the behest of Abraham Lincoln, who might as well be called the Great Protector as the Great Emancipator. Lincoln wholeheartedly embraced Clay's American System thinking and argued that "the abandonment of the protective policy . . . must produce want and ruin among our people." From the Civil War until World War I, U.S. tariffs never fell below 40 percent, as leaders like Theodore Roosevelt emphasized their support of the American "catch-up" effort. Roosevelt said at one point, "Thank God I am not a free trader."[10]

Infrastructure and Industrial Policy

A crucial element of the American System was government backing of critical infrastructure and strategic industries. The first of these was the National or Cumberland Road. Begun in 1806, it created a paved connection from Cumberland, Maryland, to St. Louis, enabling travel from the Potomac River to the Mississippi in four days. Another important early project was the Erie Canal; completed in October 1825, it was a quick and huge success.

By far the most important project of the American System was the Transcontinental Railroad. In 1850, Congress authorized land grants to Illinois, Mississippi, and Alabama for construction of a rail line connecting Chicago to Mobile. By 1857, grants totaling 21 million acres had turned several railroad companies into America's first truly big businesses.[11] Then, in the summer of 1862, Abraham Lincoln pushed the Pacific Railroad Act through Congress. The act called for the chartering of two separate companies—the Central Pacific and the Union Pacific—to lay tracks from the Missouri River to Sacramento. After much delay and stupendous feats of engineering, on May 10, 1869, the Central Pacific's engine *Jupiter* and the Union Pacific's *Engine 119* stood nose to nose at Promontory Point, Utah, and the nation was connected from coast to coast by a ribbon of steel. Amazingly, although the government had lent the companies more than $64 million, by the end of 1869 it had earned over $103 million in return. More significantly, the railroad led to the creation of huge new markets and cities and transformed the nation into a true continental powerhouse.

Technology and Education

The promotion of technological innovation was also vital. On July 4, 1836, Congress created the U.S. Patent Office, with a commissioner of patents established within the State Department. An early beneficiary of this new office was a former professor of painting and sculpture at New York University named Samuel F. B. Morse, who received a $30,000 appropriation for an experimental telegraph line. Other inventions, like the sewing machine, the reaper, and the Colt revolver, were developed with strong government encouragement and protection.

Inextricably linked with the push for innovation was support for higher education. Jefferson had presented to Congress a proposal for a nationwide network of colleges to be built on land donated by the federal government, but it wasn't until Congressman Justin Morrill proposed a bill granting the states 5.8 million acres of federal land to be used for colleges, signed into law in July 1862 by Abraham Lincoln at the height of the Civil War, that the idea came to fruition. The colleges founded by the act revolutionized American education.

The United States also stole technology from Europe. In 1787, American agent Andrew Mitchell was intercepted by British authorities as he was trying to smuggle new technology out of the United Kingdom. His trunk was seized after being loaded on board a ship. Inside the trunk were models and drawings of some of Britain's newest textile production machinery. Mitchell escaped and sought refuge in Denmark. But his mission marks the start of a sustained U.S. campaign to obtain technology from the world's high-tech superpower of the day by hook or by crook.

Mitchell was sent by Tench Coxe, a Pennsylvanian economist and businessman and a close associate of Alexander Hamilton, who was soon to become the first secretary of the U.S. Treasury. Hamilton and Coxe were both convinced of the need for America to industrialize. In the Report on Manufactures he presented to Congress in 1791, Hamilton reminded his readers of the enormous problems Americans had had during the revolution with shortages of all kinds of military supplies, from guns and ships to shoes and uniforms. Historian Doron Ben-Atar describes Hamilton's campaign as "unabashed, state-sanctioned flouting of British law."[12] Ben-Atar argues that Hamilton acted as though intellectual property, like physical property, was confined within national frontiers.

Hamilton used patents to lure immigrants with skills and knowledge to move to the United States. George Parkinson, for example, was awarded a patent in 1791 for a textile spinning machine that was really just a knockoff of a machine he had used in England. The United States paid his family's expenses to emigrate to the United States.

The British were not happy about such attempts to steal their intellectual property. Severe penalties were on the books for anyone trying to take machines or designs out of the country or trying to lure skilled workers. Indeed, it was made illegal for such workers to leave the country. Eventually, the American drive to acquire foreign intellectual property died down in the early nineteenth century as homegrown Yankee ingenuity came to the fore, supported by American venture capital. But America's industrial development in the first generation after independence was not guaranteed, and Hamilton gets credit for providing state support and protection of these new businesses, which eventually dominated the world. All of these measures worked together to produce unprecedented economic growth.[13] Between 1820 and 1870, U.S. GDP growth was, like China's today, the wonder of the world.

Britain Changes Course

The wisdom of the American System was thrown into significant question by a huge decision British leaders made in the 1840s: for the most part to abandon their long-standing mercantilist policies in favor of free trade. In those days, "free trade" meant unilateral free trade rather than the reciprocal free trade of today. Britain dropped most of its tariffs and mercantilist measures without any agreement by other countries to do the same.

Behind this fateful decision were the arguments of London banker David Ricardo, whose 1817 treatise *The Principles of Political Economy and Taxation* laid out a case against mercantilism and for open markets and the specialization of production by nations. His analysis extended Smith's in several ways and introduced the powerful and ingenious concept of comparative advantage. His chief example, which became a classic, was the trade of British woolens for Portuguese wine.

Rather than Britain and Portugal both making wine and cloth, Ricardo argued, it would optimize both countries' benefits if the Portuguese imported their woolens from Britain and Britain imported its wine from Portugal. Even if Portugal could produce both cloth and wine more efficiently than Britain, the British were still better off concentrating on cloth, because they were less inferior in woolens than in wine making. If they tried to take up wine making in addition to making cloth, they would have less of both because their disadvantage in wine was so much greater. In a classic example, England needs 100 hours to make one unit of cloth or 5/6 units of wine. Portugal needs only 90 hours to make the cloth, or it can make 9/8 units of wine in 90 hours (table 1). So Portugal possesses an "absolute" advantage in producing both wine and cloth. In the absence of trade, England requires 220 hours of work to produce and consume one unit each of cloth and wine, while Portugal can do that in only 170 hours. But if each country specializes in what it does best, England can produce 2.2 units of cloth with 220 labor hours while Portugal can produce 2.125 units of wine with 170 hours of work. If the two countries then trade with each other, both can consume at least a unit each of cloth and wine, with 0–0.2 units of cloth and 0–0.125 units of wine remaining in each country to be consumed or exported. Each thus makes itself better off by specializing in what it does best and trading for the rest.

Although it took a few years, this thinking, combined with the rapidly growing dominance of British manufacturers and British commerce, led to the almost total abandonment of the mercantilist strategy (with a few major exceptions, to be discussed later) and the adoption of the new doctrine of laissez-faire. British leaders had come to the view that as the leading manufacturers, transporters, and financiers of the world, they would automatically be the low-cost producers in a world of open markets and free trade. Switching to the laissez-faire model would thus be greatly to Britain's benefit. By 1860, Britain had virtually no trade barriers.

The new British ideal was a world in which the United Kingdom would import grain and raw materials at the lowest possible cost and then export back to the world the manufactured goods churned out by the factories that had made Britain "the workshop of the world." The British also argued passionately, pushing the analysis of Smith and Ricardo, that the rest of the world should also switch to laissez-faire—but the rest of the world was not persuaded. The Germans, French, Swedes, and Japanese imitated the Americans in resisting "free trade" and pursuing mercantilism, or

Table 1. Hours of work necessary to produce one unit

Country	Product	
	Cloth	Wine
England	100	120
Portugal	90	80

"catch-up." (Later, after World War II, the Germans, French, and Japanese repeated their earlier pattern and were joined by the new Asian Tigers of South Korea, Taiwan, and Singapore. One might call China the last Tiger, or perhaps the first Dragon.)

By the late nineteenth century, Britain had become the world's only fully free market. A highly asymmetric global economic structure was established in which the world was partly governed by free trade doctrines and partly by strategic catch-up policies.

America Becomes Number One

The golden age of British supremacy was nowhere better symbolized than at the 1851 International Exhibition at London's Crystal Palace. It was dominated by British machine tools, British locomotives, British textiles, and everything else British. At the time, Britain was by far the world's main industrial country, alone accounting for about 30 percent of world industrial output. It produced nearly twice as much as the next largest producer, the United States. British ships carried more than half the world's ocean freight. As the increasingly troubled United States moved toward civil war and Germany struggled to become a united country, Britain seemed assured of economic supremacy for the indefinite future. Yet between 1870 and 1900, America surged ahead of Britain in virtually every economic sector.

The American System began to reap vast rewards. The United States had evolved into an enormous, relatively unhindered market that afforded American manufacturers unprecedented economies of scale, which led to rapid increases in productivity. The railroad infrastructure was the lynchpin of astonishing economic growth. It also fostered the first modern business enterprises, and the model was copied to modernize one industry after another.

By 1870, America was laying 5,100 miles of track a year, more than the rest of the world combined.[14] By 1896 it had 183,601 miles of rail, not counting another 60,000 miles in sidings and yards. This came to 42 percent of the world total, in a country with just 6 percent of the global land area. The railroad system accounted for about 15 percent of national production, more than all federal, state, and local governments combined, and it employed 800,000 men, or over 2 percent of the entire national workforce.[15] By 1900 the number of American farms had nearly tripled, from 2 million to 6 million, while the area farmed doubled and production of wheat, corn, and cotton outstripped the doubling of the population to make the United States the world's largest exporter of agricultural commodities.

Yet even as agricultural production soared, it declined to less than half of total U.S. production in the face of a vast wave of industrial development that has been called the second industrial revolution. The new farms and the rapidly growing population needed the stream of newly invented machines, such as the thresher, automatic wire binder, combine, husker, typewriter, electric light bulb, telephone, and refrigeration car, that emerged from America's industrial inventors. The railroads and the building boom drove demand for steel and wood, and all producers needed the tools and equipment that would allow mechanization and automation.

In 1870, Great Britain produced 40 percent of the world's steel, followed by Germany at 30 percent and the United States at 15 percent. By 1900, U.S. production was nearly 40 percent of the world total, with Germany second at 25 percent and Britain at about 20 percent. By 1913, the U.S. was making nearly half the world's steel.[16]

If we look more broadly at total manufacturing output, we find the same dynamics.[17] By 1914, U.S. GDP stood at $518 billion, more than double that of Britain and over three times that of Germany, while U.S. per capita income was $5,307, compared to $5,032 for Britain and $3,833 for Germany. America had become the richest country in the world, and it had reached this height by using high tariffs and a catch-up strategy that resulted in an annual rate of GDP growth of over 4 percent, while free trade, laissez-faire Britain could not maintain even 2 percent annual growth.[18] In the old tariff debates, it had been argued that protection of nascent U.S. manufacturers with initially higher costs than foreign producers would impose higher prices on consumers and inhibit economic growth. In fact, U.S. producers rapidly improved quality and exploited economies of scale, becoming the world's low-cost producers even as they paid the highest wages and American consumers enjoyed the lowest relative prices.

America Tightens Its Grip

Britain's losses in the Great War, and those of the rest of Europe, were America's gains. For starters, Britain had borrowed heavily from U.S. banks for war funding, and once it had exhausted its credit with them, it turned to the U.S. government for further credit. Before extending aid, however, Washington insisted that Britain liquidate its remaining assets. From 1914 to 1919, London sold off about $8 billion of its U.S. holdings and then borrowed another $5 billion from the U.S. Treasury. By thus depriving Britain of future gains on its U.S. investments and forcing it to become a large net debtor, Washington undermined future British wealth creation and power. Other countries, like France, also borrowed from America, so that whereas in 1914 the United States had been the world's leading debtor, five years later it was the leading creditor.

Perhaps even more significant was the shift in the management of the gold standard. Before the war, most nations had adhered to the system, managed by London, whereby currencies were backed by gold and pegged to its value. Once the war started, however, all governments except the United States went off the gold standard and issued paper money with no gold backing. The result was soaring inflation, wildly fluctuating exchange rates, and a huge flow of gold to the United States. America emerged from the war as the newly dominant financial power, with New York having replaced London as the center of global finance.

The story with shipping was similar. Before the war, America had virtually no merchant marine, and less than 10 percent of U.S. exports were carried by U.S. ships. This had been a source of concern in commercial and naval circles for some time, and in the 1912 presidential election campaign, Woodrow Wilson had argued that "without a great merchant marine we cannot take our rightful place in the commerce of the world."[19] With the war as an excuse, the government established the United States Shipping Board to direct and finance a major shipbuilding program. By 1918, the board was directing the launch of 3 million tons of ships annually—an amount equal to total world production in any prewar year. By 1920, American ships were carrying 42.7 percent of American commerce, and the United States had displaced Britain as the world's leading maritime country.

Aircraft and aviation were other areas of shifting leadership. Although the airplane had been invented in the United States, its development had taken place much more rapidly in Europe under the direction of government-sponsored institutes. The outbreak of war demonstrated dramatically and concretely that European and particularly German aviation was far ahead of America's. In response, the 1915 U.S. Navy appropriations bill established the National Advisory Committee on Aeronautics, which became a key driver of U.S. aerospace technology, eventually morphing into today's NASA. The army also placed orders for aircraft, increasing U.S. production from a few hundred planes annually before the war to fourteen thousand in 1918.[20]

After the war, the Kelly Air Mail Act of 1925 gave private contractors, rather than the Post Office, the right to transport airmail. A year later, the military declared its intention to have a fleet of twenty-six hundred planes by 1931, touching off another wave of investment in aviation that was further stimulated by the Air Commerce Act of 1927, which financed the building of airports and set standards for radio communications and aircraft design and construction. These efforts and Germany's defeat gave the United States world leadership in this field as well.

Perhaps the most interesting story of shifting leadership, however, is in radio telegraphy, which was also dominated before the war by Britain and its Marconi Radio Corporation. At the Versailles Peace Treaty negotiations, President Woodrow Wilson concluded that British leaders were reading his communications by dint of a "back door" (a secret tap on the transmission line) into the then world-dominant Marconi Radio, proclaiming that "we are on the eve of a commercial war of the severest sort, and I am afraid Great Britain will prove capable of as great commercial savagery as Germany has displayed for so many years in her competitive methods."[21] He believed communications technology was the key to the future, and he wanted to use radio to break the British monopoly on cable traffic.

Navy officials were particularly worried about an attempt by British Marconi to buy from General Electric the exclusive right to manufacture and sell the Alexanderson alternator, the only key piece of U.S.-owned radio technology still in American hands. Wilson therefore directed navy secretary Franklin Delano Roosevelt to stop the sale. The navy pressured GE to halt negotiations with the British, assisted the company in a buyout of American Marconi, the owner of many key patents, and then orchestrated the formation of a consortium of other holders of important electronic technology, including GE, AT&T, Westinghouse, and the United Fruit Company. The new communications giant thus formed was called Radio Corporation of America, or RCA, with the U.S. Navy as a 20 percent shareholder.

Owen Young, the GE lawyer who became RCA's first chairman, said he "wanted to make America the center of the world in radio communications."[22] RCA undercut the submarine cable rate of 25 cents a word with a new rate of 18 cents a word. By 1923 it was carrying 30 percent of transatlantic traffic and 50 percent of transpacific traffic. U.S. GDP rose by 204 percent from 1914 to 1918 and another 63 percent by 1921.

From Number One to World Hegemon

The United States had morphed into the world's biggest economy, but Britain, still with one of history's biggest empires, remained diplomatically and militarily the world's leading power. The British leadership was determined to recover its economic leadership, at least in finance and commerce, and despite what should have been glaring evidence that the laissez-faire system had contributed heavily to British decline, so strong was the belief in the system that the emergency measures instituted during the war were reversed. Government management of the economy was largely abolished, and most (though not all) tariffs were removed.

Washington, like London, also reverted to prewar policies. But these were diametrically opposite to those of Britain. The United States raised tariffs by over 40 percent to 38.5 percent ad valorem on dutiable items with the Fordney-McCumber tariff bill of 1922. In percentage terms, this was a much bigger hike than that of the Smoot-Hawley tariff of 1930, which has long been criticized as a major cause of the Great Depression. Thus we might have expected Fordney-McCumber to be a drag on the economy and especially on U.S. international trade, given that it was enacted during a global economic downturn and risked retaliation by U.S. trading partners. Instead, trade rose and the economy picked up speed as it moved into the Roaring Twenties. The U.S. boom was powered by exports to the war-devastated European economies, rapid innovation and adoption of new technology like electricity and the telephone, and government support of easy consumer credit, which marked the beginning of America's evolution into a consumer society. In the decade of the 1920s, the United States produced more than the major countries of Europe plus Japan combined.[23]

The American boom, of course, turned to a bust with the crash of the stock market in 1929 and the onset of the Great Depression, in which the United States temporarily lost some of its new dominance. Indeed, it suffered more than the other major countries primarily because of three factors. The first was a decision by the Federal Reserve to allow the money supply to shrink by a third; the second was a wave of competitive currency devaluations that substantially affected world trade. The third factor was a premature tax increase in 1936, after recovery looked as if it was beginning. The U.S. GDP fell by half between 1929 and 1932, and the value of manufactured goods' production in 1933 was only a quarter of what it had been in 1929.[24] U.S. exports fell by 69 percent, and the U.S. share of foreign commerce fell even faster than total world trade, declining from 13 percent to 10 percent in 1932.

The catastrophe of the Depression was followed by a significant economic recovery in the United States in the late 1930s, driven by a willingness to experiment with far-reaching methods for government-industry partnership and for government intervention in managing the economy. But it was the advent of World War II that demonstrated how government policy could really boost economic growth. The most important of the new government measures was the Reconstruction Finance Corporation (RFC), established in 1932 by President Herbert Hoover. Based on the old War Finance Corporation, it was initially intended to lend up to $2 billion (keep in mind that the entire federal budget under Calvin Coolidge had been $3 billion) to large financial institutions under stress, and to railroads whose bonds were held by insurance companies and banks. The idea was to shore up the credit markets, but the structure of the RFC was extremely flexible, it had certain extra-legislative powers, and of course it was well funded.

When he became president, Franklin Roosevelt seized on this new corporation and turned it into one of the most powerful government agencies of all time. Most of the funding of the New Deal passed through the RFC, and Roosevelt didn't see it as temporary or restricted to assisting the banking sector. He wanted it to spread government capital and credit to as broad a base as possible. The first step was to use RFC money to buy shares in over half the nation's banks and thereby enable them to join the new Federal Deposit Insurance Corporation. From there, the RFC funded the Federal Emergency Relief Administration, the Rural Electrification Administration, the Resettlement Administration, the Federal Home Loan Bank, the Commodity Credit Corporation, and the Export/Import Bank.

This was only a warm-up exercise. When World War II broke out, the RFC was ready to resume its old role as the government's war finance arm. In June 1940, Roosevelt authorized it to make loans and purchase stock in any company that produced or transported war materiel. The RFC quickly created eight divisions for defense production. The Rubber Reserve Company became the only importer of crude rubber. The Rubber Development Corporation became the nation's main source of synthetic rubber. The Metals Reserve Company bought and stockpiled strategic metals, and the Defense Plant and Defense Supplies corporations each invested over $9 billion in plants and equipment for producing war supplies.

Through the Defense Plant Corporation, the government financed over 80 percent of the new plant construction and plant conversion by the auto, aircraft, and other companies for wartime production. Washington came to own 90 percent of the country's synthetic rubber, aircraft, magnesium, and shipbuilding plants and facilities; 70 percent of the aluminum factories; half of U.S. machine tool plants; and thirty-eight hundred miles of pipelines. It spent $38 billion (nearly $700 billion in today's dollars) that not only helped win the war but stabilized the economy. All of this is comparable to the role of the government in today's China, and to its state-owned enterprises.

To run the wartime economy, the White House in 1940 established the Office of Production Management, which two years later changed into the War Production Board and the Board of Economic Warfare.[25] In today's terms, one might think of this as the coordinator of a large number of what might be called state-owned enterprises, or SOEs, à la China today. The war created 17.5 million jobs in the United States as war production accounted for over 40 percent of GDP in 1943–44. Steel production in 1944 reached 80 million long tons, or over two-thirds of total world production. The merchant marine expanded dramatically, and by 1945 the United States accounted for 60 percent of the world's merchant tonnage. Having produced fewer than fourteen thousand airplanes total in the twenty years before the war, by 1944 the United States was turning out ninety-six thousand per year. On top of this was an incredible R&D effort that led to the atomic bomb, the computer, the jet airplane, and the development of penicillin and numerous other drugs and biological agents.

By 1945, after a century and a half of "catch-up," the American System of industrial policy, government-backed infrastructure, protectionism, and continual government intervention in the economy to encourage industrial development and direct war production, the United States emerged from the war as an unprecedentedly powerful hegemonic colossus. It accounted for half of global GDP, owned 70 percent of the world's gold, had a monopoly on nuclear power, was the world leader in virtually every technology and every industry, owned the world's main currency, was the leading world creditor, and had a chronic trade surplus.[26] It had more than caught up. It was all alone in a realm no nation had ever before inhabited.

Then it took a fateful new tack.

6

The False God

> Free trade is God's diplomacy and there is no other certain way of uniting people in the bonds of peace.
>
> —*Richard Cobden*

In anticipation of victory in World War II, the Allied powers convened a meeting at Bretton Woods, New Hampshire, from July 1 to July 22, 1944, to consider how to organize the global economy after the war. This gathering brought a momentous about-face of American international economic policy. After nearly 150 years of mercantilism and protectionism, Washington decided to switch to British-style free trade—and to take the rest of the world with it.

Three factors prompted this shift. One was that the United States had come to account for about half of global GDP. Having reached the pinnacle, America saw that the view from there was much different from that on the upward climb. It needed to change priorities. The United States was now number one in virtually every industry, technology, and economic undertaking. There was no more need for catching up. Rather, there was a pressing need for global refinance, reconstruction, and revitalization at a moment when the world was facing the rapid approach of a new war.

The Cold War

At the time of the Bretton Woods meeting, which set out the rules for the postwar global economy, the Soviet Union was still an ally of the West. But in the wake of the 1945 Soviet occupation of most of eastern Europe, U.S. ambassador George Kennan's "Long Telegram" forecasting increasing hostility from the Soviet Union toward the free world, and Winston Churchill's March 5, 1946, Iron Curtain speech in Fulton, Missouri, the Cold War had begun. Thus, the reconstruction of the global economy was activated in the Cold War's opening rounds. Free trade and the opening of the American market to imports were therefore seen by Washington as strategies to prevent the spread of communism and the power of the Soviet Union. When I worked for the U.S. government twenty years later, it was still repeatedly impressed on me how important Washington thought free trade was for U.S. national security.

In 1966, as a newly minted foreign service officer, I was posted to Rotterdam, the Netherlands, to serve as vice consul at the U.S. consulate there. Before I left Washington, my State Department superiors emphasized that one of my major responsibilities would be to promote Dutch exports to the United States. This was twenty-one years after the war's end, and the Netherlands, along with the rest of Europe, had long since recovered. One might have thought I should be promoting American exports to the Netherlands, but no: America needed to keep the Netherlands on its side.

In 1984, while serving as counselor to the secretary of commerce, I was seconded to the staff of Vice President George H. W. Bush to be part of his Japan Task Force. This was a group established to follow up on bilateral trade negotiations recently agreed to by President Ronald Reagan and Prime Minister Yasuhiro Nakasone. The U.S. trade deficit with Japan had been rising dramatically for a few years, and the difficulty U.S. corporations experienced in getting access to Japan's markets was thought to be aggravating U.S. unemployment in the middle of a recession. There was little question that the U.S. market was far more open than Japan's, and many Americans accused Japan of pursuing mercantilism rather than free trade. The result was growing friction between the two allies.

The goal of the task force was to negotiate a significant new opening of key Japanese markets. If we succeeded, the vice president would go to

Tokyo for a victory lap. But the task force members agreed at the start that if there was no success, the Japanese would not be rewarded by a vice presidential visit. As it happened, there was no success. A task force meeting duly ensued to decide about the visit. I thought the meeting would be short. Since we had agreed on no visit in the case of no success, I was sure we'd all quickly agree to save Bush an unnecessary trip. Instead, a long debate ensued. Toward the end of it, Gaston Sigur, senior director for Asian Affairs of the National Security Council, brought down his hands hard on both arms of his chair and said: "We must have those bases. Now that's the bottom line." He was talking about the U.S. military bases in Okinawa and mainland Japan.

There had been no suggestion in either Tokyo or Washington that the bases were in any way at risk. But the U.S. national security establishment was so sensitive to anything that might infringe on its flexibility, and yet so insensitive to any damage arising from unequal trading conditions, that it always made trade concessions to achieve geopolitical objectives. Bush made the trip. We all had a reception at the prime minister's Kantei (White House), at which the Japanese negotiators savored their victory. Had there been no Cold War, the outcome of this and a thousand similar situations over the years would have been dramatically different. The Cold War led Washington not only to adopt free trade as its policy but to adopt unilateral, one-sided free trade. But according to the trade god, that was no problem, because even unilateral free trade was said to be economically more advantageous than protectionism.

The Trade God

As we have seen, David Ricardo demonstrated that it was better for both Portugal and England to specialize their production—Portugal in wine and England in cloth—even though Portugal could produce both at a lower absolute cost than England could. Because Portugal's advantage was greater in wine and England's disadvantage was lesser in cloth, ultimately each would do better by focusing exclusively on the production it did best.

What made this concept so powerfully attractive was its implication that countries would always gain from trade because every country always made some product in which it had a comparative advantage. With each nation specializing in production of that item and importing other needed goods and services, world production of all traded items would rise and the citizens of the participating countries would enjoy greater wealth. Even if England were to bar imports of wine, Portugal would still be better off specializing in wine production and importing its cloth from England, rather than retaliating by barring cloth imports. In other words, under the Ricardian model, while reciprocal free trade is the best solution, unilateral free trade is better than no trade. This doctrine captured Britain in the mid-nineteenth century, and it tried, unsuccessfully, to convert the rest of the world. In the twentieth century, enhancements of the argument enraptured American economists and policy makers.

In the 1920s, the Swedish economists Eli Hecksher and Bertil Gotthard Ohlin developed a revised version of the Ricardian theory that has guided the trade and globalization policy of the United States and many other countries over the past sixty years and still underpins most public debate. The new model kept Ricardo's argument about the benefits of countries' specializing in the production of certain goods—the benefits of comparative advantage—but refined his analysis in several ways. While Ricardo had argued that labor is the only factor of production, and that who exports and imports what products is determined by differences in technology within countries (wine making versus production of cloth), he did not account either for a country's ability to obtain a new technology, or for how a country's capital and natural resources determine what it produces. The new model assumed that new technology would readily spread to all players, and it added land and capital to labor as the factors of production. This led to the conclusion that those factors of production, rather than a particular technology, were the key determinants of trade flows.

A country that was rich in capital and with a relatively small but highly skilled labor force is expected to produce capital-intensive, high-technology products like computer chips, and export them in exchange for commodities and low-skill, labor-intensive products, like potatoes and textiles, from countries with much land and/or unskilled labor.

In 1941, economists Wolfgang Stolper and Paul Samuelson added the notion that over time, the costs of production, such as wages, would tend to converge among trading partners. In other words, if the United States and China engaged in free trade with each other, according to Samuelson, their wages would trend toward a median level. Chinese might find this pleasing, but Americans might not. This aspect of the free trade doctrine remained little discussed until very recently.

Under this model, as under Ricardo's, comparative advantage determines one unique combination or equilibrium of production and trade that produces optimal results for each country and thus for the world. If you grant the assumptions on which this argument is based, its conclusions are mathematically irrefutable. It was this, and the stubborn faith that global trade was "God's diplomacy" and would lead inevitably to world peace, that made free trade the dominant international economic doctrine in the Anglo countries and—because of those countries' power—throughout much of the world.

God's Government

The Bretton Woods meeting led to the establishment, between 1947 and 1950, of three institutions to manage the global economy: the International Monetary Fund (IMF), the World Bank, and the General Agreement on Tariffs and Trade (GATT).

The IMF's role was to be the czar of global finance. It established a fixed-rate global monetary system based on the U.S. dollar that was tied to gold at $35 per ounce. The dollar would be the main currency in which trade would be conducted and in which countries would pay their debts to each other. All other currencies were valued at a fixed rate of exchange to the dollar—4 Swiss francs to the dollar, 360 Japanese yen, 3.33 deutsche marks, and so on. These rates would be allowed to fluctuate over six months or so, but only by 1 percent. The expectation was that each member nation's trade would be roughly balanced over time, so that no country would accumulate either a chronic trade surplus or a chronic trade deficit. The primary role of the IMF was to provide emergency loans for countries that might begin suffering from "balance of payments difficulties," meaning that they were experiencing large trade deficits and did not have enough dollars to pay for their excess of imports over exports. But there was a condition to these IMF loans. To get one, the deficit country had to agree to follow an IMF-imposed plan aimed at revitalizing its economy to prevent further trade deficits. A final aspect of the system, which would come to have unexpected significance, was that a country that accumulated a lot of dollars could pass them to the United States, which was obligated to redeem the dollars with gold.

The job of the World Bank was initially to provide loans for the reconstruction and revitalization of Europe in the wake of World War II. Once its work there had been accomplished, it widened its scope to become an economic development lender to the entire world.

The GATT was aimed at administering while also widening and deepening the initial agreement of 44 countries to pursue global free trade in goods by reducing their tariffs and quotas on imports. In a series of negotiating rounds between 1947 and 1993, the GATT reduced global tariffs by more than 75 percent, grew to include 164 countries, and extended its coverage from goods to trade in services. It also became a kind of independent arbiter of disputes and thereby helped to tamp down conflicts between nations. In 1995, the GATT was replaced by a new, more comprehensive body known as the World Trade Organization, which extended its mission to include trade in services, intellectual property, and government procurement.

Based on this system, international trade over the next twenty years seemed largely to conform to the predictions of the Hecksher/Ohlin/Stolper/Samuelson free trade model, within what came to be called the neoclassical economic system. In increasingly open markets, capital-rich countries with skilled labor forces, like the United States, tended to produce and export medium- to high-technology manufactured goods and to import raw materials and commodities. Countries with a lot of land and low-skilled labor, like the Philippines or Mexico, exported commodities and low-tech manufactured goods while importing more advanced manufactures. The United States was a bit unusual in that, being rich in land, it also exported agricultural commodities along with advanced manufactured items. Because commodities constituted a large part of global trade and national markets for manufactures remained relatively protected despite the GATT tariff reductions, there were few globally dominant producers, and global markets were fairly price competitive. It seemed that Hecksher/Ohlin/Samuelson/Stolper were right on the mark, and that free trade was always and everywhere a winning proposition.

The Golden Age

The years between 1947 and 1975 have come to be known as golden era of the American economy. U.S. GDP and productivity grew at a compound annual rate of about 4 percent for twenty-five years, while household income nearly tripled.[1] Home ownership steadily rose, as did ownership of automobiles and TVs. Moreover, the gains were equitably spread, with those at the bottom of the income distribution narrowing the gap between themselves and those in the top 10 percent.

Manufacturing was the driving force of American wealth creation, accounting for about 25 percent of GDP, 20 percent of employment, and the greatest part of productivity growth.[2] The big industrial companies were mostly union shops, and union members comprised about 35 percent of the total workforce, peaking at 21 million members in 1979.[3] Most families had one bread winner, whose earnings easily supported a rising middle-class lifestyle.

This was all made possible by the fact that America had by far the highest productivity (especially industrial productivity) of any country on earth. A good example was General Motors. In 1959, the year I graduated from high school, GM produced 1,468,962 units of its Chevrolet line of models. Remember that the high fixed costs of investment are distributed over more and more units as production rises, so that the cost of the car becomes less with each unit produced. Thus, because of its enormous volume, GM could pay the highest wages and still be the world's lowest-cost auto producer. One result was that as soon as they graduated, most of the guys in my high school class just walked a mile down the street and joined the GM assembly line, where they made wages and obtained medical and retirement benefits that allowed them, as a sole income earner, to afford a boat, a cottage at the beach, and a family with four kids.

With this kind of competitiveness, Washington could and did move strongly to expand global trade. In the early rounds of GATT trade negotiations, the United States gave a lot more than it got because, well, it could afford to. A good example was the 1947 Geneva Round, in which Washington offered Britain tariff reductions of 36–50 percent on 70 percent of traded items. In return, Washington asked for a reduction of Britain's "Imperial Preferences," which discriminated in favor of imports from the empire. In the end, Britain kept the preferences while also pocketing the American concessions. President Truman and the State Department decided for geopolitical reasons that "a thin agreement was better than no agreement."[4]

In the 1954–55 negotiation with Japan, the United States made substantial tariff cuts on 56 percent of its imports from Japan while receiving cuts on only 1.6 percent of U.S. exports to Japan. These results were deemed a great success by economists and policy makers intent on both promoting recovery from the war and binding allies to the United States. The U.S. attitude was well expressed by a State Department official who noted that "the U.S. trade surplus is a serious problem and we must become really import minded." President Truman added that "our industry dominates world markets and our workmen no longer need fear the competition of foreign workers." The President's Advisory Board for Mutual Security called for unilateral elimination of tariffs on autos and consumer electronics because "U.S. producers are so advanced no one can touch them."[5]

The Storm

America's confident dominance and rapidly rising living standards led it to overlook the early harbingers of a storm that by 1971–72 would sweep away much of the Bretton Woods system and create an entirely new dynamic. As early as 1956, Japanese textile exports to the U.S. market had made such inroads that the Eisenhower administration pressured Tokyo into a "Voluntary Restraint Agreement" (VRE) to limit its textile exports. By 1969 there was also a VRE on Japanese steel exports, which was later broadened to include European steel exports as well. Between 1955 and 1970, sales of Germany's Volkswagen Beetle grew from zero to 7 percent of the U.S. auto market.[6] But that was nothing compared to what Sony and other Japanese producers were doing in the television market: by 1972 they had captured 62 percent of sales of black-and-white TV sets and by 1976 had 45 percent of color set sales as well.[7] By then they completely dominated radio, stereo, and recorder sales.

While during the 1950s and most of the 1960s the United States had had a trade surplus, it vanished between 1968 and 1972. This had been foreseen in a 1959 National Security Council debate on international trade policy, at which CIA director John McCone argued that "the problem of foreign competition was going to grow rapidly in the future. The costs of production abroad of competitive products were shockingly lower than in the United States, mostly as a result of cheaper labor costs." Treasury Secretary Robert Anderson emphasized that the balance of payments was the "acid test" of a sound economy. Now America seemed to be failing that test, and this suggested that both its global role and its standard of living would have to be reduced. The Norwegian historian Geir Lundestad remarked, "The United States is organizing its own decline."[8]

Part of what was happening was the natural recovery of competitive positions by the formerly war-devastated industries of Europe and Japan. But other, more fundamental and important factors were also at work. By the 1960s, the exchange rates for the dollar that had been fixed in 1947 had not been adjusted for nearly two decades, despite dramatic increases in relative productivity by Japan and the major European countries. The dollar was now seriously overvalued, and U.S. producers were increasingly priced out of foreign markets.

The United States was losing its competitive advantage. During the hundred years from 1870 to 1970, the United States had run continual trade surpluses of 1 to 2 percent of GDP. But in 1971 the balance went negative.[9] For the next few years it swung back and forth, but since 1974, it has been continually negative, sometimes amounting to as much as 5 percent of GDP. As James McBride and Andrew Chatzky wrote in 2019, "Today's $621 billion deficit, representing about 3 percent of gross domestic product . . ., is down from a 2006 peak of more than $760 billion, which at the time was over 5 percent of GDP."[10] This shift had many implications, of which the most immediate came even before 1971 had ended.

In August of that year, President Nixon halted the dollar's convertibility into gold. Since the 1960s, many countries had been accumulating dollars from their trade surpluses with the United States. By adding to these countries' money supply, the dollars caused inflation, which they tried to combat by exchanging some of their dollar holdings for gold. Soon a veritable river of gold was flowing from Fort Knox to Paris, London, Tokyo, and elsewhere. Between 1958 and 1968, the United States lost half its monetary gold and faced the prospect of having to reduce spending of all kinds, including on defense.[11] Nixon not only stopped redeeming dollars for gold, he imposed a surcharge (or tariff) of 10 percent on all dutiable U.S. import items. By refusing to pay out in gold, he effectively abandoned the Bretton Woods system and allowed the value of the dollar to be determined by the demands of the international money markets. His treasury secretary, former Texas governor John Connally, famously told a group of European journalists, "The dollar is our money, but now it's your problem."[12]

That turned out not to be true. In a system of floating, market-determined currency valuations, central banks can manipulate relative values by intervening in currency markets. If, say, the Japanese government wanted to increase employment and wages by pumping up exports, it could easily do so by selling its own yen and buying dollars in the international currency markets. The value of the dollar would rise while that of the yen would fall, making Japanese products less expensive for non-Japanese buyers. Thus, while Nixon's bold moves temporarily improved the U.S. trade position, the effect did not last. By 1980, the trade deficit (technically, the current account deficit) had reached $20 billion, and it kept climbing as European and Japanese televisions, cars, steel, and much else poured into the great American market, resulting in lower prices for American consumers but also in a great dislocation of U.S. industry, loss of jobs, and lower wages for millions of American workers.[13]

This was not just a matter of currency manipulation. The god of free trade orthodoxy was beginning to fail. The unusual circumstances of the postwar period had initially made the free trade god look good, but his/her high priests were growing increasingly worried. A huge misconception of the reality of international trade seemed to be at work.

The Japanese Miracle

Even as early as the late 1950s, and certainly by the mid-1960s, there was clear evidence that the high priests might be worshiping at the wrong altar. Japan after World War II was a country with a lot of inexpensive, relatively unskilled labor and few natural resources. American leaders and economists, in keeping with the orthodox economic doctrine, advised and expected Japan to produce low-tech manufactures such as toys and inexpensive textiles. In 1955, Secretary of State John Foster Dulles advised the Japanese to concentrate on exporting to Southeast Asia and forget about the U.S. market because Japan was incapable of making products Americans would want to buy. The chief U.S. negotiator with Japan on trade, C. Thayer White, in 1954–55 advised Japan to forget about creating an auto industry and simply import cars from America.

By 1964, however, Japan's shipyards were building half the world's shipping tonnage, the United States had recorded its first trade deficit with Japan, and the "Japanese Miracle" became widely acclaimed. For example, between 1964 and 1984, Japan's auto industry captured a quarter of the world market.[14]

I went to Tokyo in 1965 to study Japanese at Keio University and got to watch the Japanese Miracle unfold. Later, during the Reagan administration, I was counselor to the secretary of commerce, Malcolm Baldrige, and one of the chief U.S. negotiators with Japan during a period of maximum U.S.-Japan trade friction. In this role, I became friends with Naohiro Amaya, a former vice minister of the Ministry of International Trade and Industry (MITI) and one of the key architects of Japan's postwar "catch-up" industrial policy strategy. He once explained to me the Japanese perspective on economic development and the Anglo-American orthodox trade theory. "We did," he said, "the opposite of what the American economists said. We violated all the normal concepts. The American view of economics may help business to increase current production or to lower current costs. But research and development are necessary for the future, and it is a gamble. Businessmen are risk averse. They hesitate to take the gamble on new developments. Therefore, if the magic invisible hand cannot drive the enterprise to new developments, the visible hand of the government must do so."[15]

One of his colleagues at MITI, K. Otabe, added: "If the theory of international trade were pursued to its ultimate conclusion, the United States would specialize in the production of autos and Japan in the production of tuna." But this would not create wealth and good-paying jobs for Japan. Therefore, the Japanese government believed that creation of certain industries was "necessary to diversify and promote the development of the Japanese economy."

But wasn't Japan a member of the GATT? Didn't it agree to reduce its protective tariffs as a condition of joining? Didn't it believe in free trade just like the United States? The answers are yes, yes, and no. Japan did become a member of the GATT in 1955 (at American insistence, over the objections of most European countries), and it did reduce tariffs, even getting most of them to zero by the early 1980s, but it didn't embrace free trade. Like the United States of the nineteenth and first half of the twentieth centuries, Japan adopted a mercantilist, catch-up strategy. The country it was catching up to was the United States. It offset its tariff reductions by selling the yen in order to maintain its undervaluation against the dollar.

Moreover, tariffs are not the only barriers to trade. They are not even the most important barriers. Customs officials can delay inspections; safety regulations can be designed to exclude certain imported products. Sales of products like autos require dealers. In the United States, by law, the dealers are independent and cannot be controlled by the auto companies. But in Japan, Toyota dealerships are owned by Toyota and sell only Toyotas. If you, as a new automaker in the Japanese market, must build out your own nationwide dealer network, the cost can be prohibitive. For example, the Korean automaker Hyundai is internationally quite competitive, yet it has withdrawn from the Japanese market. Despite being a member of the GATT and a major international trader, Japan maintained a substantially protected market for key products for a very long time.

Nor was it just Japan. The Japanese Miracle encouraged imitation. Singapore's founding leader, Lee Kuan Yew, directed his officials to study Japan rather than focusing entirely on the United States or the United Kingdom for lessons on how to achieve rapid economic development. South Korea looked across the waters and vowed that anything Japan could do Korea could do better. With no previously skilled workforce, no natural resources, and a relatively small population, it soon gained strong positions in the shipbuilding, steel, auto, and semiconductor industries, all fields that orthodox theory said should be dominated by advanced, developed countries.

Calling Japan to the True Faith

Throughout the 1980s, the United States and Japan were locked in bitter economic combat. Seemingly endless negotiations resulted in numerous agreements in industries ranging from textiles to autos to semiconductors to fighter aircraft. Perhaps the best example of how this played out is the battle over semiconductors. During that time, several Japanese electronics companies sought to catch up to and surpass the U.S. semiconductor producers like Intel, National Semiconductor, and Advanced Micro Devices (AMD). The war was first fought over dynamic random access memory chips (DRAMs or D-RAMs) and later extended to microprocessors. In 1981 the main product was called a 16K DRAM, and U.S. producers accounted for about two-thirds of the world market. But they complained that Japanese competitors like Toshiba, NEC, and Fujitsu were not only copying their products but dumping them in the U.S. market—that is, selling in the U.S. market below cost or below the price in Japan. They also complained that the Japanese government was rewarding Japanese users of the chip if they followed a "Buy Japan" policy.

The Japanese makers were also reverse engineering the U.S. chips, a practice that created a telltale buying pattern. When a new chip introduced by a U.S. maker first came into the Japanese market, it would enjoy robust sales. But a bit later, the Japanese makers' sales would soar while those of the U.S. makers would collapse. The Japanese, of course, claimed they weren't copying the American chips and that the U.S. producers' falling sales must be due to poor quality, late delivery, or some other flaw. In response, the U.S. makers noted that sometimes there were mistakes in their own chip designs and that the Japanese chips contained the same mistakes, demonstrating that they had indeed copied the U.S. chips.

In any case, this was another example of doing the opposite of what the Americans advised. The Japanese government and industry understood that semiconductors would be the critical components of much future technology and of many advanced products for both consumer and national security uses. Their experience had convinced them that the American faith in market-driven comparative advantage as a kind of law of nature was not necessarily valid. They had shown that they could create comparative advantage in chosen industries through a combination of government support and protection with industry effort and competition.

This was, of course, at odds with the theoretical underpinning of the GATT, and even more with the orthodox American view of free market competition. Japan was therefore vulnerable to the charge of trading and competing "unfairly," and we in Washington repeatedly called on it to stop "cheating" and open its market as it had promised to do when it joined the GATT.

One of our rounds of talks went by the label "market-oriented sector specific," or MOSS (some said it stood for "more of the same shit"). The idea was to identify sectors in which we *knew* the United States was competitive, and then to negotiate with Japan at the highest levels to remove all barriers to American imports in those markets. U.S. companies would move in, establish strong market shares, and act as forerunners for other U.S. corporations and products. This was presented to a small group of us negotiators in the Roosevelt Room of the White House. The moment I heard it I knew it was nonsense. The problem wasn't with U.S. products, and although we continually accused the Japanese of being unfair, they weren't really acting unfairly. The issue went back to Amaya's comment about how Japan did the opposite of what the Americans had advised. Our premise was that the United States and Japan were playing the same game. After all, we told ourselves, Japan was a democracy just like us. It had a capitalist market economy just like ours. So, we told ourselves, it should embrace open, free market trade just like us.

But those assumptions were wrong. Japan may have been a democracy, but only one party had ruled it for most of its postwar existence. Its bureaucracy was immensely powerful. CEOs in Japan did what key vice ministers told them. That was known as "administrative guidance." The CEO who received such "guidance" didn't go to court against the Japanese government or call in his lawyers or lobbyists. He tipped his hat and did as instructed. I will never forget Sony founder Akio Morita telling me once regarding a certain trade issue: "MITI must give the Japanese companies 'strong guidance.' " Most important, Japan was only a quasi-market economy. It didn't embrace the same laissez-faire spirit of the Anglo-Americans. The word *open* has a very different meaning in Japanese than in American English. It can mean open the door or open your eyes. But whereas Americans like open spaces, open personalities, and open agreements openly arrived at, those terms are understood quite differently in Japan. There, one speaks not of open relationships but of close, tightly knit relationships, of loyalty to longtime suppliers even if their present prices are a bit higher than those being offered by a newcomer, of long-term relationships rather than of the best deal today. The truth was that the Japanese were simply not playing the same game we were. Both teams were playing football, but Japan was playing American football with helmets and pads, while the United States was playing European football (what Americans call soccer), which has no protective equipment. Until we recognized that and responded accordingly, we were never going to change the situation or the negotiation.

Interestingly, the President's Council of Economic Advisors didn't at all support the U.S. negotiators. It took the pure free trade position that Japan was only hurting itself by protecting and subsidizing its industries. The council's attitude was well captured by its former chairman, Herb Stein, who once said to me: "The Japanese will sell us cars and we'll sell them poetry." Later, council member and Stanford University economist Michael Boskin was reported to have said, "Potato chips, computer chips, what's the difference?" Boskin denies saying this and I accept his word, but the comment is deeply indicative of how economists thought in the late twentieth century. Many still think that way.

And the Winner Was

In the U.S.-Japan trade war of the 1980s, the United States put numerical limits on imports of Japanese autos, created a so-called trigger price mechanism to impose tariffs on imports of Japanese steel if their price fell below a designated level, essentially forced Japan to revalue the yen by more than 50 percent between 1985 and 1987, and concluded an agreement, known as the Semiconductor Agreement, that guaranteed U.S. producers 25 percent of the Japanese semiconductor market while also obtaining a pledge that Japanese chip makers would not dump their products in the United States. There were many other measures as well, but this will give you a taste of how we U.S. negotiators were trying to persuade Japan to play football our way.

If asked today, most economists, pundits, congresspersons, and business leaders will say that America won the trade war with Japan. They have that view because in the wake of the Plaza Agreement, the Bank of Japan created extreme liquidity in order to reduce interest rates and cushion Japanese industry against the blow of the yen revaluation. They may have overdone it: by 1989, major Japanese companies were borrowing at negative interest rates, meaning that the market was paying them to take the money. An enormous stock and real estate bubble expanded and then burst in 1991, resulting in very low economic growth for Japan for the rest of the decade.

But those who would declare an American win are often not aware of the wounds on the U.S. side. We lost our machine tool industry, our forging industry, our circuit board industry, much of our semiconductor equipment industry, much of our steel industry, our entire consumer electronics industry, most of our textile industry, and much of our auto industry. It is true that Japanese companies like Toyota and Honda put auto factories in the United States, but many of the parts for the U.S. assembly lines come from Japan. The United States was able to negotiate the agreements noted above only because of the fact that acting as the guarantor of Japan's national security and providing the biggest market for Japan's exports gave Washington enormous leverage in the negotiations. Yet despite those deals, the United States did not convert Japan to the Anglo-American faith of free trade, nor did it win the trade war, as its current account deficit bottomed out and then rose again.

False God, False Assumptions

The main reason Washington could not convert Japan to its free trade faith was that the neoclassical Anglo-American doctrine was full of holes. This had been clear to the Japanese at least since the 1950s. In the late 1970s and early 1980s, it should have become clearer to the Anglophone world as well. Young economists like Paul Krugman, James Brander, Barbara Spencer, and Joseph Stiglitz had begun to question the assumptions underlying the divinity of that god. Krugman, who later received a Nobel Prize for his work, emphasized that much of world trade seemed to operate outside the theory—a discrepancy he attributed to the fact that the theory rested on shaky assumptions.

These assumptions include perfect competition (all markets are like that for wheat, in which no single producer or buyer can affect ultimate total production or final prices); eternal full employment; no costs attached to opening or closing factories; no costs for training new workers; no cross-border flows of investment; no costs of switching from production of one product (wine?) to another (cloth?); fixed exchange rates; no economies of scale (the more units of a product I make in a single factory, the lower the cost of each item); no technological innovation unique to one country; no increases in productivity; no spillovers of know-how from one industry to another; operation of factories at full capacity at all times; zero costs of entering or exiting a business; zero transportation costs; the ability of workers to switch instantaneously, with no need of training, and at no cost of moving from making, say, steel, to designing semiconductor chips; and finally, no offshoring of production (Ricardo had said in his original analysis that if British textile makers moved their factories to Portugal, his reasoning would not hold).[16]

As Krugman pointed out, merely to list the restrictive assumptions of the conventional wisdom was to demonstrate its inadequacies. The global economy no longer operates under fixed exchange rates, there are substantial costs involved in switching industries and moving people, and there are enormous cross-border capital flows, to name just a few of the more obvious problems. In an effort to improve the theory, Krugman altered the conventional trade model so that rather than assuming away economies of scale, it incorporated them (since they so obviously exist in virtually all manufacturing industries) as a major element of the equation. He argued that economies of scale could be a major driver and even a shifter of trade flows. Through economies of scale, a country's comparative advantage could change, and it could become an exporter of things it had formerly imported. It could also achieve such a low-cost position that it would come to dominate not just production but also technological advancement in its industry, giving it a virtually unassailable market-technological position worldwide—think Boeing and Airbus.

Krugman's thinking became known as New Trade Theory, or the New International Economics. As a member in good standing and even a shining star of the economic establishment, he maintained that his thinking did not undermine the argument for free trade, which he insisted was the best policy despite so many of its assumptions being at obvious variance with reality. His argument has been that free trade generates more demand and thus more large-scale production, which generates greater economies of scale and lower unit costs. It also increases consumer choices—we in the United States can buy not only Fords, Chryslers, and Chevrolets, but also Hyundais, Volvos, and Toyotas—and thereby sharpens competition. Nevertheless, he and many of his colleagues recognized that incorporating economies of scale into the model changed the theory. It was no longer about mathematical certainty but about conditionality. The ability of the old orthodoxy to explain and predict trade patterns would grow increasingly limited—if it remained valid at all.

Krugman and his colleagues were also forced to note that, contrary to orthodox theory, government intervention in trade might sometimes be in the national interest. For instance, subsidizing or protecting an industry to enable it to achieve unchallengeable economies of scale in key areas might be sensible—as Amaya had said. Think of computing, aerospace, and solar panel manufacture. Or consider the case of U.S.-based Boeing versus European Airbus: Europe has substantially subsidized Airbus in its attempt to overtake Boeing, and most analysts agree that these subsidies have benefited not only the European aerospace industry but the European economy.

In view of all this, Krugman concluded that while "free trade is not passé, it is an idea that has irretrievably lost its innocence. There is still a case for free trade as a good policy . . . but it can never again be asserted as the policy that economic theory tells us is always right."[17] When Krugman received his Nobel Prize, I wondered if Amaya felt cheated. But he was a modest, generous guy, who is probably smiling now from Takamagahara (the Plain of High Heaven).

Cambridge University economist Ha-Joon Chang takes the discussion another step forward, to perhaps its most critical point. In his book *Bad Samaritans,* he argues that a nation may decide to subsidize a given industry because it wants or needs more advanced technology, for reasons of either national security or greater productivity and economic welfare.[18] In other words, Chang totally disagrees with Herbert Stein that it makes no difference whether a nation writes poetry or produces semiconductors. Poetry may be uplifting to read, but it doesn't put much bread on the table or defend against aggression. Chang argues, in fact, that economic development is largely about acquiring and mastering advanced technology; countries need manufacturing and new technology because it is in advanced manufacturing that the greatest productivity gains are made. And because unfettered market dynamics tend to favor the early developers of a technology, countries that wish to develop the same capability at a later date sometimes have to defy the market and provide government support, even if that entails short- to medium-term losses. Chang says it's like going to school. You sacrifice present cost efficiency and income for future productivity and wealth. He points to Tom Friedman's "Golden Straitjacket" (an agreement to relinquish a degree of national economic sovereignty, maintain savings at high levels, balance national budgets, and maintain open international markets even in the face of mercantilist trade policies by other countries) in *The Lexus and the Olive Tree*, noting that if Japan had worn that straitjacket in the 1960s, there would be no Lexus today.

Religions Die Hard

Despite the practical and theoretical evidence of the past two decades, and despite the growing phenomenon of offshoring of manufacturing—something both Ricardo and Hecksher/Ohlin/Stolper/Samuelson said would never happen—U.S. economics professors, members of the Council of Economic Advisors, economics pundits, officials such as the U.S. trade representative and the secretary of the treasury, and writers of economics textbooks have found it impossible to abandon the old-time religion. Krugman himself insisted that his work was only theoretical, and that in the real world, an orthodox free trade policy was still best because political lobbying would prevent any strategic trade policy from following a sensible course. Well, perhaps. But Krugman is not an expert on either politics or trade negotiation.

The huge wave of euphoria that followed collapse of the Soviet Union in 1991 became linked to the notion that democracy and free trade had won the Cold War. This conviction, in turn, gave impetus to a project to turn the GATT into the World Trade Organization, which was duly established in 1995 with 123 member nations. Under this institution, subsidies for production, protection of strategic industries, currency manipulation, and other industrial policy measures that had enriched the United Kingdom, the United States, Japan, South Korea, Taiwan, Germany, France, Switzerland, Singapore, the Netherlands, and Sweden were strictly forbidden, not only with regard to trade in goods but also regarding trade in services such as communications, banking, and tourism.

Treasury Secretary Robert Rubin pushed for all this with the strong assistance of the future secretary of the treasury, Lawrence Summers, who had also been the youngest economics professor ever to achieve tenure at Harvard University. His support not only for the WTO but for orthodox free trade was backed by Laura Tyson, chairwoman of the Council of Economic Advisors, who had written a tract called *Who's Bashing Whom?* in which she acknowledged the efficacy of Japan's industrial policy despite economists' disapproval of it.[19] The pages of the *Washington Post, New York Times* (where Krugman became a columnist), *Wall Street Journal,* and *Financial Times* constantly sang the hymns of the old-time religion, providing little space for contrary opinion.

Similarly, with think tanks. The Brookings Institution, the American Enterprise Institute, and certainly the Peterson Institute all promoted the orthodoxy. Peterson Institute director Fred Bergsten was especially talented at developing econometric models that uncovered new benefits of free trade. Of course, the models all assumed full employment, eternal absence of recessions and financial crises, and a host of other nonexistent conditions. Now too there was the annual meeting of Klaus Schwab's World Economic Forum in Davos, Switzerland, where high-powered CEOs, journalists, and academics gathered to sing the good old hymns and praise something now called "globalization"—which included not only trade but the offshoring of investment and jobs to create "global supply chains" that inevitably undercut unions in economically developed countries by taking advantage of cheap, unorganized labor in developing countries that had no or few regulations for the environment, worker safety, or health.

At this time, it also became virtually required that any sophisticated person of affairs believe that China had turned onto the capitalist road and that free trade would inevitably turn it into a capitalist, market-driven democracy, or at least quasi-democracy. To hasten this development, the high priests of orthodox free trade began calling for China's admission to the WTO. As we have seen, this duly occurred at the end of 2001, with the enthusiastic support of U.S. trade representative Charlene Barshefsky, President Clinton, *New York Times* columnist Tom Friedman, and virtually the entire congregation of the free trade church.

Adversarial and Strategic Trade

Also, in 2001, former IBM chief scientist and Sloan Foundation president Ralph Gomory and former American Economics Association president William Baumol wrote the book *Global Trade and Conflicting National Interests.*[20] It may be the most important unread book of all time.

Baumol and Gomory developed a series of models that more nearly approximated the reality of international trade by incorporating the effects not only of economies of scale but those of rapid technological changes and sudden shifts in productivity. Such a shift might arise, for example, when a company like, say, Intel places an advanced facility in a place like China. Unlike previous models, which incorporated only a few countries and products, the Baumol and Gomory model included large numbers of products and countries. It went far beyond Krugman in demonstrating how badly flawed the conventional wisdom is. Whereas the orthodox theory holds that there is only one win-win trade pattern, uniquely optimal for all trading partners, Gomory and Baumol found that there are many possible trading patterns, of which some are optimal for one party and others for the other parties, but that none is optimal for all parties at all times. In other words, while trade can sometimes be win-win, it is more frequently adversarial or zero sum (you win, I lose).

Again, think of Boeing and Airbus. A Boeing sale tends to be a gain for the United States and a loss for Europe; an Airbus sale is the reverse. (I know this is simplistic, but you get the point.) Depending on the relative economies of scale, levels of technology, rates of productivity, and industry or national strategy, any given country might produce amounts of a product that are not optimal for other trading partners. Take the classic case in which England produces all the cloth. Suppose the Portuguese came to see cloth as a high-growth market and wine, their area of comparative advantage, as a low-growth one. To ensure full employment for their rapidly growing population they might decide to kick-start cloth production with a subsidy, a ploy that eventually leads to much larger-scale production and lower costs in Portugal than in England, even without the subsidies, which have now been discounted. As the Portuguese take most of the global cloth business, they need so many workers that they turn their wine pressers into cloth makers. With no wine coming from Portugal and no work in the cloth mills, the British workers turn to wine making, precisely their area of comparative disadvantage. Here the introduction of economies of scale has turned the areas of specialization upside down, to the disadvantage of England and the global economy but possibly to Portugal's advantage.

This example demonstrates another key Gomory-Baumol conclusion. Whether a country achieves large-scale production, innovation, or major jumps in productivity is largely unrelated to climate, geography, and national endowments like capital, land, and labor. Sometimes it results from a strategic choice to subsidize large-scale production. It may also come by serendipity—for example, if a Portuguese entrepreneur were to innovate the latest cloth fashion. The key point is that once achieved, economies of scale and technology innovations become barriers to entry for newcomers. Whether foreign or domestic, a new competitor will have to make an enormous investment to match the scale and technology of the dominant player. What makes this even more difficult is that normal market dynamics will reinforce the existing market structure. Customers will favor the lower prices (based on the lower costs arising from economies of scale) of the dominant producer, thus creating more production, leading to even greater economies of scale. As Baumol and Gomory pointed out, once a dominant market position like, say, Intel's in microprocessors is attained, it tends to generate extra-high profits, which allow the company to compete in ways that raise the barriers to entry ever higher. Under the assumptions of conventional trade theory, such barriers don't exist.

A final key point, also at odds with conventional theory, is that attainment of the level of large-scale production that yields economies of scale is very much influenced by public policy. Economies of scale are more likely to accrue if, for example, the government adopts a favorable regulatory policy, constructs supporting infrastructure, uses government procurement to provide an early market, provides a special tax incentive, or takes any of several other steps to foster an industry. Governments can also do a great deal to help companies attain and maintain market dominance, including spurring innovation. In the 1980s, Intel benefited greatly from the U.S. government's Minute Man missile program, from strong U.S. protection of patents and intellectual property, and from U.S. anti-dumping and market-opening measures toward Japan. Because countries with large numbers of dominant producers tend to be more prosperous than other countries (such producers are profitable and pay good wages), national leaders often pursue interventionist policies aimed at helping producers in their countries attain and maintain dominance. The European Airbus program, Japan's development of its shipbuilding, semiconductor, and other industries, Taiwan's semiconductor industry, China's Made in China 2025 strategy, and the U.S. Sematech consortium are all examples.

As Baumol and Gomory showed, such national promotion programs are a key reason that the fundamental premise of free trade theory—that trade never hurts any trading partner—is also wrong. I have already noted the zero-sum character of the Boeing-Airbus duopoly. The ascendance of Korea's semiconductor and semiconductor equipment makers tends to make Korea more prosperous at the expense of both the U.S. semiconductor and semiconductor equipment industry and the U.S. economy. The stark reality is that global trade can easily be adversarial.

This is particularly true in so-called dual use industries, whose technology can be used for both civilian and military purposes. Do we really want pure free trade in artificial intelligence technology today, knowing that the industry could someday be completely dominated by China or Russia? Probably not. Free trade cannot always trump national security, and the two are often not easily divided. In fact, based on their analysis of the many possible trade patterns for many trading partners, Gomory and Baumol found that a large share of trade fits into the adversarial, zero-sum category. For example, China's subsidized exports of solar panels to the United States not only killed the U.S. solar industry's sales but also its ability to maintain a competitive technological capability in a field it invented, and in which it should be competitive based on its capital, educational, and technological resources.

Economists may say that subsidized products from China are a gift, and we should accept it and turn to doing something else. But that assumes it is easy to find something else of equal value and that the potential spin-offs of solar panel technology and production have little value or national security significance. None of the assumptions are inevitably valid. That adversarial trade accounts for a major part of total trade is not surprising, given the extent of intra-industry trade between developed countries and the ambition of virtually every developing country to move into those industries now dominated by the developed countries. The wonder is not that there is conflict but that any economist could suppose there would not be.

The Origin of Innovation

Perhaps the biggest weakness of the old-time religion is that it can only measure the present. We all know that innovation is a sure thing, and we all want it to be economically advantageous, but free trade theory has nothing to say about it. It neither predicts innovation nor hints at how to develop it.

Sometimes innovation can be planned, as in the case of the atomic bomb or the Apollo project to send a man to the moon. More often it occurs unexpectedly out of the interplay of numerous skills, ideas, and improvements. To maximize innovation, it helps to have a plethora of skills, industries, and ideas, and plenty of interaction among them. This goes against the notion of specialization in some area of production like wine making or cloth production. Maybe there is a potential linkage between wine and cloth that could create a new world, but that world will never be created if a nation concentrates only on making wine.

Economists do know that what countries make tends to be both "path dependent," meaning that what I make today is highly dependent on what I made yesterday, and subject to nonmarket intervention. Finland dominates global production of icebreaker ships. It has a long history of dealing with both ice and ships. Taiwan's leadership in semiconductor foundries stems from the Taiwan government's initial financial backing of entrepreneur and former Texas Instruments executive Morris Chang's idea for the first such foundry in the 1990s. Economists also know that comparative advantage can be a handicap. Countries fated by climate, geography, or history to specialize in producing bananas, coffee, or potash are usually poor because people tend to use the same amount of these products regardless of the price, and costs tend to rise with greater production (diseconomies of scale). Free trade does not help these countries. It may do them harm as bananas (for example) from even poorer countries take over their markets.

Finally, a country's gain from trade does not necessarily mean a gain for all the people in the country. Imagine a country with a population of one hundred. Suppose the country makes a net gain of $100 as the result of adopting free trade. Further, suppose that one person among the population gets the whole $100 of gain while the remaining ninety-nine suffer a loss of 50 cents each. On paper, the country has a net gain of $50.50, but do most people feel better? This is what has been happening in most of the so-called advanced, rich countries for the past thirty years. It is a major cause of the populism and divisions that have been plaguing most of the world's democracies recently. We should remember that Paul Samuelson told us back in 1948 that orthodox free trade theory predicted that it would happen.

Globalization

The terms *free trade* and *globalization* have come to be somewhat interchangeable, especially in the wake of *New York Times* columnist Tom Friedman's best-selling 2005 book *The World Is Flat*. But this is a misleading conflation of two very different things. International trade involves importing and exporting goods and services among nations. Globalization involves trade, but it also involves investment; the location of production facilities in countries other than a company's home country; the transfer of managers and skilled people from a home corporate facility to one abroad; the transfer of technology between countries; the exploitation of low wages and lax safety standards; and the use of tax incentives, R&D incentives, capital subsidies, and a wide range of official regulations to guide or block investment, flows of funds, technology, production, and delivery in ways advantageous to global corporations and to some, but not all, countries and people.

Let me give you an example of how this can work. Intel is the world's premier producer of microprocessors for laptop computers. Much of its production is done in Arizona. Its fabricating facility (fab) there is probably the lowest-cost, highest-quality location in the world for production of such chips. A substantial percentage of this production is exported, and it can fairly be said that as a result, the United States has a comparative advantage in the production of computer microprocessors. If global trade were conducted on a comparative advantage basis, the United States would be where all such chips are made, and they would then be exported in exchange for machine tools or poetry or something else. But Intel has a fab in China. Why would it put production in China if it has a comparative advantage in the United States? Probably the Chinese gave Intel, for free, the land on which the fab is located. Probably they also offered Intel half price or so on utilities along with no taxes for ten years and maybe a $1 billion capital grant for what would be about an $8 billion fab. If Intel were to build that fab in the United States, it would not get the land or the worker training free, nor would it get utilities at half price, and it certainly would not escape federal taxes. So on a cost basis, perhaps the United States has a comparative advantage in microprocessor chips, but on a full financial basis maybe not. On top of that, Intel's customers all do their assembly in China, and they want Intel to produce close to their assembly plants. This is the globalization game, and the United States is very close to not even being in it.

Competition between Countries

A favorite argument of the apostles of orthodoxy is that "companies compete, not countries." The idea is that countries are all pals while corporations chartered by those countries duke it out. This argument has always baffled me. Have economists never heard of war? Of course countries compete, in a variety of ways, one of which is certainly economic. Power does not accrue to nations of taxi drivers. China had comparative advantages in tea, porcelain, and silk under its old regime, but it became a poor and weak country. It is powerful today because it changed the composition and structure of its economy, and it did so expressly in order to compete. The notion that we should not be concerned when certain countries gain an edge in the production of certain products and in the development of certain new technologies is romantic in the extreme. Do we not care if China becomes the dominant player in artificial intelligence or super-computing? Such technology involves leading-edge semiconductor materials and processing technology. Do we not care if we lose leadership in those technologies, which is exactly what happens when U.S.-based production and R&D close up shop and move to China or Singapore for better tax breaks or better engineers? Of course we care. Probably even some orthodox economists care. I'm pretty sure Ricardo cared about such things in his time.

Given that the free trade champion Richard Cobden, the hero of Britain's repeal of the Corn Laws in 1846, was the founder of the *Economist*, it is ironic that it was the *Economist* that broke the news on March 1, 2018, that the West's twenty-five-year bet on China had failed.[21] It was like the Vatican announcing the death of God.

7

Blind Prophets, Tycoons, and Soothsayers

> Hear now this, O foolish people, and without understanding; which have
> eyes, and see not; which have ears, and hear not.
> —*Isaiah 6:9–10*

The history of U.S.-China relations resembles nothing so much as the swings of a pendulum. In the late eighteenth century, American traders, who were locked out of many European markets, envisioned China as a new Eldorado, as the *Empress of China,* a brand-new, three-master merchantman, turned a 30 percent profit on its first voyage (February 23, 1784–May 11, 1785) from New York to China. But it turned out that the Chinese would take little except silver in return for the silks, tea, and porcelain so much in demand in America. Some U.S. traders joined the British in selling opium to millions of Chinese drug addicts, but that led to bad feelings on the part of the Chinese authorities and eventually to the Opium Wars of the mid-nineteenth century and to the establishment of rights of extraterritoriality (Chinese law did not apply to citizens of Western countries living in China), which were applied to Americans in China. In the mid- to late nineteenth century and continuing into the early twentieth century, China became a magnet for missionaries hoping to "throw Satan down from his seat in the Celestial Empire."[1] Most of China's colleges, YMCAs, agricultural extension programs, charities, and research institutes were established at this time by missionaries who were able to persuade one in eight Americans in 1900 to donate in their church collection plates to save China.

Yet the missionaries were continually disappointed as the number of Chinese converts rose only very, very slowly.

During World War II, President Franklin Delano Roosevelt (whose forebear was successful opium trader Warren Delano) tried to raise the status of China to that of Britain and the Soviet Union by convening the "Big Four" conference in Cairo that included Chiang Kaishek along with Winston Churchill and Josef Stalin. But it really didn't work and eventually President Truman more or less forced China into the communist camp by withholding U.S. aid from Chiang and forcing him into a coalition government with the CCP (which Washington at the time perceived as nothing more than a group of "agrarian reformers") at the very moment that he and his Nationalist Party had Mao's CCP on the brink of extinction.

Indeed, Truman gave Stalin and Mao exactly what they wanted. This was probably the lowest point of all time in U.S.-China relations.

Nixon Goes to China

For the next twenty-four years, China was second only to the Soviet Union on the American bad guys list. Indeed, in May 1963, President John F. Kennedy appears to have contemplated the use of nuclear weapons against China as a way of helping India to defend itself against an attack by China along the northern border of India. Told by Defense Secretary Robert McNamara that if the United States were to intervene, it would have to be with nuclear weapons, as the transport of large numbers of U.S. troops to northern India would take too long, Kennedy responded, "We should defend India and therefore we will defend India."[2]

As it turned out, the Indians and Chinese struck an agreement, and there was no need for U.S. intervention. No one knows for sure exactly what Kennedy meant. He did not directly say he would order the use of nuclear weapons. But he didn't say he would not. He seemed to embrace the necessity.

By 1969, however, the shoe was on the other foot. In his inaugural address in January, President Nixon indirectly referred to a *Foreign Affairs* article he had published in 1967 noting that America wanted "a world in which no people great or small will live in angry isolation."[3] In March, Soviet and Chinese troops battled near the border of Manchuria and

Siberia. U.S. satellite photos revealed that the Chinese had taken a beating from Soviet artillery. A bit later, Beijing heard rumors that Moscow might be considering a preemptive strike against China's nuclear facilities. Over lunch in Washington that August, KGB officer Boris N. Davydov explained to U.S. diplomat William Stearman that Moscow was indeed considering a nuclear attack on China. He wondered if the United States might like to join in.

Now it was Mao who needed protection.

Stearman replied that the United States would view any such action "with considerable concern." Then, on September 5, Undersecretary of State Elliot Richardson noted in a speech that Washington would "not let the Soviet apprehensions prevent us from attempting to bring China out of its angry, alienated shell." Henry Kissinger called this speech a "revolutionary step."[4]

In response to the threat from Moscow, Mao asked four of his most senior military marshals to reevaluate China's foreign policy and particularly to determine who the country's main enemy was. They also undertook to consider playing the "U.S. card" against the Soviets. The marshals concluded that Mao should seek a new understanding with Washington. They were aware from Nixon's writings and their own intelligence that he hoped to gain China's help in the Cold War, so they suggested that Mao negotiate a "breakthrough" that would enable Beijing to play the U.S. card against Moscow.

Meanwhile, Nixon was trying to play what came in America to be called the "China card" by establishing contact with the Chinese through the U.S. ambassador to Poland. But that didn't work. Instead it was the U.S. national table tennis team that did the trick. After meeting the Chinese team at the table tennis world championships in Japan, the team was invited to play in China. There was no way the lackluster U.S. team would have been invited to China except at the behest of Mao Zedong and Zhou Enlai. The week after the team left China, Zhou sent an invitation to the White House to send a high-ranking official to Beijing. There was no mention of the usual Chinese demand that the United States abandon Taiwan before any encounter could take place. On June 2, 1971, Zhou sent a message to National Security Advisor Henry Kissinger that Mao had approved a secret visit; Kissinger then rushed into the Oval Office and told Nixon this "was the most important communication that has come to an

American President since the end of WWII."[5] After secret trips by Kissinger and much diplomatic cable traffic, Nixon arrived in Beijing on February 23, 1972, to establish a détente with China that he hoped would enable a U.S. withdrawal from Vietnam and at least a tacit alliance that might compel the Soviet Union to engage in arms control talks.

But Nixon's and Kissinger's ambition went far beyond even that. Nixon later wrote that he had to "cultivate China" so that it would not become "the most formidable enemy that has ever existed in the history of the world." He thought that with a halfway decent government, the Chinese would be "the leaders of the world."[6]

Mao and Zhou had four problems that had made it necessary to turn to the hated America for solutions. China's economy in 1972 was coming nowhere near fulfilling the hopes and dreams of the Chinese in 1949. It was humiliating for them to look across the sea at Japan and Taiwan, both of which had flourished while China floundered. China even faced the very real prospect of a famine worse than that experienced during the Great Leap Forward. The country needed fertilizer, farm equipment, and technology. China's former comrades in the Soviet Union weren't helping, and in any case were importing food themselves. Hence the need for America.

The second problem was that China faced an enormous buildup of Soviet forces on the Manchurian border while being continually harassed by the Taiwanese in the south. Zhou complained that "no one wants to make friends with us."[7] America might be the friend in need that China required.

Perhaps above all, Mao wanted respect. He saw himself as a hero for the ages, but until he had achieved *ganmei* (catching up to America), no one else would recognize that. And perhaps Mao himself wasn't quite sure.

Finally, Mao desperately wanted to erase the "humiliation" China had suffered in the nineteenth and twentieth centuries by bringing Taiwan back under Beijing's control. He couldn't do that without a deal with America. He told journalist Edgar Snow, "I place my hopes on the American people."[8]

Who Won the Negotiations

The iron rule of any negotiation is not to pay in advance. As John Pomfret points out in his book *The Beautiful Country and the Middle Kingdom*, Mao and Zhou "sold the impending rapprochement as an act of celestial benevolence, bestowing warm relations on the barbarians" from beyond the seas. Kissinger had a reputation for high intellect combined with tough pragmatism and a strong sense of personal superiority. Some thought he fancied himself a latter-day Bismarck. He was famous for forcing subordinates to rewrite their reports several times before he would even bother to read them. But under the spells of China's ancient civilization and Zhou's patrician charm, the awkward Kissinger began to give away the store.

Without asking for anything in return, he immediately began to ease the CCP's fear of encirclement by providing intelligence on the Soviet military array facing China across its northern border.[9] He also said that U.S. support of Taiwan had been a historical mistake and that America intended to retreat from the Western Pacific. In addition to withdrawing the U.S. military from Taiwan, he also committed to winding down U.S. forces in South Korea. Astoundingly, he further agreed with Zhou's statement that once the United States pulled out of Taiwan, "unification" with Mainland China would likely follow and did not insist that such unification be nonviolent. He further assured Zhou that the United States would not assist Chiang's forces on Taiwan in any attack on Mainland China and promised that the United States would get Taiwan out of the China seat at the UN Security Council.

It would be nice to imagine that Kissinger got something big in return for all this. Nixon's conditions had been the release of all Americans in Chinese custody, Chinese help in persuading North Vietnam to accept a peace deal, and assurance that he, Nixon, would be the first American statesman to be accepted in Beijing. China met only the last condition.

It has been said in several fora that "only Nixon could go to China." It means that because he had made his political career as an anticommunist, he had political leeway that a more centrist or liberal official would not have had. Perhaps so, but once he got to Beijing, he proceeded to one-up Kissinger in giving gifts. Kissinger, according to his own notes, had advised Nixon to treat Mao like an emperor. The American diplomat U. Alexis Johnson notes that when the two met, Nixon sat on the edge of his seat while Mao reclined royally.[10] In discussions with Zhou, Nixon said he wanted a prosperous China that would be open for foreign business and could act as a second superpower in stabilizing Asia, allowing the United

States to reduce its arms expenditures. Just before leaving China, Nixon spoke in Shanghai, a city once dominated by Britain, France, and other foreign powers, whose enclaves sometimes had signs saying: "No Chinese or dogs allowed." Declaring that those days were well over, he promised that the American people would uphold China's right never again to suffer foreign occupation or domination.

He didn't leave entirely empty-handed. In the ensuing years, Beijing allowed U.S. intelligence agencies to establish watching and listening capabilities on Chinese soil for monitoring the Soviet Union and also engaged in a degree of intelligence sharing. Of course, this was the Soviet Union that would disappear within twenty years. But in another failure of Western intelligence—perhaps not so much a failure as a steadfast resistance to questioning what had become conventional, familiar, self-justifying doctrine—no one seemed aware that the danger the Soviets posed was diminishing rapidly. If one thought the Soviets were the main threat to America, one might conclude that Nixon and Kissinger had not been entirely outmaneuvered.

From today's perspective, however, it is clear that in return for being allowed to listen to and watch the Soviet Union from China and a few other tidbits, Nixon had agreed to help make China rich, powerful, and a co-regent of the world. You have to hand it to Mao and Zhou. They were very, very good.

They were so good that Kissinger and Nixon didn't even know they had been fleeced. U. Alexis Johnson noted Kissinger's "rapturous enchantment." Kissinger himself said: "No other world leaders have the sweep and imagination of Mao and Chou nor the capacity and will to achieve a long-range policy." He added: "We have progressed farther and faster than anyone would have predicted, or the rest of the world realizes. For, in plain terms, we have now become tacit allies." Nixon, even more grandly, said, "This was the week that changed the world."[11]

The Cycle Repeats

Nixon's visit to Beijing was, of course, followed by his landslide reelection and then his resignation over the Watergate scandal. It wasn't until Jimmy Carter's presidency that anyone followed up Nixon's visit to

Beijing. Carter's national security advisor, Zbigniew Brzezinski, was a Soviet expert whose top priority was undermining the Soviet Union. He saw any deal with China in the light of its effect on Moscow. His chief China hand, Michael Oxenberg, was himself enraptured by Nixon's apparent breakthrough with China, had been pleased to see China take the UN Security Council seat, and hoped to see U.S. relations with mainland China normalized.

The stumbling block was Taiwan. U.S. secretary of state Cyrus Vance wanted Beijing publicly to commit to a peaceful resolution of the Taiwan question. But when he visited Beijing for talks, he was told that that stance was U.S. aggression against China. Deng reminded him that Nixon and Kissinger had agreed the United States owed China for the sin of occupying Taiwan, and he savaged Vance's plan to keep a low-profile presence there. That was a "retreat," he spat.[12]

By the spring of 1978, Soviet-inspired uprisings in Africa and Afghanistan had strengthened support for Brzezinski's call for playing the China card against Moscow. In his own talks in Beijing, he abandoned the idea of an official U.S. office in Taiwan and the U.S. request for peaceful settlement of the Taiwan issue. Echoing Kissinger, he said that "the existence of some separate Chinese entities . . . will come to an end." He further emphasized that Carter was determined to normalize relations with the Beijing regime according to Beijing's formula. Although Brzezinski always denied having any special sentiment about China, Carter wrote that his advisor "had been seduced" by the celestial magic.[13] U.S.-China relations were officially normalized on December 15, 1978. Taiwan officials were informed of this just hours before the official statement was released.

Deng had anticipated the announcement in a speech to a Central Party Work Conference on December 13, in which he announced his policies of "reform and opening up." He emphasized what he called the Four Modernizations: science, technology, agriculture, and defense. He particularly linked this agenda to the normalization of relations with America. Senior Party leaders understood that America would give China the security, technology, and investment it needed to become rich and strong.[14]

There followed what might be called the American promotion of China period. In the wake of normalization, the first agreement the two countries signed committed America to help strengthen Chinese science. In the summer of 1979, Vice President Walter Mondale traveled to China and offered a $2 billion credit for a hydroelectric project while also announcing that Congress would approve most-favored nation trading status for China, meaning that China would get the same trading conditions the United States offered to best friends like Canada. Yet China met none of the conditions (free and open markets) normally necessary for obtaining that status.

An important reason for the granting of MFN to China was expressed by Arkansas representative Bill Alexander, who told the House of Representatives during the debate over MFN that "seeds of democracy are growing in China." The old notion that trade would lead to democracy was still alive despite its never having done so, and it would drive the U.S.-China relationship for almost four decades. Mondale also proposed providing weapons such as F-15 and F-16 fighter jets, insisting that "we believe in the importance of a strong China."[15] Following Mondale's trip, Undersecretary of Defense William Perry also visited Beijing and laid the groundwork for sales of U.S. military equipment to the PLA. Virtually every U.S. government agency was being urged to develop some tie with its Chinese equivalent.

Nor did this attitude change with the arrival of the Reagan administration. In the fall of 1982, when I accompanied Secretary of Commerce Malcolm Baldrige on the first American trade mission to China since the end of World War II, we stayed at the Diaoyutai State Guest House, and I recall almost being run down by a mass of bicycle riders all dressed in black Mao suits as I left the gate for my morning jog. We concluded several routine trade arrangements and laid the foundation for establishing offices for the U.S. Foreign Commercial Service. The service was directed to promote American investment in and exports to China, but also to promote Chinese exports. (I was reminded of my instructions to promote Dutch exports as vice consul in Rotterdam in 1966.)

Our visit brought a stream of American business leaders and investment to China. Under Reagan, Citibank opened its China branch, American Motors undertook to make its famous Jeep in Beijing, and Kentucky Fried Chicken showed up in 1987. Like our predecessors in 1783, we saw China as a place where Americans could do well—and perhaps even make the country over in our own image. And, like the nineteenth-century missionaries, we saw China as a place where Americans could do good. New missionaries flocked to China's shores, and the CCP even issued Document 19, which said that religion would continue to exist under socialism for a long time. The Party even revised China's constitution to grant more freedom of religion.

All of this ignited an explosion of U.S.-China trade. In 1972, mutual trade was only $5 million. It hit $500 million in 1978 and then doubled in 1979. China ran its first modern trade surplus with the United States in 1981. By the end of 2018, the annual surplus had reached $419 billion.[16] This giant Amazon River flow of exports to America has been the most important factor in what has become known as the "rise of China"—even if China itself doesn't like to recognize this fact.

An interesting and eventually corrupt and even un-American by-product of all this commercial activity was the rise of a new class of compradors. Henry Kissinger began making his fortune as chairman and CEO of Kissinger Associates, a consulting firm that would charge you a handsome fee for introducing you to some of Henry's nice friends in Beijing. Not to be outdone, former assistant secretary of state Richard Holbrooke, former secretary of energy James Schlesinger, and even former president George H. W. Bush got into the business, the last charging $250,000 a day. As a Qing Dynasty envoy to America once noted: "The love of God is less real than the love of profit."[17]

But there were some things China couldn't yet make—such as torpedoes, anti-artillery radar, avionics, and large-caliber ammunition. The Reagan administration issued three national security directives telling U.S. manufacturers to sell weapons to China, and it approved assistance to China's civilian and strategic nuclear programs. With this permission, U.S. sales of technology quickly rose tenfold, to over $5 billion. One example of what was happening is the semiconductor industry, the highest of high tech. In trade terms, the United States had a huge comparative advantage.

According to the prevailing free trade religion of the time, the United States should focus on the production and export of items like semiconductors to developing countries like China, which in turn should export labor-intensive products like shoes and clothing. But in the early 1980s, Washington not only allowed but encouraged U.S. manufacturers to move industrial production to China. Said my old colleague, Assistant Secretary of State Paul Wolfowitz: "Our goal is to strengthen China's ability to resist Soviet intimidation."[18] He said this only a decade before the collapse of the Soviet Union.

Without realizing it, Deng had unleashed not only freer markets but increasingly freer speech. There were protests as early as 1986, when students at the University of Science and Technology demonstrated against the Party's decision to overturn local election results. Other protests led the Party to crack down in early 1987 with an "Anti-Bourgeois Liberalization Campaign," which included harsh criticism of American values. But no one in America paid attention. U.S. leaders were less interested in human rights than in playing the China card against the Soviets and doing more business in China.

What did get attention was China's serious entry into the arms business, especially the nuclear arms business. In the early 1980s, China sent Pakistan not only the plans for one of its own early nuclear bombs but weapons-grade uranium with which to make it. Later in the decade, Beijing sold $2 billion of medium-range ballistic missiles to Saudi Arabia, in return for which Riyadh switched its diplomatic recognition of China from the Chiang regime in Taiwan to the CCP regime in Beijing. These and similar incidents led to much U.S. scolding of Beijing, but never to any serious action. As John Pomfret notes: "Most U.S. officials dealing with China believed that with time the interests of the Middle Kingdom would align themselves with those of the United States. As Assistant Secretary of State for East Asian and Pacific Affairs Paul Wolfowitz was fond of saying, China was 'not our adversary but a friendly, developing country.' "[19] As preordained since the late eighteenth century, China and America had become friends.

Washington would have done well to pay more attention to China's students. They had invented something called a "democracy wall" where they and others posted daring statements and called for dramatic changes in the way the Party governed. By the spring of 1989, protests had spread all over the country. On May 19, over a million people demonstrated in Tiananmen Square, in the center of Beijing, under the portrait of a benign-looking Mao. A few days later, students created a Statue of Liberty symbol, which they called the "Goddess of Liberty," prompting Premier Li Peng to accuse the United States of plotting to undermine China's socialist system. On the night of June 3, Deng and Li ordered the tanks of the PLA into Tiananmen Square (recall that despite its name, People's Liberation Army, the PLA fights for the Party, not the people), where they fired indiscriminately into the darkness—this was not something that would stand the daylight—at the peacefully demonstrating students. The exact death toll is a state secret. As noted above, estimates range from a few hundred to as high as twenty-six hundred, including subsequent attacks on demonstrators and students around the country.[20]

Clearly, China was not evolving into an Asian likeness of the United States.

Steady as She Goes

In retrospect, this might have been a time when Washington could have made some real progress toward realizing the ancient dream. In the wake of the brutal crackdown, foreign investment into China dried up and foreign importers stopped buying from China. The Soviet Union was on its last legs. The CCP had showed its true colors. A strong response from Washington, making clear that China could expect no American cooperation with its economic development without greater freedom of speech and political choice, might have had an impact at that moment.

We will never know, because George H. W. Bush, who thought he had absorbed some deep knowledge of the Chinese people during his seventeen months as the head of the U.S. mission to Beijing in 1974 and 1975, bet on conciliation. While he voiced regret for the loss of life, it was carefully calibrated. He refrained from criticizing Deng or any other specific Party leaders, let alone holding them responsible. He suspended further arms sales but ordered the Pentagon to go ahead with delivery of arms China had already ordered, and he specifically rejected the imposition of any economic sanctions. Most significantly, he sent National Security Advisor Brent Scowcroft on a secret visit to Beijing to maintain communication with the top Party leaders. Via Scowcroft, he promised Deng, "I will do my best to keep the boat from rocking too much." In a note to Deng, he said the U.S. Congress was trying to cut off trade but made it clear that he would not support such an effort. "We both do more for world peace and the welfare of our own people," he added, "if we can get our relationship back on track."[21]

I must pause at this point to wonder what on earth Bush was talking about. I worked on his staff for a time and still revere him, both as a man of character and as a mostly good president. Perhaps he still felt need for a Soviet listening post, but America then needed nothing from China. The first round of free Polish parliamentary elections took place on June 4, 1989, immediately in the wake of Tiananmen Square. The Berlin Wall would fall on November 9. It should have been clear to Bush and his team that the Soviet Union would no longer be a great threat and that the United States had no further need of a China card, if it ever really had. It should have been clear that without American investment, technology, markets, and education, China would have to struggle for a very long time to emerge from abject poverty. Did Bush see himself as president of the United States or as a kind of latter-day missionary?

Shortly after Deng met with the PLA leaders to thank them for the Tiananmen massacre, Scowcroft told him, "my President wants you to know he is your friend forever." Rather than pressure Beijing, Bush protected it by beating back congressional efforts to impose trade sanctions. Importantly, he also shifted the rationale for the U.S.-China relationship from one of national security to one of democracy promotion through trade. He steadfastly maintained that "as people have commercial incentives, whether it's China or in other totalitarian countries, the move to democracy is inexorable."[22]

Euphoria

The Iraqi invasion of Kuwait, a bit over a year after the Tiananmen Square massacre, quickly distracted attention away from China. Bush no doubt felt his "go easy" policy was justified by the need for China's cooperation at the United Nations when he was organizing the allied counterattack that pushed Saddam Hussein's forces back to Baghdad.

But three other major events created the conditions that made the 1990s a euphoric decade. The first was the collapse of the Soviet Union on Christmas Day 1991. This finished the Cold War, leaving the West, and the United States especially, as the big winner. Elation over this victory gave rise to the conviction that global democracy was imminent. In 1992, the American political scientist Francis Fukuyama published a best-selling book entitled *The End of History and the Last Man,* which argued that universal liberal democracy is the end point of human government.

The second key event was Deng Xiaoping's southern tour. In the wake of Tiananmen, economic growth had slowed dramatically, and hard-line Maoists were reasserting the need for central economic planning. Deng responded by touring the cities of southern China and talking up market-oriented economic reform. It was during this trip that he famously announced: "To get rich is glorious." Although he had officially retired from politics, his prestige was enormous, and the slogan sparked a renewed drive in China toward a market-based economy as thousands of peasants and entrepreneurs raced to follow his advice about getting rich.

The third event was the election in the United States of William Jefferson Clinton as president of the United States. During the 1992 campaign, Clinton had promised not to "coddle dictators from Baghdad to Beijing." In his debate against President Bush, he argued, "I think it is a mistake for us to do what this administration did when all those kids went out there carrying the Statue of Liberty in Tiananmen Square. Mr. Bush sent two people in secret to toast the Chinese leaders and basically tell them not to worry about it. . . . I would be firm. I would say if you want to continue Most Favored Nation status for your government-owned industries as well as your private ones, observe human rights in the future. Open your society. Recognize the legitimacy of those kids who were carrying the Statue of Liberty. If we can stand up for our economics, we ought to be able to preserve the democratic interests of the people in China, and over the long run they will be more reliable partners."[23]

As president, on May 28, 1993, Clinton issued an executive order linking human rights to the annual renewal of MFN for China. At the signing ceremony in the White House, surrounded by Democratic congressional leaders, Tibetan exiles, and Chinese students, he proclaimed: "It is time that a unified American policy recognize both the values of China and the values of America." The U.S. must maintain "a resolute insistence upon significant progress on human rights."

One must wonder how Clinton, a product of Georgetown University, Oxford University, and Yale Law School, could have believed that China's Communist Party would make an iota of progress on what Americans consider human rights. Certainly, China's premier, Li Peng, had no intention of doing so. He had said in 1992 that any concession on human rights "would shake the basis of our society." Nevertheless, in March 1994, Secretary of State Warren Christopher traveled to Beijing and told Li that Washington demanded "significant progress and soon." Assistant Secretary of State Winston Lord described it as "the most brutal diplomatic meeting" he had ever attended.[24] "Nuts" was the essence of Li's response.

To Beijing, this talk of human rights was equivalent to a declaration of war. The Party had realized in the wake of Tiananmen Square that economic opening and linkage with the West carried risks. Deng had anticipated that in 1978, when he noted that "opening the windows for fresh air might also allow in a few flies." The student demonstrations showed that flies had indeed entered the house, and the Party soon focused on countermeasures, including educational emphasis on Party doctrine and Chinese nationalism. In other words, the Party saw the U.S. emphasis on human rights as a cleverly veiled attack on itself—which in fact it was. But neither Clinton nor the American foreign policy and economic establishment understood this. It can at least be said of Nixon that before his death he had second thoughts regarding his China policy. During an on-the-record interview with William Safire, he wondered aloud if his opening to China had, perhaps, been a mistake rather than the stroke of genius he first imagined. Referring to China during the interview, Nixon said, "We may have created a Frankenstein."[25]

In any case, in the fall of 1993, China took a further step toward opening its economy by reducing tariffs on three thousand items and allowing repatriation of some of the profits earned by foreign corporations operating on its soil. In May 1994, when it came time to review the MFN renewal, Clinton dramatically changed his tune. Without a step of human rights progress in China, he renewed MFN and introduced a whole new theme as the basis of America's China policy. Gone was the link to human rights. In its place was something called "constructive engagement," which sounded a lot like Bush's inevitable linkage of human rights and democratization to international trade. Nor did Clinton dream this up by himself. His cabinet, his economic advisors, his assistant secretaries of state, his national security advisors, his U.S. trade representatives, and many other sophisticated people bought into this vague concept. So did the Council on Foreign Relations, the Brookings Institution, the Institute for International Economics, the American Enterprise Institute, the Center for Strategic and International Studies, and most leading academic experts in trade and international relations. Indeed, I must confess that at times I myself was tempted by this siren song.

While China continued to open its economy and welcome foreign investment and technology, it continued to swat bothersome flies carrying the human rights fever. It also refocused its sights on the return of Taiwan to the motherland and the extension of Beijing's power beyond its borders. For instance, as the U.S. Navy left the Philippines' Subic Bay and Clark Airfield in 1992, China adopted "the Law on the Territorial Waters and Their Contiguous Areas," a measure that essentially assumed Chinese sovereignty over the entire South China Sea and its islands, reefs, and even its rocks that break the surface only at low tide. In early 1996, Beijing began launching rockets in the vicinity of Taiwan. One even flew over the capital city of Taipei. Clinton responded by sending two aircraft carrier battle groups in the vicinity of Taiwan as a warning.

While it was opening to foreign investment and imports, China was also collecting mountains of intelligence and stealing oceans of technology. A favorite technique was to require that foreign companies investing in China have a partner to which technology would be transferred, or else to license their technology in return for permission to do business in China. At the same time, armies of "researchers" in the United States were scooping up anything that looked like technology. Counterfeits of everything from optical fiber to nuclear power plant parts flooded markets in China as well as outside. None of this shook the faith of the president (or anyone else in the American foreign policy establishment) in the efficacy of constructive engagement.

Clinton welcomed Jiang Zemin, resident and Party general secretary, to Washington in the fall of 1997. In his memoirs, he notes that he and Jiang had a far-ranging private discussion about "how much change and freedom China could accommodate without risking internal chaos. . . . I went to bed thinking that China would be forced by the imperatives of modern society to become more open."[26] Like most of the American foreign policy establishment, Clinton either had not read or had dismissed Richard Bernstein and Ross H. Munro's 1997 book, *The Coming Conflict with China.*

Clinton returned the visit in June 1998. He defended the decision to go despite the lack of progress on human rights, saying, "I'm going because I think it's the right thing to do for our country. If the choice is between making a symbolic point and making a real difference, I choose to make the difference." He added that "when it comes to advancing human rights and religious freedom, dealing directly, and speaking honestly to the Chinese is clearly the best way to make a difference." On the other hand, "seeking to isolate China is clearly unworkable. Choosing isolation over 'engagement' would not make the world safer. It would make it more dangerous. It would undermine, rather than strengthen, our efforts to foster stability in Asia. It will eliminate, not facilitate, cooperation on issues relating to weapons of mass destruction."[27]

Clearly, constructive engagement meant never appearing to be upset with China. From there it was only a very small step to granting China permanent normal trade relations (PNTR) and negotiating its membership in the World Trade Organization. After American and Chinese negotiators signed a document that would lead to China's entry into the WTO, Clinton said the move would "have a profound impact on human rights and liberty" in China. In selling the deal to the Congress and the American public, he wrote an article for the *New York Times* in which he said,

> The change this agreement can bring outside [of China] is quite extraordinary. But, I think you could make an argument that it will be nothing compared to the changes that this agreement will spark from the inside out in China. By joining the WTO, China is not simply agreeing to import more of our products. It is agreeing to import one of democracy's most cherished values, economic freedom. The more China liberalizes its economy, the more fully it will liberate the potential of its people—their initiative their imagination, their remarkable spirit of enterprise. And when individuals have the power, not just to dream, but to realize dreams, they will demand a greater say. . . . The Chinese government no longer will be everyone's employer, landlord, shopkeeper and nanny all rolled into one. It will have fewer instruments, therefore, with which to control people's lives. And it may lead to very profound change. The genie of freedom will not go back into the

bottle. As Justice Earl Warren once said: liberty is the most contagious force in the world.[28]

As the deal was being considered by Congress, U.S. trade representative Charlene Barshefsky told the members that China's WTO membership would "promote the rule of law in many fields now dominated by state power and control." Robert Rubin, Clinton's former treasury secretary and former head of the investment bank Goldman Sachs, told the Congress that China's accession would "sow the seeds of freedom for China's 1.2 billion citizens."[29]

In Beijing, however, Premier Zhu Rongji warned that "western hostile forces are continuing to promote their strategy of Westernizing and breaking up our country."[30] One wonders if Clinton, Barshefsky, Rubin, and company ever read Zhu's comment.

Tycoons and Soothsayers

Whenever I reread these statements by American policy makers, I find myself wondering how and why the speakers believed what they were saying. The answer, I think, is that they desperately wanted to believe for two reasons. One was that the corporations that largely run Washington saw huge business opportunities in China and were determined to cash in. The second was that the leading pundits and academics of the time told them it was all true—told them, in effect, what they wanted to hear.

We have already seen how Motorola chairman Bob Galvin rushed to Beijing in the wake of the Tiananmen Square massacre to cut a favorable business deal while China's leaders were on the ropes and in need of friends. But for steadfast persistence, he was far outdone by Maurice "Hank" Greenberg, the chairman and CEO of American International Group (AIG), the giant global insurer. AIG had been founded in Shanghai in 1919 by Cornelius V. Starr, who left his estate to the C. V. Starr Foundation, which Greenberg also chaired. A veteran of the D-Day Normandy landings and of the Korean War, Greenberg did not share the foreign policy establishment's need for a happy human rights ending to the China story. Perhaps that was because he owned the establishment. As the head of C. V. Starr, he was a major donor to the Council on Foreign Relations and even served for a time as its vice chairman. He was also a key donor to the Asia Society (where he served for a time as chairman), the Nixon Center, the Atlantic Council, the Brookings Institution, the Carnegie Foundation, the Heritage Foundation, the Peterson Foundation, the U.S.-China Business Council, and any other significant Washington influence organization that may come to mind.

Hank (I can call him that because he also donated to my Economic Strategy Institute) had an office with an outer waiting room full of pictures of the Bund (the old center of the foreign establishment in Shanghai), of himself with numerous U.S. presidents and Chinese officials, and of the old AIG headquarters in Shanghai. He was not at all into the human rights thing. He was openly sympathetic to the Chinese leaders in view of the problems they faced, and would explain that "the histories and cultures of countries are vastly different, so it is unrealistic to expect China to have a political system that parallels any other." He could be very aggressive in pressing think tanks and other institutions to share his views. At one point he threatened to cancel his donation to the Heritage Foundation after one of its scholars called on Congress to delay the grant of PNTR to China.[31] Hank wanted to go back to AIG's roots in the biggest way possible, and that meant granting China PNTR, getting it into the WTO, courting Jiang Zemin and other Party leaders, and lobbying the hell out of Washington. Hank almost always got what he really wanted, and in the case of China that was insurance sales, not human rights. Although he would not object if sales of insurance happened to lead to human rights, he did not expect them to.

Another example of what was driving Washington was FedEx chairman and CEO Fred W. Smith. Fred (also a former donor to my institute) had envisioned an aircraft-based package-and-mail delivery service while an undergraduate at Yale. In a sense, he could be called at least a father, if not *the* father, of what is known today as the global supply chain. In establishing FedEx in 1971, Fred was going up against the well-established (since 1907) United Parcel Service (UPS) and the U.S. Postal System. He became a master at playing Washington, putting ex-senators and congresspersons on his board, donating to all the influence makers just as Hank did, and making big contributions to political campaigns. If you have ever wondered why FedEx bins sit outside post offices, you are seeing the magic Fred could and can make in Washington.

Fred desperately wanted a piece of China. Like Hank, he was not primarily motivated by human rights for the Chinese. As a dynamic, successful American entrepreneur, he probably thought there might be something in the trade-creates-rights argument, but trade without human rights was okay with him too. To help him get into China he hired my former Foreign Service classmate Scott Halford, who had been a China hand at the State Department, rising to the rank of deputy chief of mission (number two) at the U.S. embassy in Beijing. Scott's job was to get Beijing's approval for FedEx to land, deliver, and pick up cargo in China.

I was at the APEC (Asia Pacific Economic Cooperation) leaders' summit in Shanghai in 2001. The actual meeting of the heads of state at these summits is always preceded by a two-day conference of business leaders, at which the presidents and prime ministers sometimes speak. Scott worked like crazy to arrange for Fred to introduce Jiang as the speaker at one of the plenary sessions. He succeeded, and I had the pleasure of listening to arch entrepreneur, free market–oriented, champion capitalist Fred Smith lavishly praise the leader of the land of socialism with Chinese characteristics. It was great theater, and it was also great for FedEx.

Four years later, as I was writing a book about the rise of China and India (*Three Billion New Capitalists*), I visited FedEx headquarters in Knoxville, Tennessee. The Knoxville airfield is virtually synonymous with FedEx. In the evening, Scott and I took an elevator to the top of the airfield tower to watch the FedEx flights converging from all around the world. They would land early in the evening, unload in literally a few minutes, reload, and be off late in the evening to get the package to your doorstep the next morning. It was an amazing sight. Across the sky, little dots of light appeared on the horizon as the planes approached the field. One of those planes flew FedEx's single most profitable route: the one from Shanghai. Like Hank, Fred had a way of getting what he wanted.

The third example is Henry "Hank" Paulson. Since I don't know him, I'll be formal and call him Paulson. In 1991, as the co-chief of investment banking at the venerable investment bank Goldman Sachs, he visited China for the first time. Mao had kept China on a wartime economic footing for forty years. All provinces and even some counties were organized to be

economically self-sufficient, with the result that by 1991 there was a pro-
liferation of state-owned companies all doing the same things. These were
also the Party's main source of income. Looking at this, Paulson came up
with an idea that would forever change China and the world. It was bril-
liantly simple—to merge some of the companies into large enterprises that
could compete on a global scale, and then monetize them by taking them
public on domestic and international stock exchanges.

It worked. The marriage of Wall Street financial smarts with the old
fantasy of the riches that might be had in China yielded a multibillion-
dollar money machine that saved the state-owned enterprises, created a
huge windfall for the Party, and further enriched Goldman Sachs, along
with the rest of Wall Street. Between 1993 and 2010, the SOEs raised over
$600 billion. In one deal alone, Goldman is thought to have reaped a $200
million profit. Importantly, those in the West who bought the shares had
little idea that they were buying the Chinese Dream. The offering documents did not reveal the Party's role in the enterprises, or that the Party
would be a major beneficiary. Paulson and the other bankers managed to
keep the words *Chinese Communist Party* out of the disclosure papers.
The value to the CCP, China, and Wall Street of this deceit was so enormous as to be incalculable. It is a near certainty that without Wall Street's
cash, most of China's SOEs would have collapsed, and taken the Party
down with them.

Paulson made more than seventy trips to China, mostly in his private
jet, and began to fancy himself an expert on the country. He wrote in his
book, *Dealing with China*, "Western bankers were Promethean figures in
the process: we jetted in and competed to show the Chinese how to kindle
the fire of capital markets. Much of what we did was educational. We might
as well have been running a school—indeed, at times it felt as though we
were."[32]

One early success was China's phone companies. In the early 1990s,
phone service was provided, very inefficiently, by a bunch of provincial
monopolies. Paulson persuaded Zhu to consolidate them into a national
phone company to be called China Mobile. When Goldman took China
Mobile to Wall Street, it was nothing but a paper company that had never
received a renminbi in revenue. That made not a whit of difference. When
the company was taken public on the New York and Hong Kong exchanges

it raised $4.5 billion. Today it is the largest mobile phone operator in the world.

Paulson thought he was educating the Chinese, but Zhu saw things differently. His goal was not to create a purely private sector economy but to save the SOEs as viable pillars of the CCP's one-party rule. Paulson did extensive writing and speaking as a self-styled China expert, yet there is no evidence that he or anyone else on Wall Street understood that far from privatizing that country, they were strengthening the Party's authoritarian rule and its ability to project its power beyond China's borders.

It is important to note that the experience of the investment bankers was different from that of companies that sold real products. If you were a Corning Glass or an IBM or a Microsoft you might be required, as a condition of producing in China, to have a partner company—one selected for you by the Chinese government and, of course, ultimately by the Party. You might be required to transfer some of your technology to that partner or to others in China. Of course, you could refuse, but then you might be visited daily by safety inspectors, health inspectors, and others who would impede your business efforts. You certainly would not be surprised to see counterfeits of your product widely used in the marketplace. This was the "death of a thousand cuts." You could not effectively resist, so you yielded. Sometimes the condition of investment was that you export a certain percentage of your production. This was an aspect of business life in China with which the Paulson gang was unfamiliar, but it was very real. It is also true, however, that the U.S. and global business communities were so eager to get into China that they resisted half-heartedly or not at all. On one hand, they were so confident of their ability to invent faster than the Chinese that they didn't worry very much about the theft of their intellectual property. On the other hand, they were so anxious to get early entry into the Chinese market that they were willing to pay whatever it cost.

Many of the corporations with an interest in producing in, selling to, or buying from China gathered under the umbrella of the U.S.-China Business Council, which became a powerful lobbying machine in Washington. The Business Roundtable also threw its immense weight into the "Go to China" effort, as did the immensely well-funded U.S. Chamber of Commerce. The president of the chamber, Thomas Donohue, always presented himself as the "voice of American business." But many observers felt he should have been forced to file officially as a foreign agent, because he was effectively a voice for Beijing.

Another important reason for the prevalence of the "liberalization via trade" faith was that it was spread by the leading soothsayers in the U.S. press. *New York Times* chief foreign affairs columnist Tom Friedman is a perfect example. In 1999, his book *The Lexus and the Olive Tree* became a runaway best seller and made him even more of a celebrity than he already was.

Friedman fell in love with the apparent liberalizing effect of the personal computer and the microchips that power them. He even discovered a new disease, which he called "Microchip Immune Deficiency" that he said afflicted old, slow, top-heavy systems like those of IBM and the former Soviet Union. These were the losers in the era of globalization, he wrote, because "in the world of the PC and the microchip it had become much more efficient to empower individuals, who could get more information and make more decisions themselves rather than having a single person at the top trying to direct everything." Friedman went on to say that "we have gone from a command and control leadership model in the Cold War to a command and connect leadership model in the globalization era."[33]

Turning to China, he insisted, "China's going to have a free press. Globalization will drive it. Oh, China's leaders don't know it yet, but they are being pushed straight in that direction." He continued, "China needs a quintuple by-pass" to get its economy running properly. "China . . . will have a difficult adjustment—not for cultural reasons but for political ones. China has the will. It just doesn't have the way. The only way China can take care of the millions who work for the SOEs is to privatize them. . . . At some point either China won't get richer or it won't be as authoritarian as it is now . . . because what the Chinese government can get away with now is very different from what it will be able to get away with once it is fully integrated into the herd."[34]

Nor was Friedman alone in declaring the inevitability of China's political and economic liberalization. The Pulitzer Prize–winning journalist Nicholas Kristof wrote in the *New York Review of Books* in June 1994, "The Communist dynasty is collapsing in China."[35] Kristof's credibility on China was strengthened by the fact that his wife, Sheryl WuDunn, is a Chinese American who won the Pulitzer Prize along with him for reporting on the Tiananmen Square demonstrations and massacre.

Writing in *Foreign Affairs* in November 2000, Samuel ("Sandy") R. Berger, President Clinton's national security advisor, said, "Just as NAFTA membership eroded the economic base of one-party rule in Mexico, WTO membership can help do the same in China."[36]

American business saw a pot of gold at the end of the Chinese rainbow and went for it, while buying the political and intellectual influence necessary to reach the goal. American pundits and academics supported this effort by telling the story they and their readers desperately wanted to believe.

Berger also demonstrates another reason why the foreign policy establishment clung so tightly to the free-trade-equals-democratization theme. After leaving the Clinton administration, he established Stonebridge International, a consulting group that advised companies on how to deal with China. In doing this, he was emulating Henry Kissinger, who established Kissinger Associates to advise on China after stepping down as secretary of state. The idea was to do well by doing the good of promoting trade with and investment in China, which would inevitably lead to its political liberalization. Whether or not Kissinger did any good, he did do very, very well. So did Clinton's secretary of state Madeleine Albright with the Albright Group, former senator and secretary of defense William Cohen with the Cohen Group, former U.S. trade representative Carla Hills with Hills & Co. (Hank Greenberg was her particular champion and put her on AIG's board of directors), and former national security advisor Brent Scowcroft with the Scowcroft Group. Former U.S. trade representative Mickey Kantor took a couple of China hands from the Office of the Trade Representative with him and did very well advising on China with the law firm of Mayer, Brown, Rowe, & Maw, and former U.S. trade representative Charlene Barshefsky did exceedingly well doing the same at the law firm of Wilmer Hale. But one did not even have to establish a firm and be visible as an advisor on China in order to do well. Many former officials went into seemingly mundane jobs in academia but still found ways to profit from their China experience. When Ken Lieberthal is quoted in the press, for example, he is usually identified as a University of Michigan China expert or as a former National Security Council official. He is indeed both of these things, but what is usually not mentioned is that he also served as a senior director of Stonebridge International.[37] Robert Zoellick, a strong advocate of economic coupling with China, is usually identified as a former president of the World Bank or deputy secretary of state, but he also works as an advisor with the Brunswick Group and as nonexecutive chairman of Alliance Bernstein—both of which groups work on China in some way.

In order to maintain their own self-respect, these and many others like them must sincerely cling to the faith that trade with, investment in, and transfer of technology to China will turn it into a more capitalist and more politically liberal country. They have wholeheartedly embraced the twentieth-century secular version of the old missionary dream of converting China to the true religion.

Distraction, Reassurance, and Doubts

Once China was accepted into the WTO, the predictions quickly began to prove inaccurate. As we have seen, U.S. trade representatives Mickey Kantor and Charlene Barshefsky had forecast a swift rise in U.S. exports to China and a dramatic decline in the U.S. trade deficit with China. Not only did this fail to materialize, it quickly went the other way. The deficit eventually topped $400 billion in the wake of massive offshoring of production from America to China by U.S. multinational companies. They couldn't wait to produce in China, where the cost of labor was a fraction of that in the United States, and regulation, especially regarding pollution and worker safety, was essentially nonexistent. Even more anxious to buy in China were big U.S. retailers like Walmart (which once had a Made in the USA policy), Best Buy, and Costco.

Little of this was in line with Ricardo's theory of comparative advantage. Recall that Ricardo himself had warned that if you can move investment and production from one country to another, all bets are off. That did not stop the guild of professional economists and pundits from presenting free trade and globalization as inevitably "win-win" propositions.

George W. Bush at first seemed to share his father's views. In a speech at the Ronald Reagan Library on November 19, 1999, he noted that "economic freedom creates habits of liberty that create expectations of democracy." He added: "Trade freely with China, and time is on our side." Bush's first national security advisor, Condoleezza Rice, was also in tune with the old-time religion. She wrote in the *New York Times* on December 11, 2002, that China's "WTO membership will inevitably lead to an appetite for U.S. values and interests. It will strengthen an entrepreneurial class that doesn't owe its livelihood to the state and that will set China free."[38]

Bush did, at one point, call China "a strategic competitor," and he contemplated more hedging by such means as greater arms sales to Taiwan.[39] But this Bush administration became fatally distracted early in its term by the events of 9/11 and the war on terror. In order to fight that war, the administration needed China's support on the UN Security Council, and in any case, business between the United States and China was booming. By 2004, two-way trade between the two countries had nearly doubled, to $231 billion, since China's WTO entry. The U.S. trade deficit had also doubled, to about $160 billion, but few noticed. Former British prime minister Tony Blair, visiting Beijing in 2005, cheered the "unstoppable momentum toward democracy" he found in China.[40] Even as he spoke, former premier Zhao Ziyang was in his fifteenth year under house arrest because of his sympathy for the students calling for democracy in Tiananmen Square. Blair, of course, did not have the opportunity to meet Zhao.

The skyrocketing U.S. trade deficit with China finally began to catch some people's attention when it topped $200 billion, as not only U.S. factories but also high-paying manufacturing jobs and skills left America for China. The administration's position was well articulated in a statement by Deputy Secretary of State Robert Zoellick, who said, "It is time to take our policy beyond opening doors to China's membership in the international system. We need to urge China to become a responsible stakeholder in that system." After heaping praise on China, he noted that it was showing "increasing signs of mercantilism with policies that seek to direct markets rather than opening them." A responsible stakeholder, he continued, "shouldn't tolerate rampant theft of intellectual property and counterfeiting. . . . China needs to fully live up to its commitments to markets where America has a strong competitive advantage." It needed to stop undervaluing its currency, stop trying to lock up global energy supplies, and start negotiating multilaterally rather than using bilateral fora that make it easy "to maneuver toward a predominance of power." Zoellick also called on China "to avoid partnerships with regimes (like North Korea) that would hurt its reputation."[41]

This was a bit of a shift. Previous commentators had described the path from trade to free markets to democracy as natural and irreversible. Now Zoellick was suggesting that it wasn't, and that the world and China must work together to keep (or put) China on that path. But he didn't mention any consequences for noncompliance. His speech called on the world to continue playing the same old game with China, and on China to abandon the "catch-up" strategy that was working so well in favor of becoming "a responsible stakeholder in the international system." But China had had no role in building that system and felt no responsibility for protecting and preserving it. In the end, the speech showed only that leading American experts still did not understand what China under the CCP was all about. Zoellick failed to see that the Central Party School and other key Party organs knew very well that becoming a responsible stakeholder in the international system presented a risk to their power. They were doing all they could not to become such.

The year 2005 also produced another best-selling book from Tom Friedman, *The World Is Flat*. It was a catchy title. The book explained how technology was shrinking distance and time and removing barriers to trade and finance in such fundamental ways that, in effect, the world had become flat. Friedman's analysis of how this was working did make him wonder sometimes if Ricardo had gotten it right. He sensed that "flat world" globalization could bring a lot of job displacement, but in the end he kept the faith, reasoning that the global pie was going to get continually bigger and thus provide sufficient welfare for everyone. In *The Lexus and the Olive Tree*, Friedman had developed the McDonald's theory of conflict avoidance: no two countries with McDonald's restaurants would go to war with each other. That balloon had burst when the United States and several EU countries went to war with Serbia in 1999. Now, Friedman presented the Dell theory of conflict avoidance. Dell computers were then being assembled in China with parts from all over the world. The notion was that no two countries sharing a supply chain would go to war. Since China shared supply chains with every major country and many smaller ones, Friedman argued, there was no need to worry about future military conflict with China.

By 2005, however, not everyone was still convinced. As we saw in chapter 3, China's five-year plans, catch-up strategies and goals, and aggressive technology acquisition were completely unaltered by its entry into the WTO, as were the rise of the U.S. trade deficit with and the export of jobs to China. There was no sign that China wished to become a "responsible stakeholder in the international system" and increasing evidence that it did not. James Mann, former bureau chief of the *L.A. Times* in Beijing, published a book in 2007 called *The China Fantasy* in which he skewered much of the old conventional wisdom and pointed out that what had been predicted was not coming true. He also explained why it was not likely to come true: it was based on false assumptions about both international economics and the Beijing regime. He showed that China was, in a paraphrase of Japan's catch-up architect Amaya Naohiro, "doing what the Americans told us not to do." He also refuted the view, held by Harvard professor Joseph Nye, *Washington Post* columnist Robert Samuelson, and others, that "if we treat China as the enemy, it will become the enemy."[42] Mann observed that this statement silently implied its opposite: if you treated China as a friend, it would become a friend—and that this had been the bedrock of U.S. policy since Nixon, or perhaps since Wilson. The truth, said Mann, was otherwise. China was not especially intent on being our friend or anyone else's. As a Leninist party, the CCP couldn't really have friends.

The Pivot

In the wake of the Great Recession of 2007–9, Beijing became convinced it was not a good idea for China to become a capitalist state like America, where crooked real estate agents combined with crooked loan companies and crooked banks using crooked property valuers to create crooked financial instruments, which they then sold to innocent investors.

The fault did not lie entirely with the United States. Beijing's rapid-growth policy had raised the Chinese savings rate to above 50 percent of GDP. The resulting trade surplus funneled dollars into China's financial institutions, and these were invested in U.S. Treasury bonds, a step that contributed to the very low U.S. interest rates that had sparked the real estate bubble. But very few in Beijing believed that. To them, it seemed that the Americans didn't know how to run their own economy, let alone the world.

A lot of Americans were thinking the same thing. Their jobs kept disappearing while everything they bought had a "Made in China" label. Then the former Goldman Sachs banker Hank Paulson, in his new role as secretary of the treasury, organized a $700 billion bailout of U.S. banks (including Goldman Sachs), followed by an $80 billion bailout of the U.S. auto industry. No one went to jail, and the banks and auto companies remained under essentially the same management that had gotten them into the mess. Unemployment kept rising. The Economic Policy Institute has estimated that between 2001 and 2011, 2.7 million U.S. jobs went to China.[43] All this, of course, put Barack Obama in the White House in 2008.

One of Obama's early questions about China to his economic advisor Larry Summers and his treasury secretary Timothy Geithner was: "Did you guys give too much away?"[44]

One thing that became clear shortly after Obama's election was that Beijing was in no way becoming liberalized by trade. In December 2008, a group of Chinese liberals led by Liu Xiaobo formed what they called Charter 08 and issued a manifesto calling for freedom. Liu had been a student in Tiananmen Square on the night of June 3, 1989, and had negotiated a peaceful withdrawal of students from the square in the early morning of June 4. By doing so he saved hundreds of lives. For his trouble he was sentenced to twenty months in jail. Now, on December 8, 2008, he was arrested even before the charter was published and sentenced to eleven years in prison. When he was awarded the Nobel Peace Prize in 2010, Beijing reacted by detaining his wife and halting its imports of Norwegian salmon. In the ceremony at Oslo, he was represented by an empty chair. The Party would not allow him to go to Norway to accept the prize.

U.S.-China relations went downhill quickly. China began harassing Japan by sending hundreds of "fishing boats" to the waters around the Senkaku Islands, which Japan administers. It also began demanding that other Southeast Asian nations recognize its territorial claims in the South China Sea, and it elevated these to the level of "core" interests like those it claimed to have in Tibet and Taiwan. Chinese hackers had already stolen the production plans for the F-35 Lightning II (America's most advanced fighter in production) and modeled their J-31 on it.[45] Then, in October 2011, Secretary of State Hillary Clinton used the word *pivot* three times in an article, "America's Pacific Century," in *Foreign Affairs* that announced a "strategic turn to the Asia-Pacific region." The word stuck, and the policy became known as "the Pivot." The United States increased its troop and naval vessel deployments to the region with new bases in Australia and ships in Singapore. The policy committed the United States to joining the East Asia Summit (the major regional organization) and to negotiating a Trans-Pacific Partnership free trade agreement.

Not to be outdone, in November 2012, the Chinese Communist Party's newly elected general secretary, Xi Jinping, took the seven-member Standing Committee of the Politburo on a tour of the National Museum of China's exhibition *The Road to Rejuvenation*. Here he emphasized that the "Chinese Dream" involved the "great revival of the Chinese nation." In April 2013, the Party issued Document 9 listing seven political perils, among which were the promotion of universal values, a free press, and a privatized economy.

The hacking intensified. In the spring of 2015, Chinese spies stole sensitive personal information on more than 20 million U.S. employees, including information on every person who had received a high-level security clearance since 1986.[46]

Three years later, in March 2018, the voice of the global economics establishment, the *Economist,* declared the free world to be on the losing side of an important bet.[47] The free world had bet that globalization would not only open China's markets to free trade and competition but would also liberalize China's political environment. China had bet the opposite: that it could use the technology and markets of the free world to become a rich and powerful nation without yielding an inch of political liberalization. The *Economist* announced that China had won the bet.

Disturbingly, most of the free world bettors seemed unaware that a wager had existed.

PART

Nothing to Fear from 100 Battles
—Sun Tzu

8

Lay of the Land

> For now we see dimly, but then face to face.
> —*Corinthians 13:12*

In an important sporting event, the players often try to survey the field of competition before play begins. They want to know where they will find the sticky and slick spots, the hard and soft spots, the areas that may enhance their strengths and those they should avoid. So let us look at the playing field, both physical and mental, for China and America in the decade of the 2020s.

The World Is Round

Because of the blindness of China experts, economists, pundits, and business leaders, inhabitants of the free world have been living in a fairyland for forty odd years. Despite much evidence to the contrary (for instance, World Wars I and II were fought between countries that were best trading partners), the free world (particularly America) was guided by Cobden's notion that "free trade is God's diplomacy." It embraced Tom Friedman's exciting, reassuring conclusion that "the world is flat" and accepted the premise that free trade and globalization are always and everywhere win-win propositions in which the few losers will be compensated for their relatively small losses out of the gains of the many winners. It condemned "protectionism" and "mercantilism" as relics of a benighted past. It overlooked the CCP's massacre of Chinese students at Tiananmen Square and proceeded to help enrich and empower China and the Party because it believed trade and foreign investment would inevitably "plant the seeds of democracy." It believed that China's becoming a "responsible stakeholder in the global order" was inevitable and would liberalize and eventually democratize the country, thereby making China just like us.

Free world leaders further misunderstood the nature of the CCP. They did not grasp that the Party well understood the danger to its power implicit in the free world's "hug them to death" gambit, and that it had taken strong measures to contain any political or cultural impact. The free world's leaders and intelligentsia failed to see that the Party understood their offers of a seat at the free world's head table as an attack on its very foundations. Nor did they understand the quasi-religious nature of the CCP and the importance to the Party of inculcating and keeping the faith, of broadcasting propaganda, and of strictly controlling the distribution of information. Everyone laughed when President Clinton likened any attempt to control the internet to nailing Jell-O to a wall. How silly of Beijing to imagine it could do something like that.

It is now clear that the free world should not have been so quick to abandon its old friend Columbus. He was right in his time and remains right today. The world really is round.

The New Econ 101

We have also seen that free trade in the conventional sense is quite limited today. What we are mostly experiencing is not free trade but globalization, especially the cross-border financial flows that free trade doctrine assumes do not occur. Globalization is about economies of scale and scope that also do not fit nicely into the conventional theory taught to university students in Economics 101. Contrary to the view of the economics establishment that university undergraduates need only be taught conventional free trade wisdom, students need to know a lot more than conventional free trade theory.[1]

One thing they need to know is that in lieu of a meaningful, enforceable international economic agreement, mercantilism works. No country has ever become rich except by mercantilist practices. Economic theory cannot predict innovation, and it therefore cannot tell a country how to become rich. Think of recent examples such as South Korea, Taiwan, Japan, and China. None of them had many natural resources. None of them "did what the Americans said." None of them adopted the "Washington consensus." All of them succeeded by using mercantilist strategies.

It is important for students—and everyone else—to discard a common trope of free trade economics. The notion that corporations compete economically but countries do not is simplistically wrong. It might be true if wage levels were guaranteed to be equal everywhere and if countries were all democratic, operated under rule of law, maintained no armed forces, had no reason to fear one another, and shared the same political, social, and economic values. But this is not the world in which we live.

The CCP Party/state's values are not only different from those of the free world but are hostile to them in fundamental respects. Leadership in key technologies like computer chips is not just an important matter for companies like Intel or Qualcomm. It is also important for national security, for both China and the free world. It would not be a positive development for the free world for all its countries to lose leadership in such an important technology. Countries do compete economically and technologically because they don't share values, and they fear the forceful imposition of foreign doctrines and practices as well as the possible necessity to pay tribute of some kind.

It is important for Americans especially to understand that economic and technological advance are not achieved solely by entrepreneurs taking advantage of free markets. In the first place, a completely free market is a jungle. It requires government to establish and police what we consider to be a free market. Consider: the New York Stock Exchange is a market and so are the Moscow and Shanghai Stock Exchanges. On which do you think you'd prefer to trade? Did you say New York? If so, the reason is that it is better regulated. Beyond that, as we have seen in the cases of semiconductors, aircraft, and many other technologies and products, government support of R&D, procurement, and protection have been critical to success. Almost everything Apple sells, for instance, came out of some U.S. government program.

In this round world, we have also recently discovered that globalization can be weaponized. If Manila does something Beijing dislikes, bananas from the Philippines can be left rotting on Chinese docks. If South Korea allows a missile-tracking device to be installed on its shores, sales of Lotte (a Korean company) products to China can dry up because "the feelings of 1.4 billion Chinese are hurt," and Lotte Mart will have to close the hundred-odd stores it had invested in establishing in China. Major global corporations, if they are dependent on Chinese markets, can be forced to change their operations. In September 2019 the head of Hong Kong's Cathay Pacific Airlines was forced to resign because Beijing disliked the fact that some Cathay personnel supported demonstrators in Hong Kong. United and other international airlines have changed the booking code of their Taiwan-bound flights from "Taipei, Taiwan" to simply "Taipei" (despite the fact that Taipei is not governed by Beijing) in response to the threatened loss of air routes to major Chinese cities.

When the deeply held values of countries clash, globalization can intensify rather than modulate the conflict.

Finally, while there has been much talk of the gains of trade and the benefits of globalization, their costs have been ignored or downplayed. Typically, the analysis holds that while a few workers in an industry such as the auto industry may take a hit when imports take their jobs or reduce their wages, this loss is greatly outweighed by the benefits of lower prices to consumers, who far outnumber the autoworkers. Moreover, it is argued, the former autoworkers will find other jobs, so the net loss is only their wages for whatever period they were out of work and, of course, any continuing negative pay differential. There are several holes in this argument, but an important one is that the models used to analyze gains and losses of trade assume full employment. In the absence of full employment, loss of jobs in one industry tends to lower wages in other industries. Thus, the trade-off is not autoworker jobs versus all consumer prices, but all consumers versus all workers' wages. That is not a slam-dunk for globalization. On top of that, the equations and models do not consider the global warming impact and cost of all the air travel and sea shipping entailed in globalization. Nor do they consider the cost to future innovation of the loss of important skill sets entailed by many aspects of today's globalization.

Consider further the differences in the quality of pain and pleasure. Of course, it is nice to save a few dollars when buying shoes or a washing machine. But that pleasure does not equal the intensity of the complete loss of a job, or of a school system in a factory town when the factory closes. Moreover, the pleasure of inexpensive socks is fleeting, while the pain of the factory, school, and local water system going down is long lasting and has severe knock-on effects. These elements are never captured in the econometric models used to evaluate the gains and losses from trade, yet they are the most important elements. Look at the generations of costs incurred when a city like Detroit loses its businesses and its schools, and then its sanitation and much more, and consider that those costs are not just local. They ultimately hit the whole country.

Another way of considering the question is to look at the gap between rich and poor. It has widened dramatically in the United States and most other free world countries in lockstep with globalization. Even if there appear to be overall economic gains from globalization, the winners are clearly not compensating the losers, with the result that the society has become poorer even if the GDP numbers say it hasn't. Some economists such as David Autor at MIT, Robert Scott at the Economic Policy Institute, David Dorn at the University of Zurich, and Gordon Hanson at the University of California–San Diego have recognized that neoclassical free trade and globalization doctrine is badly flawed and is a major factor in growing economic inequality and the rise of populism. But the mainstream of professional economists has yet to grasp reality. Because their models don't incorporate the proper assumptions, the economists don't see and therefore tend to reject these conclusions. But that doesn't make the conclusions wrong.

Another key element never mentioned in the discussion of globalization is that investing in China, producing in China, and buying from China are all actions that directly strengthen the CCP and all of its activities, including the internment of Uighurs, the dredging and arming of artificial islands in the South China Sea, the attacks by Mainland Chinese students on Hong Kong students in Australia, and the spreading of propaganda through the distribution of *China Daily* via the *Washington Post*, and the recent denial of free speech and rule of law in Hong Kong. The total costs of all this and more that I could cite might make the price of "free trade" look like not such a great deal.

Indeed, a very important revelation of the COVID-19 pandemic has been that of the true costs associated with the China-anchored global supply chain. Heretofore it was widely believed that the most efficient and cost-effective way to supply many world markets was to produce components in a variety of global locations, fly or ship them to China (or, increasingly, manufacture them in China) for assembly by inexpensive or specially talented (or both) Chinese labor, and then ship them by boat and airplane to the world's markets. The coronavirus, along with China's Made in China 2025 drive for making all cutting-edge high-tech products in China, has sparked a deep questioning of the true costs and rationality of the global supply chain. Excessive reliance on supply from China has been seen to carry potentially high costs with it. Needed products might not be available. Or, if China is angry with you, they might be withheld. In addition, the air and sea shipping inevitably involved account for about 8 percent of global greenhouse gas emissions—and that number is rising. The costs of this have never been incorporated into the pricing of the supply chain. In the future they must be, and they could be prohibitively high. As European Bank for Reconstruction and Development economist Beata Javorcik says: "The quest to find the most cost-effective suppliers has left many companies without a plan B. Businesses will be forced to rethink their global value chains."[2] Because of this and also because of new technologies like three-dimensional printing (a ball bearing, for example, can be printed at the auto plant just like a book instead of being manufactured in a factory and then shipped to the auto plant), future supply chains are likely to be more diversified and located much closer to the place of final sale than has been the case for the past thirty years.

Of extreme importance in considering the landscape is Beijing's decision on May 1, 2020, to pass a so-called national security law covering Hong Kong. Passed by China's National People's Congress over the head of Hong Kong's legislature, it was a blatant violation of the special administrative status granted for fifty years to Hong Kong in 1997. It told the world that Communist China cannot be trusted to keep commitments. Indeed, it said far more than that. The move will essentially destroy Hong Kong's status and value as a major international financial center. The basis of that status was the rule of law left behind when the UK turned the territory over to Beijing. Now that Beijing has made clear that this was only a head fake, the money will move to safer territory. Bret Stephens of the *New York Times* called this "the Rhineland moment," referring to Hitler's illegal occupation of the Rhineland in 1936.[3] The lack of a strong UK-

French-U.S. response at the time is often credited with contributing to the later outbreak of World War II. Stephens was clearly calling for a strong international response. So far, the United States has canceled the special and favorable trade treatment it had always accorded Hong Kong, and the United Kingdom has announced that it would welcome about three hundred thousand holders of British overseas passports in Hong Kong to come live in Britain.

The new law will have a significant negative impact on China, whose large corporations tended to use Hong Kong as the main place to raise new capital. That Zhongnanhai made the move despite the likely negative financial impact demonstrates how clearly making and keeping all of China authoritarian and communist outweighs all other considerations for the CCP. Indeed, the attitude of Zhongnanhai toward any who questioned it was defiant and sarcastic. For instance, the Chinese state media referred to Australia as "a giant kangaroo that serves as a dog for the United States" and that "chews gum stuck on the soles of Chinese shoes."[4]

While this was going on in the Asia-Pacific region of the world, emerita professor Lucia Dunn wrote a letter to the editor of the *Washington Post* on May 27, 2020, noting that as an advisor to the campus Falun Gong chapter at Ohio State University, she had seen their posters defaced and email hacked, while the campus Chinese Student and Scholar Association demanded that they not be allowed to use campus email. She wondered if it is worthwhile to bring thousands of Chinese students to U.S. universities because "the process brings its own costs."

These issues, attitudes, and questions must always be kept in mind by anyone, any corporation, or any government considering dealing with China. Now that we know what the playing field looks like, let's compare the lineups of the contestants.

China

There is no contest between the Chinese people and those of the United States. The tug of war is between the United States and the CCP Party/state that tightly controls China and its people. Not only are the Chinese people subject to strong police control, but because the internet is controlled by the government and much of the foreign press is blocked in China, the Chinese people have great difficulty obtaining a perception of reality that is independent of the Party's views. This was vividly demonstrated in January 2019 by the overwhelming reelection of democracy advocate Tsai Ing-Wen as the president of the Republic of China in Taiwan, and again over the summer of 2019 by the massive demonstrations of citizens of Hong Kong against the rule of its CCP-appointed government. One important point is that the perceptions of what was happening in Taiwan and Hong Kong were entirely different among Mainland Chinese from those of the citizens of Taiwan and Hong Kong. The second point is that the citizens of both Taiwan and Hong Kong made it abundantly clear that they do not want to be ruled by the CCP.

The Party was founded as a communist party and still uses those words in its name. But Marxist communism placed a strong emphasis on equality, even if that meant equal poverty. The Party under Mao deliberately pursued class warfare, killing not only rich Chinese but even supposedly "rich" peasant farmers who were just a bit above the average in income and wealth. That disappeared when Deng led the Party into "socialism with Chinese characteristics." Some say that one of the characteristics is inequality. Thus, the Party is no longer truly communist, but it does remain a Leninist party in that it follows Lenin's concepts of how to obtain and maintain absolute power. Power is its highest priority.

The Party is not subject to the rule of any laws, and it brooks no opposition, no interference, and no expressions of disagreement. It monitors the people constantly and comprehensively. It does not confine itself to the political sphere but enforces its will in art, religion, philosophy, and all other aspects of life. For instance, after kidnapping the duly selected Panchen Lama, it went on to choose its own replacement Panchen Lama, even though the current Dalai Lama does not recognize the legitimacy of the Party's choice. This is not a situation unique to the religious hierarchy's political role in Tibet, where the Dalai Lama was once head of state. China is also the only country in the world where the government (that is, the Party) names the priests in the Catholic Church. Or, to take another example, look at something as mundane as the translation of books. In response to the U.S. imposition of tariffs on some imports from China in 2018, Beijing simply halted the translation of all books originating from the United States. There was never any policy announcement or other kind of notification. The whole translation process just stopped.[5]

Having abandoned communism, the Party has adopted Chinese chauvinism and the restoration of China's ancient greatness as its raison d'être. Xi's "Chinese Dream" is for China again to become the dominant power in Eurasia and Southeast Asia—and eventually in the rest of the world. The United States is seen to be the main obstacle standing in the way. But for the rulers of China, the problem the United States presents goes far beyond just being a rival great power. America's founding principles and present values are diametrically opposed to those of the CCP, and their possible spread to the rest of the world is just as much a threat to Beijing as the CCP's values are a threat to America. It is for these reasons that the Party considers America its chief enemy. No posture the United States can take and no policy it can adopt will change the Party's perception of it. As noted previously in chapter 3, in Document 9, "Communiqué on the Current State of the Ideological Sphere," cadres are ordered to arouse "mass fervor" and wage "intense struggle" against the following "false trends":

1. Western constitutional democracy—"an attempt to undermine the current leadership";
2. Universal values of human rights—an attempt to weaken the theoretical foundations of Party leadership;
3. Civil society—a "political tool" of the "Western anti-China forces" to dismantle the Party's social foundation;
4. Neoliberalism—U.S.-led efforts to "change China's basic economic system";
5. The West's idea of journalism—attacking the Marxist view of news, attempting to "gouge an opening through which to infiltrate our ideology."

A good example is the current unrest and demonstrations in Hong Kong against possible interference in Hong Kong affairs by Beijing. A Hong Kong man killed his pregnant girlfriend in Taiwan and then fled back to Hong Kong. Taiwanese authorities wished to extradite him from Hong Kong for trial in Taiwan but could not do so because the two governments do not have an extradition treaty. This led the Hong Kong government to consider establishing a kind of extradition procedure that would apply to all jurisdictions worldwide with which Hong Kong did not have such arrangements. But such a step would also inevitably include Mainland

China (People's Republic of China), of which Hong Kong is a Special Administrative Region, and with which it did not have any kind of extradition arrangements. In February 2019, Hong Kong chief executive Carrie Lam submitted a general extradition bill to the Hong Kong legislature and the bill was made public in early March 2019. When the citizenry became aware that this bill might make Hong Kong citizens vulnerable to extradition to Mainland China, millions of them began daily marches and protests in the streets. Eventually Lam was not only forced to withdraw the bill but also witnessed her political party's loss of elections in virtually every Hong Kong voting district. The central problem is that the residents of Hong Kong fear that they will lose significant freedoms as Beijing tightens its control over their city; for Beijing, the problem is how to bring Hong Kong under its control without sacrificing the city's value as a world financial center or—now that millions have taken to the streets—allowing the protests to be seen as successful, which could inspire similar demonstrations elsewhere in China. No outside intervention is needed to make this disagreement deeply divisive and perhaps unresolvable without violence, yet Beijing has tried to blame the protests on "the black hand" of America. Because it can think only in terms of striving for power, the Party cannot accept or understand any gesture as something other than a stratagem aimed at holding China back and ultimately engineering the Party's demise. It cannot recognize that Hong Kong citizens might have their own grievances, or that these might be legitimate.

China's is a highly centralized and coordinated society in which the Party makes itself aware of a much wider and deeper range of activities, meetings, discussions, and communications than does any free world government or political party. U.S. states or major cities often have "sister" city or state relationships with Chinese cities and provinces. When they visit these sister entities, American governors and mayors do not coordinate their trips with Washington, and they often assume that they are building independent and even confidential relationships with their counterparts in China. But this is not at all the reality.

If it chooses to, Beijing can know virtually every word of a conversation between a local official and a foreign representative within hours of its taking place. I recently saw on television an American governor saying, with some condescension, that he didn't need to bother talking to Washington in order to build the great relationship he enjoyed with his opposite number in China. He appears to have had no idea that his Chinese interlocutor would carefully brief Beijing both before and after his visit.

The Party's modus operandi is being vividly demonstrated again in Hong Kong. In a story for the *Wall Street Journal* on September 3, 2019, entitled "Hong Kong and the Truth about China," Claudia Rosett reported that she was present in Tiananmen Square on July 3–4, 1989, and the demonstrations in Hong Kong had convinced her that the nature of the communist regime had not changed from the "brutal, dehumanizing tyranny that would rather destroy people than give them a say." On September 4, 2019, the lead editorial in the *New York Times* emphasized that "Hong Kong just wants the promise kept of free election of its legislature and Chief Executive made at the time of Beijing's takeover of the city in 1997." It went on to note that China (meaning the Party and the Beijing government) "has reams of information on Hong Kong but doesn't understand the people of Hong Kong." On September 5, 2019, a *Financial Times* headline declared: "China Mobilizes Social Media to Aim at Demonstrators." The international significance of all this was captured in a *Financial Times* headline the next day: "Merkel Faces Hong Kong Dilemma in Beijing." The piece was about a trip by a group of top German business leaders headed by Chancellor Angela Merkel, but the dilemma it mentioned was one that all business and political leaders in democratic countries need to contemplate. In the face of the demand by the young people of Hong Kong for such core liberties as free speech and free elections, how could Merkel and her coterie of business leaders representing a major Western democracy do deals with the CCP leadership as if nothing significant were going on in the Special Administrative Region of Hong Kong? The question was only sharpened by a *Financial Times* editorial on September 7, 2019, which noted a recent speech by President Xi invoking *chuxin* (original aspirations) and exhorting Party and government leaders to be "commanders and warriors."

Clearly, Xi seems to feel that he and his country are at war, and beyond exhorting his "commanders and warriors" he is employing classic Chinese strategy. His game is not the direct confrontation of Western chess, in which the conquered king is eventually knocked out. Rather, he is playing *weiqi*, in which the object is to surround the opponent and completely block his ability to move. The key element of this strategy is the absence of rule of law in China and the Party's position as the final authority on everything. There is no rule or agreement that cannot be avoided or gutted. Informal administrative power or "guidance" is a secret weapon that can empty agreements and understandings of any meaning.

For example, China has agreed to a variety of open-market business practices in conjunction with its membership in the WTO. These can easily be undermined in practice by imposition of such things as frequent "health inspections," investigations for building code violations, and unexplained delays of permits with which China can easily bend any corporation to its will. The corporation would never try to fight such measures in court, and if it did, it would never win. Thus, the heads of global corporations like Apple, Cisco, and General Electric are effectively hostages to Beijing. They may be perceived as the heads of American companies, but they fear Beijing far more than they fear Washington. In Washington they are powerful, with legions of lawyers and lobbyists and the ability to sue the government and win. In Beijing, they never sue the government because they know not only that they wouldn't win but that the government would retaliate against them for trying.

As with business corporations, so with the internet and the media. All are controlled by the government and the Party. The Party line is sent each day to the leading press outlets, which communicate it to the country and the world. News of things like demonstrations against the government in Hong Kong is suppressed or written to reflect the Party's views. Massive surveillance is used to intimidate even free world journalists, while Party-line publications report within the guidelines of the Party. Perceptions in Mainland China of what is happening in Hong Kong are thus wildly at odds with what the rest of the world sees. It turns out that Bill Clinton was wrong. The Chinese can nail the internet to the wall whether it is made of Jell-O or not.

China's industrial policy of driving for leadership in 5G, artificial intelligence, aviation, semiconductors, and other critical industries is part and parcel of its political efforts. Beijing's extensive efforts to squeeze technology out of the free world by any available means are essential to realizing the Great Chinese Dream, and no trade deal with the United States or the European Union will change that outlook. Similarly, despite much expert talk of the eventual demise of SOEs, they are not going away either. Rather, they are growing, and they now constitute approximately 30 percent of China's GDP while serving as the main vehicles for China's economic expansion abroad.[6] Beyond their business objectives, these enterprises have two critical functions. The first is to fund the CCP, and the second is to be a tool of Great China strategy. Thus, if Beijing wishes to pull, say, Portugal into its orbit, it may have an SOE bid to buy a major Portuguese electricity-generating company. In the case of Greece, Beijing might have an SOE buy or contract to manage the port of Piraeus. The Belt and Road strategy of China is built on the backs of the SOEs.

Beyond the SOEs, the Party's power of coercion is such that it can effectively direct corporations and even individual spending and buying decisions. If Beijing is unhappy with, say, Singapore, it can quickly stop the flow of students to Singapore's universities, which depend on these students for their funding. If Australia's praise of China is not sufficient, Beijing can halt the flow of tourists going there. China scholars all over the world need visas to visit China from time to time. It has recently been revealed that China plans to restrict visas for those who say negative things about it.[7] In short, any company, country, or person with any dependence on China may find itself subject to coercion, and the more the dependence, the more the potential for coercion. This is the great problem of the "global supply chain." Because much of that chain runs through China, many corporations and countries are vulnerable to substantial coercion by Beijing.

China's global strategy for surrounding and displacing the United States has two main anchors. One is the Belt and Road program, facilitated by global investment by SOEs in fundamental infrastructure like pipelines, ports, and telecommunications. We saw in chapter 3 the extent of this investment and the influence it has brought. The other anchor is a massive military buildup that includes aircraft carriers, other warships, anti-ship missiles, coast guard vessels, paramilitary naval units, and copies (literally) of the latest U.S. military aircraft. China has also become highly skilled in cyberspace and has many strategic satellites, including "grabber" satellites that can reach out and literally grab other satellites to disable them. "As of 2018, the Chinese Navy consists of over 300 ships, making it larger than the 290 vessels comprising the deployable battle force of the US Navy."[8] When China's maritime militia is taken into account, the Chinese navy may have about twice as many ships as the U.S. Navy.[9] Many of these are not modern, but the whole force is rapidly becoming state-of-the-art.

As we have seen, the PLAN and PLAAF—the Chinese navy and air force, respectively—have taken substantial control of the South China Sea and are now making similar efforts in the South Pacific. They are also investing in what the Chinese government calls a "string of pearls" of ports in the South Pacific and across the Indian Ocean to their base in Djibouti.

China has had no formal allies since its split with the Soviet Union in 1960. But in September 2019, the PLAAF and the Russian air force teamed up in a flyover of the Takeshima Islands, known to South Korea as the Dokdo Islands. Were this cooperation to broaden into a military alliance between Russia and China, it would enhance the substantial threat China already poses to the free world.

In lieu of formal allies, China has substantial influence in a large network of states and regions. Cambodia, Laos, Mongolia, and Myanmar are almost extensions of China itself. Malaysia, Thailand, and Singapore are significantly dependent on China and increasingly under its military eye. India is less reliant on China and is suspicious of Beijing's increased naval activity in the Indian Ocean, but Pakistan is tightly tied to China, and Saudi Arabia is becoming more so. China practically owns sub-Saharan Africa and has been strengthening many dictators there. In Europe, we have already seen how SOEs have spread China's influence in southern and eastern Europe, and how that investment has neutered the European Union on matters of foreign policy. We have also seen how Beijing has expanded its influence in Australia and New Zealand through SOE investment, the flow of Chinese students, political donations, and coordination of propaganda. China's investment into and buying from the key countries in South America is extensive and growing.

All of these strategies share the common themes of repressing free speech, promoting authoritarianism, suppressing potential criticism of China, and surrounding the United States by splitting its allies away from it. Once the United States is completely blocked, China will be able to create a new authoritarian global system guided more by coercion than by law.

United States

Politically, culturally, philosophically, and economically, the United States is the opposite of the CCP's China. It has a much more fully free market economy that is mainly run by the private sector. It is a democracy based on free elections in which a high degree of open public debate is not only tolerated but encouraged. It is a highly diverse society ethnically, racially, socially, religiously, politically, culturally, and philosophically. It is a society that enforces strict limits on central power and in which power is dispersed. Compared to China, it is a substantially uncoordinated country whose central government is far less powerful.

The United States is under the rule of law. This does not mean that justice is always done, but it does mean that an individual can often challenge the government in court and win—something that does not occur in the CCP's China. As a result, citizens and corporations may resist and defy government direction. Nor can the government control the press and public debate. Freedom of speech is guaranteed by the Constitution and is highly protected. Not only is the internet not controlled, it is subject to little government regulation. This has its downside, but it is surely a very open public square.

The United States has also made many very harmful mistakes such as the Vietnam War, the invasion of Iraq, and the so-called war on terror. But it has also occasionally investigated itself, and it has allowed the press and citizens to investigate it and make public their critical findings. Often these findings have resulted in public acknowledgment of error and changes in laws and procedures.

The U.S. economy is about 35 percent bigger than China's at market exchange rates. Before the onset of the coronavirus pandemic the Chinese economy was growing at a bit more than twice the rate of the U.S. economy. The virus has thrown both economies into steep recession, but in the longer term the United States is likely to recover better than China. This is because on the one hand China is much more dependent on exports to the world than is the United States, and on the other hand, the developing economies are likely to recover less quickly than either the U.S. or the Chinese economy. In addition, the rapid aging of China's population will be a drag on its longer-term recovery. Nevertheless, it is important to note significant U.S. economic weaknesses. For example, compare America's gross savings rate of about 21 percent of GDP with the rates of China (45 percent), Japan (27 percent), and Germany (27 percent).[10] As a share of GDP, the U.S. national debt was over 100 percent and rising rapidly despite full employment and good economic growth before the pandemic. The impact of the virus will push U.S. debt to levels not seen since World War II. The U.S. rate of investment before the virus was around 21 percent of GDP and was among the OECD countries' lowest rates. Whether it be airports, dams and bridges, highways, water systems, railroads, or the electricity grid, American infrastructure is poor compared to that of other developed countries and has been deteriorating for some time. The effects of globalization and skewed tax rates have substantially increased the gap between rich and poor and led to political distemper. The impact of the virus will not help any of this, although it might stimulate more investment in infrastructure as part of a job creation and recovery strategy.

Unlike China's economy, which is heavily oriented toward investment and government spending, the U.S. economy is driven by individual consumption. Private consumption accounts for 69 percent of American GDP, compared to about 40 percent for China.[11] As noted earlier, the U.S. economy is about a third larger than China's, with per capita income at about $65,000 versus about $10,000 for China at market exchange rates.[12] The United States has hardly any state-owned enterprises (although important defense companies like Boeing and General Dynamics might be considered quasi-state-owned corporations) and no five-year economic plans, industry or technology targets, or government coordination of the economy beyond macroeconomic measures like the setting of interest rates by the independent Federal Reserve system and the establishment of the government budget, spending, and taxes by the president and the U.S. Congress. To be sure, there are military, energy, health, and other programs aimed at specific goals like defense capability and advancing science and medicine. But these are not part of any overall national plan or target.

U.S. corporations don't invest abroad, or domestically for that matter, as part of any U.S. government strategy. The American corporation is uniquely independent in that it has the right to make political donations and can employ armies of lawyers and lobbyists to write proposed new laws and to influence regulatory agency rule-writing to eviscerate established laws and prevent their enforcement. Corporate money has enormous power in Washington, and the heads of major corporations have easy entrée to the president and his cabinet members.

Moreover, it is wrong to think of a global corporation that has its headquarters in the United States as an American company. It has interests and employees in many countries, and many members of its board of directors may not be U.S. citizens. It does what it thinks is good for the company, not necessarily what might be good for the United States. This was not always so. For many years, the Business Roundtable published guidelines for the major tasks of a CEO. These included making the best products, maintaining the best workforce, taking care of the towns and cities where the company was located, contributing to the national welfare, and last on the list, earning a good return for shareholders. This concept was abandoned in the mid-1990s in favor of what was called "shareholder value," which defined the CEO's job as maximizing returns to shareholders. The emphasis was generally on doing so in the short term since the markets and CEO rewards are strongly organized around short-term returns. In 2019, the Roundtable reversed itself and trotted out a redo of the old guidelines, but these seem to have had little impact. Shareholder value, regardless of the effects on employees, customers, local communities, or the nation, remains the order of the day.

Yet the global corporation is vulnerable in one critical place. In Beijing, it has no political influence and is subject to the bureaucracy's coercion. It may therefore act in ways that are good for China while not optimal for the corporation. An important cause of this situation is China's technology leadership policy, the Made in China 2025 program. Since the U.S. government has no industrial or technological targets, it has little power to direct corporate effort toward anything except higher profits for shareholders. Nevertheless, due to the momentum of earlier policies and programs in response to the Soviet threat during the Cold War, and strong American incentives for risk taking and for funding new ventures, the U.S. high-tech industry generally remains the world leader. But that leadership is being increasingly challenged by China as U.S. government support for technology development and scientific infrastructure has declined while transfer of technology to China (through both voluntary and involuntary methods as well as cyber theft) has mushroomed.

Despite its apparent shortfalls, the United States remains the world's largest economy, and the U.S. dollar will likely remain the major global currency and reserve store of value far into the future. This gives America a unique power that no other country can approach. The United States also has an unrivaled overall military capability. It accounts for about half of all global defense spending, and its armed forces have been fighting continually for the past twenty years. Its eleven major aircraft carriers compare to China's two, and one each possessed by the United Kingdom, France, India, and Russia. U.S. armed forces are present in about 150 countries.

The United States' many allies and mutual defense treaties are hugely important. They include the North Atlantic Treaty Organization (NATO) with thirty countries, the U.S.-Japan Mutual Defense Treaty, the U.S.–South Korea Mutual Defense Treaty, the U.S.-Philippines Mutual Defense Treaty, the U.S.-Australia Mutual Defense Treaty, and the U.S.–New Zealand Mutual Defense Treaty. Of special importance in the Asia-Pacific area is the U.S. Indo-Pac Command, based at Pearl Harbor and responsible for patrolling the Western Pacific Ocean, the South China Sea, the South Pacific, and the Indian Ocean. These are the U.S. and allied forces that confront the rising Chinese naval and air forces in the Asia-Pacific region.

While most countries in the Asia-Pacific region see China as their biggest export market, that is not true in all cases. For instance, many of the electronics components exported by Malaysia to China go into products that are then reexported to the United States. Thus, America is more economically significant to many countries than they know.

It is important to remember that while the U.S. political and economic system may look disorganized from the outside—and perhaps *is* disorganized—it was this system, together with America's allies, that steadily fought and won the Cold War with the Soviet Union over a period of forty-four years. A new and similar challenge may perhaps spark the same kind of constant, coordinated, sophisticated response.

The Longer Term

China

There can be no doubt that for the next thirty years or so, the CCP Party/state will pose a challenge to America and its allies perhaps greater than that of the old Soviet Union. In the longer term, however, it faces serious problems. Many analysts have forecast that by 2050 China's economy will be at least twice as large as the U.S. economy. The problem is that these forecasts tend to be straight-line projections that take China's current GDP and multiply it by the current growth rate prior to the pandemic, about 6–6.5 percent, on a compound basis until 2050. But real-world economies don't act that way. Indeed, the pandemic we have all recently been suffering is the best possible example of that. Before the pandemic, China's GDP growth was already slowing substantially. *Bloomberg* cited economists' projections that it would soon fall to about 5 percent.[13] Michael Pettis of Beijing University told me he estimated that China's real growth rate before the pandemic was at best about 3 percent. In the wake of the pandemic, it will be quite some time before China's GDP is back even to that. The best long-term forecast to date is that of the Centre d'études prospectives et d'informations internationales. Its *World Economic Horizon 2050* report of October 2016 forecasts that by 2050 the Chinese GDP will be a bit more than double today's figure of $14 trillion, at about $31 trillion. This implies a compound growth rate of 2 to 2.5 percent—which is almost surely on the high side given the enormous challenges China is facing as a result of rapid aging, global warming, and rising pollution.

Of course, the most serious problem is the aging of China's population. China's labor force is already shrinking, and its total population will begin falling after 2029. The average age in China is following in the steps of South Korea and Japan, where aging and declining populations are already dramatic. By 2050, the country's population may have declined by more than 100 million, to about 1.34 billion.

Things could easily get much worse. Jared Diamond pointed out in his 2005 book *Collapse* that the Yellow River had 230 "no flow" days each year. In the 2008 Olympics, water from Hebei and Shanxi provinces was diverted to Beijing. By 2050, Tibet's glacial water flow will have fallen by two-thirds, and China will be getting very thirsty. This is not to mention the compounding problems of rising seawaters near cities like Shanghai and Hong Kong or the effects of widespread ground, water, and air pollution. Even hitting the present international target of a rise in temperature of only 2 degrees Celsius would leave much of downtown Hong Kong and Shanghai underwater. With a rise of 4 degrees Celsius (the present trend), both cities would be completely underwater.[14]

United States

While China's population declines, that of the United States will continue to grow through immigration and, perhaps, organically. By 2050 it will reach about 450 million. If we add the populations of Canada and Mexico (all members of a common economic area), the total will be 620 million, or a little under half that of China. But the U.S. population will be substantially younger. The United States will also have water and climate issues, but probably not on the scale of China's.

As for the United States' GDP, a *Bloomberg* report of March 8, 2019 ("Will China Overtake U.S. GDP?"), shows that U.S. GDP in 2050 is likely to be about $40 trillion, still substantially larger than China's likely $35 trillion, and with a younger population that, unlike China's, will still have plenty of water. Of course, this was a pre-pandemic forecast, but that may mean it was on the optimistic side for China. In any case, it is far from earlier forecasts based on straight-line projections of China growing forever at 8–10 percent annually. But China's growth has always been partly a matter of building excess capacity and of benefiting from a young and growing workforce. As noted above, these factors have already changed significantly. Another factor should also be added. The United States, Canada, and Mexico form what is effectively a single market. If we look at the numbers of these three combined, their total GDP in 2050 will be around $55 trillion.[15] This reflects the fact that China is already experiencing population decline that will continually accelerate over the next thirty years, while the U.S. population will continue to grow and remain younger than China's by dint of immigration. U.S. technology development is also expected to remain strong, while that of China will slow down a bit because it will already have achieved the easier gains of catch-up copying.

9

A Long Telegram

> Our respective views of reality are simply incompatible.
> —*George Kennan*

In the wake of the *Economist*'s March 2018 conclusion that the free world had made the wrong bet on engagement and coupling with China, three lines of discourse have emerged. They can be described as the establishment, the decouplers, and the middle-roaders.

The Establishment

The proponents and executors of positive engagement have recently defended the essence of the effort while admitting to excessive optimism and lax oversight. They now call for more of the same but with stricter enforcement of trade rules, even to the extent of imposing tariffs. Their chief concern is not to alienate China, and their chief gripe is President Trump's unilateral resort to tariffs. They acknowledge that tariffs may occasionally be a useful tool but insist that any use of that tool must be multilateral, with the wholehearted support of allies.

The establishment dramatically stated its views in an open letter to the president signed by China, trade, and foreign policy scholars and commentators on July 3, 2019. It begins by recognizing that "China's troubling behavior in recent years . . . raises serious challenges for the rest of the world" that "require a firm and effective U.S. response" but added that the "current approach to China is fundamentally counterproductive." The letter goes on: "We do not believe Beijing is an economic enemy or an existential national security threat . . . or that the views of its leaders are set in stone. . . . Chinese officials and other elites know a cooperative approach with the west serves China's interests. . . . Washington's adversarial stance toward Beijing weakens the influence of those voices."[1] In short, the argument seems to be that even though the hard-liners appear to be in charge, the United States should do nothing that might further undercut the pro-Western voices in Beijing that already appear to have been largely hushed.

The rest of the letter argues that efforts to decouple the American and Chinese economies would be costly to both and in any case could not effectively slow China down—certainly not without damaging the United States itself. (The nature of that damage is not addressed.) Further, "If the United States presses its allies to treat China as an economic and political enemy, it will weaken its relations with those allies and could end up isolating itself rather than Beijing." In any case, the fear that Beijing will replace the United States as the global leader is exaggerated since most "other countries have no interest in that outcome and it is not clear that even Beijing itself sees that goal as necessary or feasible." It is true that China "has set a goal of becoming a world-class military power by mid-century" and that its "growing martial capabilities have already eroded if not completely nullified the United States' long-standing military preeminence in the Western Pacific." But this is no reason, the letter advises, for an open-ended arms race; instead, Washington should work with allies to maintain "deterrence" (area denial, resiliency, ability to stop attacks on U.S. and allied territory) "while strengthening crisis management arrangements with Beijing."

The letter closes by admitting that "Beijing is seeking to weaken the role of Western democratic norms within the global order." But it asserts that China "is not seeking to overturn vital economic and other components of that order from which China itself has benefited for decades." In other words, China only wants to get rid of the democratic stuff, its "engagement in the international system is essential to the system's survival," and "the United States should encourage Chinese participation in new or modified global regimes. . . . A zero-sum approach to China's role would only encourage Beijing to either disengage from the system or sponsor a divided global order that would be damaging to Western interests."

If this sounds ambivalent to you, that's because it is. Also, there is one omission that cries out for attention. Nowhere do the learned solons use the words "Chinese Communist Party." They speak of Chinese officials and elite voices, but the CCP, which stands behind the officials and elites and corporations, is absent from the scene. They also speak of the increasing challenges posed by China and the need for a firm and effective U.S. response, but fail to detail what the response should be while emphasizing how important it is to stay on good terms with China. One wonders if it is possible to be "firm and effective" while also remaining on good terms with China.

Ambassador Charlene Barshefsky, the former U.S. trade representative who negotiated China's entry into the WTO, is a typical member of what might be called the "hard-ball" side of the establishment. In a meeting with the American Chamber of Commerce in Shanghai on January 13, 2019, she emphasized that bringing China into the WTO in 2001 was the right move and that China has now become an essential member of the organization. But she noted that Beijing had failed to "maintain a reform and opening agenda" after it joined the team. By 2007, she said, the familiar phrase "reform and opening" had been shortened to just "reform." Somewhere along the line "opening" got lost. She also noted that once in the WTO, China had delayed implementing the measures to which it had agreed. It still, she emphasized, "has to cease its discrimination against foreign multinationals, curb its subsidies to homegrown industries, and halt forced technology transfer and theft of intellectual property."[2] To ensure that this occurs, there would have to be a U.S.-China deal with agreed-upon metrics, timetables, and punitive measures (such as tariffs) in the event of nonfulfillment. Barshefsky noted that China had used a series of high-level talks known as the Strategic and Economic Dialogue to delay action for many years and that this had now backfired with the election of Trump and America's rising disenchantment with China.

She also strongly criticized the George W. Bush and Obama administrations for not using the provisions of the WTO protocol of accession to enforce China's commitments regarding technology transfer and the behavior of state-owned enterprises, especially the rules prohibiting direct or indirect government involvement in the commercial decisions of state enterprises.

Yet she strongly rejected any suggestion of decoupling the two economies. Such a move, she warned, would raise "a dangerous specter of isolationism and genuine 'beggar thy neighbor' outcomes." It would be "better for the two economies to operate on a more equitable basis and particularly if the Chinese economy adhered to market-based economics rather than state-led economics."

Of course, this assumed that China could and—under the right kinds of pressure (not too hot, not too cold, but just right, as Goldilocks would say)—would shift entirely to a market-based economy. Once again, the words "Communist Party" were not spoken.

A day later (January 14, 2019), former U.S. trade representative Robert Zoellick (whom Barshefsky had indirectly accused of failing to adequately leverage the WTO provisions on China) told the *South China Morning Post* that "you can't contain China" and that the decoupling he believed the Trump administration was aiming for "would be very difficult."[3] Like Barshefsky, he thought Beijing needed to be less interventionist and should be held to account for forced technology transfer and intellectual property theft. But, he added, "you don't change the types of issues I talked about overnight. It's about making people see some mutual interests in transparency rules and norms." There is something to that, of course, if both sides are interested in reaching a truly meaningful agreement. But as Barshefsky suggested in her remarks on the Strategic and Economic Dialogue, Zoellick had years in which to arrive at a sharing of mutual interests with China and somehow failed. One begins to wonder if the nod to doing something about intellectual property and state intervention is just that, a nod, while the real objective is simply to keep the process going.

Perhaps the best summation of the establishment position is the February 2019 Asia Society task force report, *Course Correction: Toward an Effective and Sustainable China Policy,* which notes that "the United States and China are on a collision course" and that "the foundations of goodwill that took decades to build are rapidly breaking down." Some would say that China has simply decided to stop "hiding and biding." The task force agrees that the Trump administration has been justified in "pushing back" against unfair Chinese trade actions but notes that "pushback alone isn't a strategy." It calls on the administration to "spell out specific steps that could restore equity and stability to the relationship." This is mystifying given that on March 22, 2018, the administration did that with the publication of its *Section 301 Investigation into China's Acts*. Nevertheless, the task force warns against an "irreparable, and possibly avoidable, rupture in this crucially important bi-lateral relationship." To avoid that, it calls on both countries to seek "negotiated solutions to priority issues" and to "erect prudent guardrails to keep the relationship from running further off the tracks."[4]

This ambiguity persists throughout the report. On one hand, "Efforts to decouple our two deeply intertwined economies should proceed with great caution." On the other hand, "The United States must safeguard its national security and the key technologies that underpin it." But "national security restrictions on trade and investment should be highly selective, and policy makers should be mindful of their costs, including to America's own innovation ecosystem." Furthermore, "disruption of production chains could hurt global economic stability and growth," and "U.S. alliances could be weakened if friendly countries believe they must choose sides between two valued trading partners."[5]

This, however, is followed by a strong statement that "many of China's recent actions require a firmer U.S. response and greater insistence on fairness and reciprocity, and there is no guarantee that China's leaders will be willing to respond to this challenge in a constructive way." Then comes a retreat: "The United States has as much to lose from overreaction as it does from under reaction."[6]

On balance, however, the report was relatively hard hitting. It identified "China's pursuit of a mercantilist high-tech import-substitution industrial policy" as not only a problem but as an effort to promote Chinese corporate control of key technology sectors. Moreover, it noted China's moves to project power and influence in Asia and its hardening authoritarianism at home, calling for tough U.S. responses that would ensure essential reciprocity of treatment. For instance, it recommended that Washington "pressure China into adopting trade and investment policies that give international firms the same access and competitive conditions that Chinese firms enjoy in developed country markets," raise "the cost to China of its anti-competitive and market-distorting industrial policies," and demand that China finally take the steps required by its accession to the WTO in 2001: it must stop making market access conditional on technology transfer, allow SOEs to make business decisions solely on commercial grounds, and not allow SOEs to be directly or indirectly influenced by the Chinese government or the CCP.[7] (This is the first time the CCP is directly mentioned in the report.) The task force even went so far as to suggest a possible "nullification and impairment" case against China at the WTO. This would charge that China had de facto acted to nullify its nominal trade concessions and as a result the United States and other countries would be justified in withdrawing all trade concessions they had made to China.

Of course, the task force didn't expect America ever to have to go there. It concluded the economic section of the report by emphasizing that "it is still possible for China to pursue its ambitious agenda while playing by rules of fair competition."[8] In other words, the task force believed that with just the right kind of negotiation, China can and will abandon its Made in China 2025 industrial policies, along with strategic CCP and state guidance of SOEs, in favor of the full adoption of the free world's standards and norms for free trade and globalization.

Regarding the military situation in the South China Sea and the Western and South Pacific, the task force was less optimistic. It called for substantial strengthening and deployment of more U.S. and allied nation forces.

In short, the establishment has been shaken by China's failure to evolve as expected, but believes that with just the right approach, the anticipated economic evolution may still occur. It particularly believes this because it sees the costs of decoupling as enormously high and geopolitically dangerous. That is why the establishment clings to its faith that the original free trade/globalization model is still achievable.

Of course, this policy report was done before the advent of the coronavirus pandemic and its partial destruction of the China-centered global supply chain. Those who believed the costs of moving or reconstructing it would be prohibitive suddenly discovered the extremely high but until now hidden costs it had already imposed on the global economy in the form of absence of flexibility and emergency backup supply sources. This revelation has dramatically changed the picture and the argument.

Decouplers

Prior to the arrival of the pandemic, the foreign policy establishment held that decoupling was the brainchild of a few disgruntled American China hawks associated with the Trump administration and that it would be extremely costly to everyone involved if really executed. In an important sense, however, decoupling has been China's strategy from the beginning. Beijing never allowed foreign companies simply to enter China to do as they pleased. At first, it generally required a foreign company to have a Chinese partner, to transfer technology to the partner, and to export a substantial portion of its China-based production. The quite reasonable idea was that eventually Chinese companies would be able to do the production themselves and perhaps underprice the foreign companies. As I have pointed out earlier, it was made clear to top foreign executives like GE's Jeff Immelt and Intel's Andy Grove that if you wanted to sell in China, you had best produce in China.

The advent of the internet should have made the reality of the situation in China (as opposed to the tone of the endless high-level talks between Chinese and free world trade negotiators) quite clear. On January 23, 1996, long before it joined the WTO, China passed the Temporary Regulation for Management of Computer Information Network International Connection—its first step toward censorship of the internet and toward building the Great Firewall between China's internet and that of the rest of the world. Nor has Beijing ever allowed Google, Amazon, Facebook, or any other non-Chinese company to enable searching on the Chinese internet. This was a major step toward decoupling, taken five years before China joined the WTO. Membership did nothing to change Beijing's mind. If anything, control over the Great Firewall became tighter even as China's economy and technological ability grew.

Analysts today cite the Made in China 2025 policy statement issued by Prime Minister Li Keqiang in May 2015 as the launch of the Chinese policy of autarky and self-sufficiency in key technological and industrial areas. But Made in China 2025 was not the start of the policy, just the latest step. It had forerunners in the five-year plans dating back to 1949 and especially since 2006—a moment when the U.S.-China Strategic and Economic Dialogue was supposed to be at its height. Today, realization of President Xi Jinping's plan for the "Great Rejuvenation of the Chinese People" must, inevitably, mean a high degree of self-sufficiency and even of exclusivity in a wide variety of critical industrial, scientific, and conceptual fields.

In one sense (that of Anglo economists), this is a costly approach. By a strict dollars and cents accounting, it would probably have been less expensive to allow Google to extend itself into China than to create Baidu as a Google clone. But there are different ways to look at costs and benefits. Had Beijing simply invited Google in, China would probably not have reached the same level of search engine expertise as quickly as it did by building its own. It also would have had less ability to control the outside information presented to Chinese netizens. Was decoupling like this really a cost to China, or an investment in China? In any case, Baidu is now the world's second-largest search engine, and no one in China appears to be complaining about the cost of having duplicated Google. Rather, there is pride in having done so. Few if any Chinese think of Baidu as having been particularly costly to them.

Since the ascendance of the Trump administration in 2017, many in the media and in think tanks have attributed the decoupling strategy to U.S. trade representative Robert Lighthizer and presidential counselor Peter Navarro, whose 2011 book *Death by China* described China's theft of intellectual property from and discrimination against non-Chinese corporations.[9] In conversations with me, however, both have explained that their purposes are not decoupling per se but defense of free world national security and of free market rights as negotiated under the WTO and other agreements. Barshefsky, as we saw, says the WTO rules that China agreed to in 2001 have never been even partially enforced. Lighthizer says his objective is simply to strike a deal with China under which the rules will in fact be applied, with heavy penalties imposed for violations. This raises the interesting questions of whether China ever intended on coupling and whether it can survive in a truly free market environment.

Navarro told me that many people both inside and outside the administration are concerned about the long-term national security implications of ever-tighter coupling. For example, on September 14, 2019, the assistant secretary of state, Christopher Ashley Ford, head of the Bureau of International Security and Nonproliferation, spoke during the Multilateral

Action on Sensitive Technologies Conference about the administration's placement of Huawei, China's leading 5G telecommunications company, on the U.S. Commerce Department's "Entity List," which imposes certain restrictions on Americans dealing with the company. Ford noted that it was placed on the list in January 2019 for "theft of trade secrets" and also because of "a significant risk of its being involved in activities contrary to the national security of the United States." He emphasized that the problems the United States had with Huawei are not only or mainly economic but deeply related to national security. And this point applies more broadly: Chinese tech giants like Huawei do not only create technical or trade problems, they pose a geopolitical challenge. While they may formally be designated as private companies, they are not what private companies are commonly understood to be and do not make decisions entirely for commercial reasons. Sometimes they act as arms of the state and the Party. Ford went on to explain that the UK's best computer experts have been unable even to assess the vulnerabilities to UK security created by Huawei coding and architectures used in the company's 4G network, never mind its new 5G line. For example, the code provided to the UK experts for study did not even match the code that was eventually deployed in Huawei's routers. The NATO Cooperative Cyber Defense Center of Excellence, he said, has warned that "the issue of Huawei 5G deployment must be assessed in the broader geopolitical context and that 5G rollout needs to be recognized as a strategic rather than merely a technological choice."[10]

This is where the rubber meets the decoupling road. Products and services freighted with national security significance cannot be valued on the same cost-benefit model as soybeans. The value of some things cannot be measured in terms of the dollar or yuan exchange. One of the best explanations of the decoupling urge has come from former Australian prime minister and China expert (and Mandarin speaker) Kevin Rudd. In a speech to Australia's Lowy Institute on June 13, 2019, he argued that America's first steps toward decoupling were not made by the Trump administration but by the Obama administration with its "pivot to Asia" policy.

More important, he noted, decoupling of the internet is occurring as a natural consequence of the two countries' political systems, with other countries "increasingly caught in no-man's land in between." Digital payment systems like Alipay, WeChat Pay, Visa, and Master Card have already divided the world into different spheres of influence, and this division, he argued, is likely to widen in the digital global economy. Likewise, "the decoupling of the two countries' telecommunications systems is also well under way." But he added that these decouplings inevitably worry the managers of global supply chains and raise the notion that it might be safer to have alternative supply chains or perhaps no supply chains. And this, he noted, is before considering the likely economic, political, or strategic impact of artificial intelligence. "Are we," he wondered, "at the beginning of the end of globalization?" Is the big question not where decoupling starts, but where it is likely to stop?

The Middle Way

Between the modified "engagement" views of the establishment and the growing trend toward global fragmentation, some analysts think they see a pathway in the middle. Writing in the September/October 2019 issue of *Foreign Affairs,* former assistant secretary of state Kurt Campbell and former State Department director of policy planning Jake Sullivan suggest what they call "competition without catastrophe."[11] They resist the neo–Cold War thoughts of some in the establishment as not reflective of the real U.S.-China relationship, noting that the Cold War was a "truly existential struggle" and that the U.S. containment policy was built on the premise that the Soviet Union would eventually fall of its own weight. In the case of China, no one foresees an eventual collapse. Moreover, while China is a much more formidable rival than the Soviet Union ever was, the competition is less existential. Therefore, they conclude, it should be possible to establish favorable terms of coexistence militarily, economically, politically, and in terms of global governance. Moreover, they note that while the Soviet-U.S. confrontation was truly global, the U.S.-China confrontation is chiefly limited to the South and East China Seas, the Taiwan Strait, and the Korean Peninsula.

Campbell and Sullivan call for extensive bilateral agreements with China, like the Incidents at Sea Agreement of 1972 between the United States and the Soviet Union. They also call for more frequent meetings and interaction between Chinese and U.S. officials to engender mutual confidence. The United States, they write, should adopt an approach of "deterrence without dominance" in the China Seas and the Indo-Pacific area. The emphasis would be away from expensive, vulnerable platforms like aircraft carriers and toward cruise missiles, submarines, and unmanned aircraft.

This all seems quite promising until one turns to economics and trade. The authors rightly note that China views geo-economics as the main field of competition and that it is investing heavily in advanced technology industries while denying reciprocal treatment to companies and products from outside. They rightly explain that this structural imbalance has eroded support for the old free trade approach of supply chains anchored in China. Then, however, comes a questionable step. Solving this problem of reciprocity, they argue, will require "making China's full access to major markets around the world contingent on its willingness to adopt economic reforms at home."[12] But this is precisely what the Trump administration has been trying to do for the past three years. Perhaps its approach could have been less clumsy and better coordinated with allies. But it is exactly the fear of real U.S. enforcement of reciprocity through denial of China's market access that has unleashed what is seen as the globalization wrecking ball of decoupling. So, the Middle Way turns out to be Trump with better manners and more attention to allies and details. But that begs the question of realistic implementation. It continues to assume that the United States can fairly precisely control China's access to various world markets and that China can—and, under sufficient pressure, will—play the free trade game our way. Both of these assumptions have proven false in the past and are highly questionable now.

The Bottom Line

The Chinese Communist Party controls virtually all aspects of Chinese life. The Party's presence is often unstated, but it is constant and ultimately always controlling. Thus, nothing in China is exactly as it appears. For instance, the country has a president, but the most powerful office is that of the general secretary of the CCP. There are newspapers and websites but they leave out information on a wide variety of topics easily accessible outside China. There are corporations, both state-owned and private, but they often do not make business and investment decisions based on profit and loss. This is because permeating all these organizations is the Party.

Although the Party calls itself communist, it is really a Leninist party, in that its primary purpose is to hold absolute power over the society it rules, leaving no recourse to human rights, religion, or law. The essential condition of any Leninist party is that it is always at war, both with internal dissidence and with any country or external body that might have the power to prevent it from achieving its goals. These are not necessarily hot wars; they can be permanent states of hostile mistrust.

Some of the Party's goals have shifted since its founding, but others have remained absolutely the same. During the Maoist period, there was huge emphasis on creating a completely new society based on equality and the new communist man. That emphasis died with Mao. But Mao also said that "China has stood up." Like Sun Yatsen, Chiang Kaishek, and many others, he envisioned a future in which China would regain its ancient glory as the Middle Kingdom and restore its rule over Tianxia (all under heaven). He foresaw a day when China would surpass first Great Britain and then the United States. That drive toward what it sees as China's rightful place in the sun has become the Party's overriding purpose and is now articulated as the Great Chinese Dream or the Great Rejuvenation of the Chinese People.

The greatest external obstacle to achieving that dream is the United States, with its completely opposite concepts of human rights, rule of law, free press, individualism, private property, private business organizations, free markets, and constant public debate. For the Chinese Communist Party, the United States cannot be other than a dangerous foe that must be constantly watched and kept under control. While the Party may not need to destroy the United States, it is essential that the Party surround it, keep it distracted, deprive it of allies, and work constantly to weaken it and to ally with others who also want to weaken it. The Party is always ready to make necessary accommodations depending on the balance of power and correlation of forces, but it essentially does not believe in the concept of win-win. Remember too that China has been a hierarchical society since ancient times. The concept of equality is difficult to grasp. One is either older or younger, richer or poorer, up or down, bigger or smaller, stronger or weaker.

In its drive to equal and surpass the United States, China carefully studied the examples of other countries that had achieved a high level of economic development, including the United Kingdom, the United States, Germany, and particularly Japan and Korea. It realized that all had adopted protectionist and mercantilist policies to jump-start industrialization and become workshops of the world. Party members grasped the importance of manufacturing, economies of scale, technological advance, and the development of retainable industries. They understood that the Anglo-American ideal of free trade and globalization was a false god, and instead paid attention when Singapore's Lee Kuan Yew advised them to study Japan and the "east Asian tigers."

In doing so, however, China realized it could not exactly duplicate the other nations' model of keeping foreign capital out of their markets while they pursued export-led growth policies. China was too far behind to industrialize all on its own, as they had done. It desperately needed American and other free world technology quickly, and the only way to get it fast was to encourage foreign investment and make sure that the investment brought technology with it. On top of that, it was necessary to run a trade surplus in order to accumulate the capital necessary for further investment. But how could they do that without losing control and winding up with their markets at the mercy of foreign capitalists? Deng was willing to allow a few "flies" in as he opened the windows. But there was never any willingness to surrender control.

The Party rightly bet that foreign businesses would be willing to take big risks and accept an unusual degree of interference in their operations in exchange for a crack at what could become the biggest market the world had ever seen. So it consciously adopted a strategy of what might be called "coupling." It would not only allow the foreign devils in but even bribe them to come, provided they were willing to accept certain conditions: joint ventures with Chinese firms, transfer of technology, requirements that substantial percentages of China-based production be exported, and so forth. It turned out that capitalists who would have caviled at such conditions had they been proposed by, say, Mexico, could not wait to accept them from China. The rest is recent history.

It turned out even better than the Party expected. Because of the political power of American corporations and the lack of coordination endemic in American policy making, coupling with U.S. companies had the added benefit of creating hostages and a Beijing lobby in Washington. The combination of no rule of law in China with a strict U.S. rule of law that allows corporations to take the government to court and win made U.S. CEOs more afraid of Beijing than of Washington. And giving U.S. investment banks a bit of Chinese business brought Wall Street along as a major cheerleader for Beijing.

Joining the WTO was a key move—not so much for trade purposes, as Americans like Charlene Barshefsky thought—but to make China bulletproof as a place to which to outsource manufacturing production and thereby make China the new workshop of the world. Of course, Beijing had to agree to a lot of annoying conditions, such as state-owned enterprises operating on strictly commercial considerations and no forced technology transfers. But it had no intention of keeping those agreements given that the United States and the WTO were unlikely really to enforce them. What foreign CEO was going to complain about a violation when he could be shut up by nothing more than a friendly call from the local Party secretary hinting at possible unexpected inspections or other difficulties? On top of that, the WTO operates at a slow crawl. Maybe China would be rapped over the knuckles eventually, but by then whatever violation it had committed would be a fait accompli. The technology would have been transferred, or the dumping would have put the foreign competitor out of business.

On top of that was the series of high-level meetings known as the Economic and Strategic Dialogue, which ran from 2009 to 2016. These show that the United States was not only convinced China's economy would eventually be marketized and its politics liberalized, it also wanted to demonstrate its goodwill and support of China's efforts by teaching Beijing how to do things and avoid pitfalls. It would have set a bad tone if one of these meetings were preceded by some suggestion of Chinese cheating or foot-dragging, or by someone's bringing a complaint before the WTO.

In retrospect, it is incredible to think that U.S. and other free world negotiators really believed China would conscientiously observe the conditions attached to its WTO entry card. After all, the Party names the heads of all the SOEs. Did free world negotiators really think these CEOs, once named, would ignore Party considerations in order to run their SOEs to satisfy the WTO? It is to laugh.

Nor does China intend to abandon its Made in China 2025 program to achieve leadership and self-sufficiency in artificial intelligence, semiconductors, telecommunications, biotechnology, aviation, and every other technology it considers significant. It is a mistake to imagine that U.S. trade actions might drive China to move more quickly to industrial and technological autarky. It has always been moving in that direction as quickly as it could and will continue to do so. Playing as it does to Chinese pride and to the highly hyped sense of historical humiliation, this drive continues to enjoy enormous public support. Whereas U.S. economists would see the policy as a costly matter of the government "picking winners and losers," Chinese economists and the Chinese public see it as a public investment in their future. They interpret U.S. nagging about market forces and talk of China's becoming a "responsible stakeholder in the rules-based global order" as attempts to slow the country's progress. The Party can never imagine that, in a dog-eat-dog world, another actor really believes in "win-win" solutions or would make a truly generous gesture. It will always assume a hidden agenda. The more the free world tries to hug China, the more suspicious and defensive it will become.

Yet Beijing will lament decoupling and will try to maintain and even extend coupling, especially its easy access to U.S. educational, research, media, business, and legal institutions. It is advantageous to Beijing to keep China controlled and coordinated while the United States persists in atomization. Thus, for example, U.S. and other foreign asset managers have recently been given access to the management of Chinese asset funds. Superficially this may appear to be an instance of opening and liberalization by Beijing. It may indeed be that, but it will also keep Wall Street coupled and hostage to Beijing. Moreover, as China increasingly becomes a technological, industrial, and scientific leader, the relationship will change from what we now call coupling to what will increasingly become dependency on China. Decoupling in terms of truly shared endeavors will advance as China becomes the dominant producer and the rest of the world becomes the consumer.

Any reduction in the free world's openness to China will be declaimed by Beijing and its acolytes as "protectionist," "racist," or "chauvinistic." But it is important to understand the dangers of too open or too much association with things ultimately tied to the Party. Chinese students, for example, come to U.S. and free world universities with the very attractive benefit that they pay full fare. Most of them are, of course, simply students trying to get an education. Some are not, but it should be possible to winnow out the intelligence agents. A more important issue is that, as we have seen in Australia and Singapore, the students can be "weaponized," meaning that Beijing can simply stop them from coming. Even some quite important universities would be in serious financial trouble if that were to occur. And while most students are themselves innocent, they have families in China who can be made vulnerable if the Party decides it needs to activate a student.

This leads to a further point about decoupling. In free world media, academic, and political circles, it is associated with high costs: to consumers, to businesses that may have to move supply chains, to workers who may lose jobs, and possibly to investors as asset market prices adjust. These are all legitimate concerns, but they must be considered in different lights. The current structure of coupling feeds capital and technology to a China that is actively opposed to free world values and striving not to become a responsible stakeholder in the liberal global order, but to recast the global order in an authoritarian, Leninist frame. U.S. corporations, technologists, and consumers are feeding the Beijing machine that suppresses Tibetans in Tibet, Uighurs in Xinjiang, and demonstrators in Hong Kong; that jails its Nobel Prize winners, feeds lies to the global media, hacks the accounts of free world credit card holders and government employees, and spends billions of dollars annually to drive division between the United States and its allies. Those are costs too, and they should weigh in the discussion. Previous generations of Americans took huge casualties and paid huge costs to protect the rule of law, the right to a trial by a jury of one's peers, and freedom of speech. Are those things now without value?

Oddly, in today's debate the costs and the allocation of any gains from establishing the supply chain through China are never discussed. It is taken for granted that the chain represents "win-win" globalization. In fact, as Stewart Paterson argues in his book *China, Trade and Power*, the overall effect was to impose huge deflationary pressure that brought the world economy to the brink of its worst financial crisis since the Great Depression of the 1930s. More than 5 million U.S. jobs were lost between 2001 and 2006, while wages stagnated in the European Union, the United States, and Japan. Median U.S. household income, which had grown at a rate of 5.3 percent in the last thirty years of the twentieth century, fell 10 percent in the decade after China's entry into the WTO. Over the same period, U.S. corporate profits doubled. Obviously, the creation of the China-centric supply chain was a great boon to big business and Wall Street, but not for the average household.[13]

Perhaps most important, as noted above, the pandemic has brought to the surface some of the real but previously unseen business and economic costs attached to the supply chain. It is fragile and without redundancy. Moreover, it is not even necessarily the lowest-cost way to run the global economy after all the real costs are recognized. Initially, cheap, unorganized, quasi-indentured labor was the main reason for global corporations to offshore some of their production to developing countries, especially China. Later, China worked hard to induce corporations making capital-intensive and high-technology products to move production to China by offering not only inexpensive labor but free land, reduced utility prices, capital grants, and other financial inducements to go along with the attraction of the rapid growth of Chinese markets. It was this immense package of inducements that led to the great wave of offshoring of U.S., European, and, to some extent, Japanese manufacturing to China between 1991 and 2018, and the great expansion of what we now know as the global supply chain.

Weaknesses and shifts in the chain were becoming evident even before the outbreak of the pandemic. Chinese labor was becoming more expensive. Chinese regulations and CCP actions were becoming more intrusive and burdensome. Theft of intellectual property and government support of Chinese corporations in key targeted industries such as semiconductors and artificial intelligence were becoming more onerous. Automation was making inexpensive labor less and less important as a cost factor. Indeed, some companies began moving production out of China to places with lower-cost labor like Indonesia, or even bringing it back home to the United States, like tool maker Stanley Black & Decker, which said the hidden costs of having production far from its domestic market made the move very profitable.

Never considered by any corporation but of extraordinary importance to every society on earth are the costs of the supply chain in terms of global warming. The chain necessarily involves a great deal of shipping by both air and sea. Combined, this accounts for about 6 percent of global emissions of greenhouse gases. In addition, it is generally known that because of their high altitude, aircraft emissions of carbon have an especially potent impact on the increase in global warming. The cost of these emissions to the global community is incalculable, but as an example, let's take the cost of offsetting the emissions of a single passenger flying from New York to Tokyo in business class. It would be about $34.[14] For sea shipping, the cost of offsetting emissions can be $45 per ton.[15] Multiply those numbers by billions of air-freight shipments and billions of tons of container shipments and one can immediately see that the price is steep. Worse, it has been rising rapidly.

Beyond these factors are three others of immense importance. One is the incalculable cost to a major country that defends liberty and free speech, like the United States, of falling behind in development and production of cutting-edge technologies. Over the past century, the United States has made every effort to become and remain the leader in those kinds of technologies because it knows that not to do so would be extremely dangerous to the survival of itself and other like-minded countries. To cede this kind of leadership to a global supply chain in order that corporations might make a few million or even billion more dollars could turn out to be extremely expensive to the country and its ideals.

The second factor is that in order to remain at the cutting edge of key technologies it is not enough to have good universities and laboratories. Much technology evolves in the factory or workplace. It is an iterative process. Moreover, the more industries a country contains the more potential it will have for iteration, combinations of different ideas and skill sets, serendipity, and technological advance thereby. Economics does not have an equation for innovation, but we know that a variety of skills and means of production helps. To lose that for the sake, again, of a few immediate extra millions of profits entails huge ultimate losses.

Finally, there is the cost of the possible failure of the supply chain. This was never considered in the past. Big, sophisticated global corporations like Apple, Cisco, GM, and on and on never considered it, and neither did major governments like those of the United States, Germany, Japan, the United Kingdom, and on and on. But, since the advent of the coronavirus pandemic in mid-January 2020, we have begun to pay the heretofore hidden cost. It is and will be immense. Surely, there must be a better way.

Indeed, the better way has already been advancing. Over the past several years there has been a decline of global exports for three major reasons. First, as China has become increasingly autarkic, it has been making more and more of its total product domestically. Thus, the chain has been gradually dwindling to the link between the production base in China and the location of the consumer. China will continue to import raw materials, but not key components. Second, the popular picture of the Chinese part of the supply chain—millions of manual laborers painstakingly assembling parts by hand—is false. The assembly of Apple iPhones in China, for example, is highly automated, and the same goes for almost everything else made in China. Labor costs in China are no longer low, and for an increasingly large range of products they are not a decisive factor in the location of the supply chain. Much more decisive are the investment subsidies, absence of labor unions, and absence of meaningful environmental, health, and other regulations, combined with a managed currency exchange rate that keeps export prices competitive. The third and most important factor ending the role of the supply chain is the combination of automation, artificial intelligence, and technologies such as 3-D printing that enable inexpensive production close to the customer. The global search for cheap labor will go out of fashion.

All the above is already occurring and will continue to occur and doubtless speed up in the wake of the pandemic. It is critical for U.S. leaders to understand that they cannot change China. They cannot persuade or entice it to develop a market-oriented economy without central guidance and coordination. They cannot stop it from expanding its military capacity or from attempting to create a global authoritarian order. They must recognize that wishing for China to become like us or thinking we can somehow force it to do so is fatuous. Had Washington acted decisively in the wake of the Tiananmen Square massacre, or enforced compliance with China's WTO deal, the situation today *might* be different. But the waters have long since passed under those bridges.

The only thing America can do today is recognize the immense depth, breadth, and power of the challenge posed by Beijing and change its own policies, structures, coordination, and alliances to meet whatever comes. The experts all say that China will not collapse the way the Soviet Union did. They are probably right, but then none of them predicted the Soviet collapse. Certainly, in the long term, China will face daunting problems. But we cannot count on that to preserve our freedom and that of our allies in the next thirty years. We must, as we have done in past moments of decision, recognize the challenge for what it is and gather ourselves to face it squarely.

10

The Plan for China

> The call for free trade is as unavailing as the cry of a spoiled child. . . . It doesn't exist; it never existed.
>
> —*Henry Clay*

Sun Tzu famously advises his students to "know the other [challenger]." Before doing that, however, it is necessary to recognize that there is a challenger. Neither America nor the rest of the free world today is fully aware of the dimensions of the challenge China poses. As I write, today's newspapers carry a story about Houston Rockets general manager Daryl Morey withdrawing a tweet in support of anti-Beijing demonstrators in Hong Kong that said: "Fight for freedom, stand with Hong Kong."[1] This withdrawal came in the wake of an uproar of criticism from Beijing and from Brooklyn Nets owner Joseph Tsai, a Canadian citizen of Taiwanese origin, who said Morey was damaging the National Basketball Association's lucrative relationship with China. To his credit, NBA commissioner Adam Silver confirmed that Morey has a right as an American to say what he pleases in America. But Morey deleted his tweet anyway. You can be sure he will not tweet about Hong Kong or China again.

The tweet and the CCP response focused a sudden shaft of light revealing the true and fundamental nature of China's challenge to the United States and the free world. The competition takes place through trade, globalization, technology theft, investment, and other activities. But those are all sideshows for the main act, which pits authoritarianism against free speech, rule of law, and democracy. For the past forty years, the free world has acted on the conviction that embracing China economically and welcoming it as a full partner in globalization would not only yield mutual economic benefits but also liberalize China philosophically and politically. While no one expected it to become fully democratic, most free world analysts and leaders expected it to evolve in that direction.

As the *Economist* made clear in March 2018, this was a false hope. Indeed, as Council on Foreign Relations China expert Elizabeth Economy says in her book *The Third Revolution,* China has become less liberal, more centralized, and more authoritarian as it has become richer and more powerful in recent years.[2] It is also clear that there is no comfortable middle ground. The more one invests and produces in China, the more one feeds the CCP-dominated machine while making oneself hostage to coercion by the Party. It is now self-evident that the United States and the free world cannot continue to drift in this direction.

By the time you read this, the United States will have elected a president in November 2020. The first thing that president must do is to use his inaugural address as a wake-up call to the nation and the free world fully to recognize the China challenge. He (it will be either Joe Biden or Donald Trump) must explain and emphasize that we are talking about the most difficult and dangerous external challenge the United States and the free world have ever faced. He must make clear that the interests of the country and of freedom outweigh those of global corporations and investment bankers, and he must explain that the Cold War with the Soviet Union was just a warm-up game for the main match now coming.

This speech (a suggestion for which comprises the afterword of this book) should also present something like the following plan.

In discussing how to deal with China realistically, we must insist on being honest with ourselves about how Beijing may or may not agree to act. For more than twenty years, American political leaders and the foreign policy elite have argued for what they call "positive engagement." In practice, this has meant trying in endless high-level meetings and talking sessions to convince Beijing that the best path forward for it is to abandon its government interventionist ways in favor of becoming more like us in America and the free world. As the *Economist* has pointed out so well, this approach has not worked and is not going to work. We must therefore accept two truths. First, we are not going to change the CCP or its policies by talking and persuading. Second, China's system and policies are ultimately harmful to us and the rest of the free world. Therefore, we must adopt policies and take actions that will prevent and offset the costs China is likely to inflict on us. In doing so, we must make clear to all concerned that we have no animus toward China or the Chinese people. Indeed, we should take a line from Michael Corleone, who famously noted of some of his actions: "It's not personal. It's just business." Indeed, we could say that we admire Beijing's policies so much that we have decided to play like Beijing and become more like them.

Reciprocity

The openness of U.S. society combined with the tightly closed nature of China enables Beijing to exploit American openness in ways that undermine free world values generally, and American economic, technological, and military strength specifically. To offset this dynamic, we must adopt the simple principle of reciprocity.

If the *New York Times* cannot be distributed in China, the CCP should not be allowed to own newspapers in America. If Amazon is limited in China's market, Alibaba should be similarly limited in the U.S. market. If GE will have to move its avionics division into a joint venture with state-owned Avic, Washington will halt the move unless Avic drops state ownership and enters into joint development, production, and sales ventures with Boeing and Airbus for its planned new aircraft. Just as U.S. universities, nonprofits, and religious organizations are restricted in China, so Confucius Institutes and Chinese Student and Scholar Associations will be restricted or banned in the United States.

In October 2019, the Trump administration adopted a policy of requiring all Chinese diplomats to notify the State Department before meeting with American local or state officials or with educational and research institutions. This was in response to China's long-standing requirement that U.S. diplomats get permission from Beijing before traveling inside the country or meeting with local officials and academics. The U.S. rule is not as restrictive as China's policy, but it is a step in the right direction, and further such steps should be considered so that U.S. policy essentially mirrors that of China.

Chinese entities wishing to operate in the United States should be required to clear the same hurdles as free world entities wishing to operate in China. The same should apply to entities from other nonmarket economies. All investors from China and other nonmarket economies must be required to provide detailed data on their ownership structure, their investors' and decision makers' past and present political affiliations with the Communist Party, and their funding sources. Chinese-owned publications, educational programs, cultural exchange operations, and editorial contributors must be required prominently to disclose their funding or other ties to the CCP and the Chinese government. The disclosure would read something like this: "WE ARE FUNDED BY AND LINKED TO THE UNITED FRONT WORK DEPARTMENT OF THE CHINESE COMMUNIST PARTY." The same rule must hold for entities such as the Confucius Institutes, Chinese Student and Scholar Associations, and all others that are engaged in presenting China to the U.S. public. The U.S. Foreign Agents Registration Act must be upgraded so that it applies to these groups. The current act, which contains exemptions for religious, scholastic, or scientific groups such as the Confucius Institutes purport to be, must be broadened to encompass all avenues of propaganda and influence.

In addition, representatives of corporations and organizations that do extensive business with China should be required to disclose this whenever they discuss China or the U.S.-China relationship in public. For example, the heads of the U.S. Chamber of Commerce and of the Business Roundtable often present themselves as the "voices of American business." But many of their members are tightly tied to China and vulnerable to pressure from Beijing. When they testify before Congress, they do not necessarily present what is best for America. They are often thinking of what is best for their business in circumstances under which Beijing has them by the balls while they, by dint of their legally unlimited political donations to U.S. politicians, have Washington by the balls. They should be required to make full disclosure of their political donations and of their ties to China when they testify, speak, or write for public consumption.

Recent news (October 15, 2019) provides a good example. Apple deleted from its app store an app that protestors in Hong Kong were using to track the Hong Kong police.[3] Beijing suggested to Apple that it might want to get rid of the app, and Beijing's wish turned out to be Apple CEO Tim

Cook's command. The public must know that when Cook talks about China, he is a hostage to Beijing because of Apple's extensive production operations there. Nor is Cook alone in that position. It seems that Google (whose motto, you may remember, is "Don't do evil") also recently deleted from its Play Store a game named *The Revolution of Our Times,* which dealt with the Hong Kong protest movement. The list goes on: Mercedes Benz, Delta Airlines, the Gap, Activision Blizzard, Medtronic, Marriott, and many others have changed their advertising or websites, or made apologies, because their product lines, the behavior of their employees, or their commercial message was improperly aligned with the Party line in Beijing.

This must all be made known to the public whenever such organizations speak on China, and they should be discouraged from meekly complying with Chinese interference in their freedom of speech by the imposition of large fines by the U.S. and other free world governments when they do so.

Shift the Supply Chain

As we have seen, a global supply chain for manufacturing has become centered on China over the past thirty years. This situation arose from the confluence of cheap Chinese labor, the eagerness of global companies to get into the Chinese market, the offshoring of production by global manufacturers, cross-fertilization of production techniques, and tight linkages that yielded rapid delivery through global distribution channels. The United States and other free world countries must significantly reduce their dependence and that of free world corporations on this supply chain.

I know that in many instances this will be a major and expensive undertaking. But in the wake of the pandemic it should be obvious that CEOs must reconsider the costs of not shifting the supply chain in comparison to the costs of doing so. The Trump administration's imposition of tariffs on imports from China demonstrated that investing in a China-centered supply chain is not without risk, as did the measures Germany and other countries began to take in the past few years to limit Chinese investment in some of their critical industries like robotics. Nevertheless, companies like Apple, Cisco, and many others insisted that moving their production out of China would be essentially impossible because similar pools of skilled labor and mass-production facilities simply don't exist elsewhere. Of course, the outbreak of the coronavirus has begun to undermine these arguments. Foxconn (the actual maker of most Apple products) has been unable to get its Chinese workforce back on the job in the face of tough quarantine measures to contain the disease. The virus is revealing that the impossible might not be so difficult after all.

Many free world corporations now understand that their overreliance on manufacturing in China is a serious vulnerability and are already trying to move at least some future production to other locations. Of course, this is not easy or inexpensive, especially for capital- and technology-intensive industries that rely on workforces trained in a narrow set of industry-related skills. The U.S. government should offer to help U.S. corporations in two ways. It could offer tax incentives, temporary relaxation of antitrust rules, and the financing of worker training and even of worker relocation to assist the companies in moving certain of their operations back to the United States. Or, if careful analysis reveals that this is not a realistic possibility, Washington can nevertheless offer introductions and even financial incentives to help move the production operations to places like India, Indonesia, the Philippines, Mexico, and Central America.

The U.S. Commerce Department should analyze and establish a policy for each significantly affected industry. Apple might be a major target and collaborator with the department. It could become an important model for others. I know that Apple CEO Tim Cook will likely object by saying that he just can't find the number of engineers and skilled workers in America that he can easily recruit in China. My reply is that when Cook first went to China he couldn't find them there either. He provided the demand and much of the training and upskilling. He doesn't have to leave China all at once. He could do it gradually while providing training and upskilling to American workers. But he doesn't even have to come back to America. There are a lot of engineers in India, Mexico, and elsewhere. He is sitting on hundreds of billions of dollars in tax havens around the world, like Bermuda, Ireland, the Bahamas, and Singapore. He engages in fancy tax avoidance maneuvers like the "Singapore Sling" and the "Double Irish with a Dutch sandwich." He might use some of that to support the move and ensure the safety of a new supply chain now that he has seen the cost of total dependence on China. Let me emphasize that this doesn't have to be an exclusively American process. Countries like Germany and Japan will face the same questions and will also want to attract U.S. and other companies away from China. Indeed, Japan has already announced a program to subsidize the return of Japanese production facilities from China to Japan. Similarly, Germany has passed legislation to allow the state to invest in corporations in order to prevent their being taken over or unduly influenced by foreign interests. There can be a significant degree of free world cooperation and coordination among countries in protecting themselves from Chinese coercion by shifting the global supply chain, or even hastening its end by moving production ever closer to the consumer. This trend is already emerging because of new 3D printing capacity, which enables local production of items that formerly could be made only in large production facilities and then shipped to markets.

Of course, many companies will want to keep producing in China to supply the domestic market. Assuming they are not transferring vital national security technology or concretely aiding the development of China's authoritarian model, they should be free to do so. If Starbucks and KFC can make a good go selling coffee and fried chicken in China, so much the better. On the other hand, it would be odd to see Google working with the PLA, given its apparent qualms about working with the U.S. Defense Department.

As we have seen, the potential costs of overdependence on China can be substantial. Even before the appearance of the virus, we saw it in the case of Morey's tweet supporting demonstrators in Hong Kong. Beijing went ballistic and immediately demanded of the NBA that he be fired. It also halted all airing of NBA games in China, where the NBA has had a very profitable business. The NBA refused to fire him, and as of this writing most NBA games are still not being aired in China, and the few that are heavily censor the English-language commentary. As I write this, all Houston Rockets games remain banned.[+]

None of this should come as a surprise. We have already noted how Philippine bananas were left to rot on the docks of Shanghai at a moment when Manila irritated Beijing. And we have seen how South Korea's Lotte lost its business in China when a U.S. missile detection system was installed in Korea. Highly coupled companies like Apple face constant theft or forced transfer of technology as well as the risk that a statement like Morey's will be seized on as an excuse for a "Buy China" campaign. A coupled company in an industry targeted by the Made in China 2025 initiative knows that Beijing is going to pull out all the stops to erase it from the global market. But the biggest, most fundamental cost is the loss of free speech, of the right to live under a rule of law, and ultimately of the company's self-respect. They know that they are already tools of the Party and will only become more so.

Is this a lower cost to pay than that of moving production out of China to Malaysia, India, Mexico, or even to the United States, the European Union, or Japan? Of course, the answer depends on how much one values a rule of law and free speech. The vast majority of free world citizens would answer that the cost of moving the supply chain is trivial compared to the cost of remaining coupled to a CCP-controlled and autocratic China. They know that the more dependent one becomes on China, the more one is subject to the diktat of the Party. The question is not "if" but "how fast?"

We must remember that, despite denials by many of those who promoted coupling at the turn of the century, the strong premise of the original decision to merge the American and Chinese economies was that this coupling would marketize and liberalize China. There was no thought that coupling would cost America its technological and economic productivity and innovative power or its fundamental freedoms. But the more dependent one becomes on communist China, the more one is subject to loss of both rights and assets. Because there is no rule of law in China, one is constantly vulnerable to hidden pressure and coercion. To understand this, one need only look at the efforts by wealthy Chinese to move their money, themselves, and their children out of China. Indeed, as soon as Beijing passed legislation affecting Hong Kong, an exodus to Vancouver, San Francisco, London, and other free world centers began.

Moreover, those who do business with China know that it is often slow to fulfill its promises. For instance, after eighteen years, it has still not fulfilled its initial undertakings to the WTO to refrain from requiring technology transfer as a condition of market access, to significantly reduce intellectual property theft and violations, to significantly reduce production and export subsidies, to liberalize foreign film distribution, to join the WTO's Government Procurement Agreement, to require state-owned enterprises to make purchases based on commercial considerations, to extend national treatment to foreign banks, to open telecommunications markets to foreign producers, or to stop manipulating technology standards to favor domestic producers.

In view of this track record, we cannot avoid the conclusion that because the economies of the United States and China are built upon diametrically opposed underlying values, closer coupling will not lead to a more peaceful and mutually beneficial relationship. Rather, it is likely to result (as has been becoming clear in recent years) in a relationship of increasing tension and conflict. Business and investment arrangements will be ever more at odds with national security and the fundamental freedoms of American citizens and those of other free world countries.

One alarming example is that a high percentage of the ingredients in drugs and much medical equipment widely used in America are now largely produced in China. Again, the pandemic has demonstrated why this is not wise or economically healthy for America. First, it imposes a strategic vulnerability on America, and second, China's regulation of medical materials production, storing, and shipping is shockingly lax. There are many instances of major harm resulting from contaminated drugs in China. It is dangerous for America to be so reliant on China for medicines and medical materials.

We must recall the sudden restriction by China in 2010 of exports of rare earth materials critical to the production of many electronics products. China was then disputing Japan's administration of the Senkaku Islands, and many believe it cut rare earth exports as a way of disciplining Japan. Of course, the move also harmed the U.S. and European makers of certain electronics goods. Eventually, China removed the restrictions in response to a condemnation by the WTO in 2014, but not before the United States and other free world countries began new investment in production of rare earth materials outside of China, which at the time accounted for 97 percent of global production. Just as overreliance on China for rare earths was dangerous, so is overreliance on China for drugs and other critical products and materials.

In the past, Washington offered special tax incentives for drug makers who produced in Puerto Rico, and many drug companies had factories there. Since those incentives were halted in 1996, much of the production has migrated to China. It would be much better to have it back in Puerto

Rico, where the companies are subject to U.S. manufacturing standards, or else in Mexico, the Philippines, or anywhere that the drugs are unlikely to be withheld as part of some geopolitical dispute or gamesmanship.

As noted earlier, the supply chain cannot be moved all at once, and it should not be done emotionally. Rather, the U.S. trade representative or secretary of commerce should meet with her or his Beijing counterparts and explain that the United States understands China's drive to become a leader in key technologies such as semiconductors and artificial intelligence. However, he or she must also point out that the United States has similar objectives and will therefore compete in the same way China has been doing. U.S. officials should even thank China for giving them a better understanding of how to compete. Possible frictions might be foreseen, and ways found in advance to temper them. It should be emphasized that the objective is not to go to war but, like tennis champions such as Rafael Nadal and Roger Federer, to play the same game to the best of one's capability.

No U.S. Money in Chinese Funds or Unaudited Corporations

China has recently decided to lift all caps on foreign ownership of asset fund management companies, a move that Wall Street has desired for a long time. But here again, the interests of American financial companies and those of American citizens diverge. American and Chinese markets are already dangerously conflated. To date, 159 Chinese companies, with a market value of about $1.1 trillion, are listed on various U.S. stock exchanges. Alibaba alone is valued at about $400 billion. Yet China does not allow these firms to be audited in the same manner as U.S. firms. For instance, the U.S. Public Company Accounting Oversight Board (PCAOB) is not allowed to audit the books of Chinese companies listed on U.S. exchanges because, according to Beijing, there is a risk that the PCAOB might uncover "state secrets." Yet accounting and other irregularities are widely known to have occurred in some of these companies.[5]

This is an unsupportable situation. Any Chinese company listed on an American exchange that is not open to the same level of audit as a U.S.-listed company should be delisted. Moreover, the U.S. Congress should pass legislation now being proposed by Senator Marco Rubio that would make it illegal for any public or private pension fund to invest in Chinese assets of any kind. As for the notion that U.S. asset managers would own and manage more Chinese funds, it should be suspended until these funds are subject to complete international accounting transparency. They contain what is essentially Chinese Communist Party money and are thus subject to the Party's influence. In August 2019, Senators Marco Rubio and Jeanne Shaheen wrote to Michael Kennedy, the chairman of the Federal Retirement Thrift Investment Board (FRTIB, which manages the retirement money of federal employees) to request that he reverse a decision to put more than $50 billion in an index fund that has been increasing its weighting in Chinese investments. This, of course, meant that the fund was essentially investing in Chinese companies, some of which are tied to the PLA, espionage, and other activities contrary to American interests.

A greater role for Wall Street asset managers in owning and managing Chinese funds will only make them and their investors more subject to Beijing's guidance. This is completely contrary to American interests and should be banned by Washington.

Submit a Nullification and Impairment Case to the WTO

WTO rules allow members to file formal complaints against other member nations whose trade and industrial policies broadly violate the WTO's fundamental principles and thereby nullify the benefits it was designed to provide. The United States should try to persuade the European Union, Japan, and other free market countries to file such a case jointly against China. But even if they decline, Washington should go it alone. The WTO increasingly becomes a joke as the Chinese Party/state violates key free trade principles while claiming it is acting in accord with the law.

If Washington wins the case, China will have to change its policies dramatically or withdraw from the WTO. If Washington loses, it may still generate support for system reform. A loss would also justify Washington in taking the decision for the United States to exit the organization and free itself of any restrictions on its policies vis-à-vis China and other mercantilist countries.

Democratic Globalization Organization

In any case, it would be wise for the United States to lead a movement for creation of a democratic globalization organization (DGO).

The creation of the WTO in 1995 was supposed to lead to better rules and more order, but it has failed for four main reasons. First, currency manipulation and chronic trade imbalances have never been addressed. Second, globalization, well established by the mid-1990s, is something quite different from the international trade concepts on which the WTO was founded. Globalization is about cross-border investment, technology flows, and industrial policy, all of which the reigning neoclassical international trade doctrine assumes do not occur. While the WTO managed to adopt some superficial measures to protect intellectual property and discipline certain subsidies, it established no rules regarding cross-border investment flows and subsidies. The third reason was that it never established an effective governance system. Decisions are by consensus of the 164 member nations, which means that in practice there are no decisions, no guidance, and no effective management. Finally, bringing China into the WTO more or less guaranteed that it wouldn't work. Rather than evolve into the free market, Western-style system for which the WTO was designed, the Chinese economy has become a unique amalgam of business and state interests completely suffused by the Party. Subsidies, market protections, administrative guidance, and other government interventions are everywhere, but they are difficult to observe and measure, and thus hard to discipline by an unwieldy outside body like the WTO. Having failed to compel China to meet the WTO obligations it signed up for and having pretended for nearly twenty years that China soon will become something it never intended to become, the WTO has made itself ineffective. It can no longer assure free trade in any meaningful sense, especially because the fundamental principles of its second-largest member are completely at odds with those of its largest member and of its own founding principles. The WTO simply has no way of dealing with politically guided and coercive trade, investment, and industrial policies, any more than the IMF can deal with the issues of chronic undervaluation and overvaluation of currencies and of chronic trade surpluses and deficits.

In view of this situation, the United States must lead the establishment of a new body, a democratic globalization organization. Its members would include only democratic governments operating under rule of law. The range of the DGO's activity would include trade, investment, data transfer and storage, anti-monopoly regulation, intellectual property protection, capital and technology flow oversight, subsidies of all kinds (trade, investment, and R&D), and cyber operations. The key founding members would be the United States, Canada, Mexico, the European Union, the United Kingdom, Japan, South Korea, Australia, India, Brazil, South Africa, and Nigeria. It would make decisions based on weighted voting. Bigger economies and countries with big populations would have more weight than those with smaller populations and economies. The dispute-settlement mechanism would be run by in-house professional trade lawyers and economists rather than part-time panelists culled from member countries for temporary duty. In addition to settling disputes among members, the DGO would have the power to impose high tariffs, quotas, or even outright bans on imports of all goods and services from nondemocratic, non–rule of law countries. It would also aim for balanced trade with no major countries having chronic surpluses or deficits in their overall trade balances.

Apply Trade Laws to the Fullest Extent Possible—Self-Initiate

Production and export subsidies along with currency undervaluation all tend to lead to the dumping of products in export markets, especially in the U.S. market because it is the easiest to enter. Under U.S. law as well as WTO rules, dumping is banned and can result in the imposition of countervailing duties. But there is a problem with the way these rules are typically enforced. A company usually must complain to the Commerce Department, which makes an initial assessment of the viability of the complaint. If it is found viable, the department will launch an investigation that can take several months. If it makes a positive finding, it submits that finding to the independent International Trade Commission, which may or may not find that there was injury to the complainant and that the injury was great enough to warrant the cost to consumers of imposing countervailing duties. This can all take a long time, during which the dumping may continue. A complainant could be driven out of business before a final judgment was made—which is exactly what happened in the case of solar panels in 2014. Chinese producers were heavily subsidized and were dumping panels in the U.S. market at far below the cost of production. U.S. maker Solar World filed and won its anti-dumping case, but it had been so weakened by the dumping over a long period that it was forced out of business soon after winning in court.

Under U.S. anti-dumping law, the secretary of commerce has the authority to initiate cases without first receiving a complaint from private industry. Historically, commerce secretaries have seldom done this, but it is not unprecedented. By the very nature of the Chinese government programs aimed at achieving Made in China goals, and by the nature of its currency-management policies, we know there is a substantial subsidy for Chinese exports. In view of that, the new Department of Commerce should begin systematically initiating anti-dumping actions on various imports from China.

Similarly, the Committee on Foreign Investment in the United States (CFIUS) should broaden and deepen its restraint of Chinese investment into the American market. As presently written, the rules pertain to technologies that are considered important to national security or key enabling technologies. To this should be added a prohibition on exports to or investment in any country that either formally or informally compels technology transfer from foreign corporations to its domestic companies.

Such a step should be taken in conjunction with proposals for the WTO to be more explicit in its requirements regarding reciprocity of free trade. It must also keep in mind that all Chinese investment is ultimately subject to influence by the Party, and that in the United States, investment tends to create political influence. In the 1980s, Japanese auto companies were careful to scatter their U.S. investments in as many states as possible to influence state governors and members of Congress regarding trade issues with Japan. At least Japan is an ally. China is certainly not, and its accretion of influence in U.S. politics should be severely restrained by CFIUS. Essentially, the only Chinese investment allowed should be in U.S. government bonds. As Josh Rogin noted in his *Washington Post* column, "China is building leverage over all Americans."[6]

Take Care with Students

The question of Chinese students in U.S. colleges and universities must be considered carefully. Let's begin by affirming that the vast majority of the 360,000 Chinese students who come each year pose no personal threat to America. I have already mentioned that a few are not innocent and that all of them are vulnerable to pressure from Beijing. But perhaps a more important point is that, in totality, they represent a lot of tuition and room and board money, on which even some top-tier schools have become quite dependent. That means the students can be weaponized by Beijing. It could decide it doesn't like some professors or some lines of teaching, and make it clear to the offending institution that if there are no changes, the students and their money could disappear. In any case, while it is beneficial for an American college or university to have some foreign students, they need not come from a particular place. If the Chinese students all leave, they may be replaced by Indian, European, African, Latin American, Middle Eastern, and other foreign students. In any case, schools with large numbers of Chinese students should be required to buy insurance policies against the risk that Beijing could cut off the flow unexpectedly.

Second, the students should be carefully vetted to weed out those who are tied to the Chinese government and the CCP. Once in the United States, they should not be left to themselves but should be required to participate in seminars aimed at well acquainting them with America. They should be taught about the rights of Americans and the rule of law and generally be made familiar with how the American System works. They should especially be taught the meaning of free speech. Further, they should not be quartered together but assigned living space among non-Chinese students. In short, they should be discouraged from becoming a separate segment of the university community.

Great care must be taken in admitting Chinese students to advanced graduate programs, especially in the sciences and engineering, and in avoiding classes that are predominantly Chinese. Of course, these students are attractive to universities wanting to maintain strong graduate studies programs in technological areas. The kids are smart and they pay full fare. But they can also be dangerous to America's health. We should not exclude them, but we should keep an eye on them. We should not let them become a powerful force in our educational system, and we should attempt to diversify so that we get smart Indians, smart Japanese, and smart others as well.

A Free World Infrastructure Development Team

We have seen that China's authoritarian system is extending not only its economic power but its diplomatic and military influence. The One Belt One Road program, the massive modernization and buildup of its armed forces, and especially the expansive claim to South China Sea islands and reefs, where it is building military facilities, are all indicators of China's grasp for international power. Not only was the international foreign policy establishment wrong about how China would evolve economically and politically, it has also been proven wrong about China's military and geopolitical ambitions. The United States and the free world need to respond.

The first step in that response could be a cooperative program by the United States and key free world governments to develop coordinated and competitive infrastructure development programs targeted at key countries, to be accomplished without putting the recipient country into great debt and without the suspected corruption that has accompanied many Chinese projects.

Japan's prime minister Abe has been promoting "quality infrastructure" as a key building block of Asia's future. Japan's postwar approach to development assistance anticipated China's Belt and Road concept. As articulated in the "flying geese paradigm" (other Asian countries would emulate Japan like geese in flight), Japanese infrastructure investment in Asia would enable the new geese to fly. At the end of 2016, Tokyo announced that by 2020, it would increase its Asian infrastructure investment by $116 billion. It also noted that whereas China had contributed only $58 billion to Asia in direct foreign investment, Japan had contributed $260 billion.[7]

In October 2018, President Trump signed into law the Better Utilization of Investments Leading to Development (BUILD) Act, aimed at reforming and strengthening American development finance capacities under the new Development Finance Corporation (DFC). The DFC opened its doors in October 2019, giving the United States $60 billion of new development finance capacity. This remains far below China's capacity, but is of a different quality, and when combined with that of Japan and other free world countries, it will be significant.

Washington should collaborate closely with Japan, the European Union, Australia, and South Korea to create joint investment and economic development programs for key countries. They should start with the Philippines, which is a treaty ally of the United States, a long-time recipient of Japanese development assistance, and the home base of the Asian Development Bank. The country's location, across the South China Sea from China and just to the north of the Straits of Malacca, with the great natural harbor of Subic Bay (formerly a U.S. Navy base), is highly strategic. And it has a pressing need for economic development.

In view of this, Washington should create a consortium of the U.S., EU, Japanese, South Korean, and Australian development and infrastructure banks along with the Asian Development Bank for the purpose of modernizing the Philippines by 2040. This project would be coordinated with programs aimed at aiding transfer of supply chain production from China to less risky countries. It would include installing a truly high-speed, modern (meaning 100 percent fiber-optic) internet, upgrading and extending road systems, high-speed rail from Clark Air Base to Manila, building a metro system in Manila, investment in wind and solar farms, and redevelopment of Subic Bay's shipbuilding capacity along with its connection by high-speed rail to major metro areas. The whole project could cost in the neighborhood of $100 billion and would create a stronghold for free world values in Southeast Asia while halting the Philippines' slide into Beijing's arms.

Of course, this would be only the first of many similar projects.

Open Seas and Stronger Alliances

It is highly desirable that the United States and its free world allies have unimpeded passage of the South China and surrounding seas for both their commercial and security purposes. At the very least, they must keep China from absolutely dominating these seas. Beijing's buildup of airstrips and military structures on various islands and reefs in the South China Sea must be answered by a substantial free world response. A first step would be the creation of a Fisherman's Protection Flotilla that would fight harassment of fishermen in the waters of the Philippines, Malaysia, Indonesia, and Vietnam. This flotilla would consist of vessels from those countries' navies and coast guards, aided by vessels from Japan, the United States, France (keep in mind that a whole département of France is in the South Pacific), and Australia. It would also prevent illegal and environmentally harmful dredging operations in the South China Sea and the South Pacific.

Fundamental to this and other steps that may need to be taken must be a rejuvenation and strengthening of U.S. alliances with Japan, the Philippines, Australia, and India along with the evolution of a mutual support arrangement with Vietnam. It is important to understand that for a long time some of these alliances have been operating in a manner far from the mutuality mentioned in their formal titles. In fact, the muscle in many of them has been mostly American. Now Washington must not only up its game, but as a condition of doing so must insist that others up their game as well. In fact, to some extent this is already occurring. Japan has not only taken steps to strengthen its forces but is aiding and working more closely with others like Vietnam, the Philippines, and India. It must go further to commit itself to spending 2 percent (instead of 1 percent) of GDP on defense. Australia and India also have taken steps to strengthen their forces and cooperation.

Assuming the allies do their part, the U.S. Navy should increase its presence in the region by shifting an aircraft carrier battle group from the Atlantic or the Mediterranean to Singapore. At the same time, the Pentagon should respond in kind to China's buildup of medium-range and anti-ship cruise and ballistic missiles, as well as to its greatly increased use of unmanned carrier-based strike aircraft, unmanned underwater vehicles, and hypersonic strike weapons. U.S. forces should also conduct joint exercises with Indonesia, Malaysia, and Vietnam, and provide them with "counter-intervention" tools. These would include, among other things, surveillance drones, sea mines, anti-ship missiles, fast-attack missile boats, and mobile air-defense capabilities. Japan, Australia, and India should be included in these exercises. These allies should also offer support to certain islands owned or administered by friendly countries. Some Spratly Islands are occupied by Vietnam, and Thitu Island is owned by the Philippines. Natunas Island, at the bottom of the South China Sea, belongs to Indonesia and would be an ideal location for an allied presence.

A final consideration is Taiwan. If it were ever to be occupied by the PLA, its strategic location would greatly complicate the defense of Japan, South Korea, the Philippines, and the rest of the region. Washington should encourage and help Taiwan's leaders to make the island into a kind of Switzerland, in the sense of being extremely difficult and costly to invade. Former U.S. military members now working in private consulting firms could be retained by the Taiwanese government to help design defense systems, train defenders, and advise on locating and building facilities in mountains and difficult coastal areas. They could also advise on delayed-effect weapons and techniques in order to make Taiwan so costly to invade that Beijing will never seriously consider doing so.

11

The Plan for America

Winning isn't everything. It's the only thing.
—*UCLA football coach "Red" Sanders*

The other major part (actually more major than China) of the problem is the United States, which has steadily lost economic, industrial, technological, and governance competitiveness over the past fifty years. To some degree this was inevitable and even desirable as other countries recovered from World War II and as formerly underdeveloped countries like South Korea, Singapore, and China got on the path to development. But to a very large degree, America's loss of leadership has come from poor, sometimes simply wrong, short-term-oriented, ill-coordinated, and often narrow and even selfish government, business, military, and academic policies. In short, Americans haven't been playing the game as well as the Germans, Japanese, South Koreans, or Chinese. The most important step is therefore to raise the American game.

Market Access Charge

An important source of U.S. decline has been the chronic over-valuation of the dollar for most of the past seventy-five years. To address this problem the United States should impose a market access charge (MAC) on all capital investment coming from abroad, unless it is direct investment in new productive facilities. This charge would vary from zero

to 4 or 5 percent, depending on the size and trend of the U.S. trade deficit. It would have the effect of offsetting the dollar's overvaluation and
would thereby encourage more exports while somewhat reducing imports
and establishing a more balanced trade situation. This would stimulate
U.S. employment and halt the rise of U.S. debt to overseas creditors.
Because the biggest part of the U.S. trade deficit is with China, the MAC
would tend to reduce Chinese exports to the United States, perhaps increase U.S. exports to China, and cause Chinese investors to pay something
for the privilege of access to the safe, liquid U.S. capital markets. If it were
set at 3 percent today, the MAC would generate about $10–$15 billion of
annual revenue, which could go into a fund to finance renewal of U.S.
infrastructure or a program to strengthen U.S. technology and U.S.-based
production of advanced products and services.

Perhaps more important, the MAC would tend to promote U.S. exports,
jobs, and fiscal income while reducing imports and job loss.

The MAC has been proposed in a Senate bill introduced by Senators
Tammy Baldwin and Josh Hawley. It should be adopted by the Congress
and put into action as soon as possible. It is perfectly legal under U.S. and
international law and does not contravene any rules of the WTO or other
agreements. It can be done at once and should be. I should emphasize
that such a charge is perfectly in keeping with the spirit of the liberal trading order planned at the Bretton Woods meeting of 1944 and established
after the end of World War II. A key figure at the conference, the famous
economist John Maynard Keynes, emphasized that trade should be roughly
in balance for each country over time and that chronic surpluses were as
bad as chronic deficits. I suspect that Keynes, were he alive today, would
strongly endorse the MAC.

Impose a Value Added Tax

Virtually every major country in the world operates a value
added tax (VAT). This is like a sales tax, but it is rebated on exports.
That the United States lacks a VAT puts it at a disadvantage in global
markets. The VAT is rebated on goods exported to the United States, so
that they tend to sell at a lower price in the U.S. market than in their home
market unless a U.S. state imposes a sales tax equivalent to the producing

country's VAT. On the other hand, U.S. exports to most countries have a VAT added to their retail price. Since there is no rebate of their U.S. taxes, the addition of the foreign VAT tends to inhibit sales of U.S. exports in foreign markets. By introducing a VAT, Washington could level the playing field while reducing both the U.S. trade deficit and the budget deficit.

The Great Rejuvenation

In order to meet the challenge posed by China, the United States must dedicate itself to maintaining the world's most competitive economy. Like Germany and China with their Industry 4.0 and Made in China 2025 programs, America should launch a comprehensive American Rejuvenation Program dedicated to world leadership in all key technological, infrastructure, and high-value-added fields. The program must be introduced as fundamental to long-term national security and as a response to the greatest challenge the United States has ever faced short of the Civil War. It must be designed and organized to be comprehensive and strongly coordinated within the U.S. government and between government, business, academic, labor, and state and local government organizations.

At its core should be something like the National Defense Education Act that became law in September 1958 in the wake of Sputnik. It provided massive scholarship funding for students in a wide range of fields. I myself studied Japanese at the East-West Center and at Keio University in Tokyo partly on the basis of this funding. It particularly aided students in the sciences and engineering with the objective of matching and overcoming Soviet technology capabilities. It worked. Today, China is awarding four or five times as many science and engineering degrees as the United States. Of course, it has about four times the population, but the United States also lags behind most other advanced countries in producing science and engineering graduates. Washington needs to do again what it did after Sputnik. On top of that, America should make it easy for students from Europe, India, Japan, and elsewhere who gain technology degrees from American universities and colleges to stay in the United States. One idea is to attach a green card to every technology doctoral degree awarded to a non-American student.

National Economic and Security Council

As a start, the National Economic Council and the National Se-curity Council should be merged into one body—call it the National Economic and Security Council (NESC). For too long, U.S. national security policy has focused on military and diplomatic issues, without much concern for industrial, financial, technological, and economic matters. But such matters are now as important to national security as the narrow military/diplomacy issues. The head of this council should be someone with very broad global experience and knowledge of business, economics, and international affairs.

Department of Competitiveness

A further major step would be to merge the Departments of Commerce, Energy, and Transportation, along with NASA (National Air and Space Administration) and DARPA (the Defense Advanced Research Projects Agency, progenitor of the internet, the semiconductor industry, the relational database, most of the products sold by Apple, and much more) into a new Department of Competitiveness, whose primary mission would be to achieve U.S. and free world leadership in all major technolo-gies and industries, and to upgrade America's infrastructure to first-class modern status. For example, true high-speed rail service (two hundred miles per hour) would be established between Boston, New York, and Washington DC, as well as in other heavily traveled corridors such as Houston-Austin, New York–Chicago, and San Francisco–Los Angeles. The telecommunications network would be made fully fiber-optic in all areas of the nation. Financing for much of the infrastructure upgrading would flow from the market access charge, in conjunction with a new Infrastructure Bank established to fund a broad array of infrastructure projects. The present Fannie Mae, which supports home building through its purchase of mortgages, could be transformed into an Infra-structure Bank.

The new department would dispose of enough funds to increase U.S. government spending on R&D to 2 percent of GDP, or about $450 bil-lion. On top of private industry spending, that would put total U.S. R&D

investment at about 4 percent of GDP and make the United States the undisputed world leader in R&D. On top of this, the Department of Competitiveness would also dramatically increase funding to its DARPA and NIST (the National Institute of Standards and Technology) arms to provide investment incentives and venture financing for key ground-breaking projects and as offsets to investment incentives offered by other countries.

The 5G Example à la Woodrow Wilson

A concrete example of how this might work is the rollout of 5G telecommunications systems. As I write, it seems that China's Huawei is in the lead in the development and deployment of this technology. Beijing is doing everything it can to get Huawei systems sold and installed in as many countries as possible. This presents both a national security risk and a technology risk to the United States and to other free market countries. At this moment, no U.S. company is in the running. Cisco somehow missed the boat. Lucent was sold to France's Alcatel and seems to have lost its innovative flair. Finland's Nokia and Sweden's Ericsson have the technology but are handicapped in competing with Huawei because their governments are not giving them the subsidies and easy financing that Beijing provides to Huawei.

In this situation, the U.S. Department of Competitiveness should recall how Woodrow Wilson and Franklin Delano Roosevelt led the creation of RCA to counter British Marconi as the leader in telegraph and then radio deployment. It should call together the leaders of Nokia, Ericsson, Cisco, and other companies with related technology and declare that it will back (financially and through regulation) a joint venture aimed at outcompet-ing Huawei. It should not only offer this support but make clear that it will bar Huawei from the U.S. market and provide whatever funding is necessary to offset the subsidy Huawei receives from Beijing. It could then take similar action in other key industries. Of course, the United States would do all in its power to include allied governments and corporations, such as those of Japan, Germany, France, Sweden, Finland, the United Kingdom, Australia, South Korea, and Italy, and urge them to cooperate and contribute.

Respond to Made in China

In addition to the 5G program, the United States should undertake its own program in combination with allied countries to take leadership in high-tech industries like robotics, artificial intelligence, semiconductors, bio-technology, aviation, space research, undersea exploration and mining, and other technologies we know will be key to the future of humankind. Senators Chuck Schumer of New York and Todd Young of Indiana have proposed a $100 billion funding and reorganization of the National Science Foundation to aim at assuring U.S. tech leadership far into the future. This kind of bill and program should be adopted.[1]

Copy Singapore and Ireland

As a model for much of its activity, the Department of Competitiveness should look carefully at bodies like Singapore's Economic Development Board (EDB) and the Irish Development Authority (IDA), which do extensive analysis of their own economies and those of other leading countries. Their objective is to raise both the amount and the value of their nation's economic output, which leads them to constantly reach for higher ground in technology and value added. If they see a company like Intel, for example, they will approach it to learn of its investment and expansion thinking and will offer it an attractive deal to locate a fabrication facility or lab in their country. They may offer it free land, no taxes for ten years, or utilities at half cost, essentially to bribe it to bring investment, technology, and skills to their economy.

China does the same thing, with the added persuader that the company might find its sales in China not doing so well if it doesn't invest there. The Department of Competitiveness should offset this and better it. It must carefully and continually study the U.S. economy and those of other leading countries, make itself aware of the state of advance in a wide variety of technologies, and learn the market dynamics of major industries and the costs incurred in various markets as well as the incentives industries are receiving in these markets. It must have a good knowledge of the costs of development and production in the United States compared to those abroad and of what might be done to make the United States the low-cost, high-productivity location for product development and production. Part of the department must associate with venture capitalists and think like venture capitalists while also considering the national interest.

Create Wealth and Good Jobs Will Follow

The Department of Competitiveness's key objective must be wealth creation. Economic welfare is often translated as jobs—political leaders always say they want to create good jobs—but that is not exactly what we need. Of course, good jobs are fine, but the real necessity is wealth creation, which is something different. As a boy I used to visit steel mills with my dad. It was very exciting, with lots of machines clattering and steam hissing, red ribbons of molten steel running through the factories, and hundreds if not thousands of men doing strong-back manual work. These were good jobs at the time. But today, steel mills have no steam and no clatter. The few people inside are not found on the mill floor but in the control room, manning the computers and other electronic gear that run the mill. Most of the jobs are gone, but the value created is much greater than when I was a boy, and the productivity of the few remaining workers is far, far above that of the workers of old. More wealth is being created today.

A semiconductor fabricating facility costs about $8 billion but employs just six hundred to a thousand people—far, far fewer per dollar of sales than, say, a textile mill. The product sells for a very high price and creates enormous wealth, while the cost of the labor is only 3 to 4 percent of the production cost. Yet that labor is extremely well paid. A governor would far rather have a semiconductor fab in his or her state than a textile mill, because the fewer jobs pay extremely well and the product yields much more profit and thus more tax revenue than a textile mill.

Over the past forty years, offshoring of production has become a common practice for American and other global corporations. For instance, Ford can make a car in North America with $30 per hour labor or in Mexico or China with $3 per hour labor. Ford has the technology for making cars and can deploy it anywhere in the world it chooses to do so. If the labor input in making a car is substantial, it is obvious that Ford would rather make it in Mexico or China than in North America unless the North American workers can add some magic unique to them, which today they do not. But if production can be automated and the number of workers substantially reduced, then the cost comparison between production locations comes down to the cost of capital, proximity to the market, the effect of taxes and tax offsets, and other factors.

Let's go back to semiconductors. The cost of labor is not a factor in deciding where to put a fab. Because the United States has workers experienced in producing the semiconductor chips and has the most advanced fabs, it can be, depending on various circumstances, the low-cost, high-quality, high-productivity location in the world for making the chips. For example, U.S.-based chip production is competitive with that in South Korea and Taiwan even though U.S. wages are higher. As manufacturing production becomes increasingly automated, and as new technology reduces the need for vast amounts of production to achieve adequate economies of scale, production from a U.S. location should not only be cost-effective but desirable for serving the market, fostering rising technological capability, and creating wealth.

Reshore Production—Make Manufacturing 16 Percent of GDP

Another major task of the Department of Competitiveness must be to maximize the "reshoring" of production. This should apply to any kind of wealth production, but certainly to manufacturing. Why? Because manufacturing production (broadly defined) has been the greatest wealth producer of all time. A key reason is that manufacturing, unlike farming or hair cutting or cancer surgery, enjoys economies of scale. The more units you make, the lower the production cost of each unit, while you can still sell them for the same price. Economies of scale can yield enormous productivity gains. In 1975, manufacturing as a percent of U.S. GDP was about 21 percent. Today it is 11 percent. We have already seen that in Germany, Japan, Italy, and other countries, it remains around 22 percent. Of course, the U.S. economy is more diversified than most others. Nevertheless, because of the importance of manufacturing for wealth production, the department should strive to raise U.S. manufacturing (broadly defined) to at least 16 percent of GDP.

Focus on Manufacturing Support

To support manufacturing, funding for the National Science Foundation's National Robotics Initiative should be raised to at least $600 million annually. Ten new public-private institutes under the Manufacturing USA program should be established and a ten-year investment tax credit provided. At least twenty universities should be designated "manufacturing universities" eligible to receive federal support for their programs. At the same time, the Defense Department's Defense Manufacturing Technology program should be dramatically expanded to completely rebuild the old defense industrial base. Today's temporary R&D tax credit should be made permanent and should include expenditures for workforce training. A new investment tax credit is needed, and it should include investment in software.

In addition to creating the new Department of Competitiveness, the U.S. Congress must also create a Congressional Competitiveness Office (CCO) similar to the Congressional Budget Office. Like the CBO, the CCO would be a nonpartisan body focused on evaluating how various bills and other proposals would affect U.S. competitiveness. It would be an authoritative, impartial evaluator and storehouse of knowledge on the competitiveness of the United States and other countries.

Saving—Investment—R&D—Infrastructure

Wealth creation is the name of the game. A country cannot be safe without some degree of wealth that is roughly evenly shared. It is impossible to create wealth without investment, in both infrastructure and productive industries, and it is difficult to have investment without savings. As a country becomes more developed and less able simply to absorb existing technology from others, spending on R&D becomes essential. On all these measures, the United States is doing poorly. Its net national savings rate in 2017 (the most recent year for which data are available) was 2.9 percent of GDP, down from 4.1 percent as recently as 2015 and from 12 percent in the 1960s.[2] Compare this with Germany, which is at about 11 percent, South Korea at 17 percent, the Euro area at about 6.6 percent, Japan at about 6 percent, and China at 45 percent.[3]

The story is the same with investment. Japan's investment as a share of GDP was about 24 percent in 2017 (the last year for which data are available). In 2018, Canada was at 23 percent, France at 23.46 percent, Germany at 21.3 percent, and the United States (also for 2017) at 20.6 percent. China was at about 45 percent.[4] In 1984, the U.S. rate was 25 percent, and despite some ups and downs, it has fallen steadily since then.

As for research and development spending, South Korea is the world champion at 4.3 percent of GDP, followed by Japan at 3.4 percent, Germany at 2.9 percent, and the United States at 2.7 percent. China is at 2 percent but climbing very rapidly.[5] Historically, American R&D spending hit 2.8 percent in the 1960s, fell under 2.2 percent in the 1970s, climbed back to 2.6 percent in the 1980s, fell to 2.3–2.5 percent in the 1990s and early 2000s, and has finally come back to about 2.8 percent now. Since the 1960s, however, the source of American spending has changed dramatically. In the 1960s and 1970s it was the U.S. government. This has fallen steadily, from about 1.8 percent in the 1960s to about 0.6 percent today, and has been replaced by business spending.[6] In most other countries, the government share is much higher.

The picture for infrastructure is even darker. In its 2017 report, the American Society of Civil Engineers gives U.S. infrastructure a grade of D. This means conditions are "mostly below standard, exhibiting significant deterioration with a strong risk of failure." The report puts the price of fixing the "infrastructure gap" at about $1.5 trillion by 2025. In its 2016 Competitiveness Report, the World Economic Forum ranked the United States tenth in the world in infrastructure quality—down from fifth in 2002—and well behind countries such as France, Germany, and Japan. Not surprisingly, infrastructure investment in most major countries is substantially higher than in the United States.

If we consider health care as part of essential infrastructure, the American picture is even uglier. Americans pay more than twice as much for health care as citizens of other advanced countries (18 percent of GDP versus an average of 8 percent) and have worse results. For example, the CIA fact book ranks the United States fiftieth among countries for life expectancy at birth: 78.11 years versus Japan at 82.2, Canada at 81.1, and South Korea at 78.72.[7]

A glance at the Congressional Budget Office Long Term Budget Outlook, released on June 25, 2019, only further darkens the picture.

Spending is on track to continue rising faster than revenue. By 2049, today's federal debt of 78 percent of GDP will become 144 percent. Today's federal spending of 21 percent of GDP will hit 28 percent in 2049, but revenue will climb only to 19.5 percent. Annual deficits will more than double, from today's 4.2 percent to 8.7 percent of GDP.[8] Consequently, most of the country's major trust funds are headed for insolvency. The Highway, Pension Benefit Guaranty Corporation, Multi-Employer, Medicare, Hospital Insurance, Social Security Disability Insurance, and Social Security Old-Age and Survivors Insurance trust funds will all be exhausted within the next thirteen years in the absence of action to stabilize their finances. Any extensions of some programs now scheduled to end will only make the situation worse. As it is, this rising debt will reduce income growth by about $9,000 per capita, raise interest payments, place upward pressure on interest rates, reduce the government's ability to respond to a recession, heighten the risk of fiscal crisis, and unduly burden future generations.

Reverse the Trends

America will simply be unable to compete with China if these trends are not reversed. Regarding health care, there are many models, such as those of France, Germany, Canada, Australia, and Singapore, from which Washington can choose. Any of them would be better than the present U.S. system.

The overall focus must be to get the U.S. government on a path of fiscal sustainability that will keep the trust funds healthy and enable increases in spending on research, infrastructure, and expansion of wealth-producing capacity. There will have to be an increase in government revenue, which means an increase in taxes. Given that extreme economic inequality is dangerous to democracy and that the U.S. already has the most unequal income distribution of any advanced country, that increase must fall more on the wealthy than on the poor and middle classes. A look at the historical progression of the U.S. tax structure reveals an ugly picture. Over the past seventy years, the richest Americans have come to pay the lowest taxes. In the 1950s, those between the ninety-fifth and one-hundredth percentiles paid 30–70 percent of their income in taxes. By 1978, that was down to 30–45 percent, and today it is 21–28 percent. The top income earners pay less than those in the tenth percentile.[9]

A new system would impose a marginal tax rate of 70 percent on those in the top 1 percent of the income distribution and of 50 percent on those in the top 5 percent. This may sound extreme, but it is less than the rates existing in the 1960s. Income from capital gains, carried interest, and other kinds of income available only to the well-off would be taxed as ordinary income. Finally, the deduction of mortgage interest from taxable income would be halted, since it is nothing but a subsidy to the housing industry and to the middle and upper classes.

The corporate tax must also be rethought, and here we have two options. One would be simply to return to the previous model of taxing U.S. corporations on their global earnings, but with a credit for taxes actually paid to foreign countries. The rate should be about 21 percent. This new tax law would have to be combined with strong rules preventing "inversions"—the reincorporation of a U.S. company in another country (like Ireland or Singapore) with lower tax rates and less stringent corporate obligations. A second option would be to do on a global basis what U.S. states do now on a national basis: divide up the global corporate tax base in terms either of sales or sales plus employment. Thus, for example, the profit on pharmaceutical sales by U.S. pharma companies would be taxed by the United States even if the manufacturing were done in Puerto Rico. By the same token, France, for example, would get to tax the euros that, say, Google would make from its sales in France.

A New American Corporation

The most politically and economically powerful forces in the United States are its major business corporations, which are extremely wealthy. Apple, for example, is sitting on an estimated $252 billion of untaxed and untaxable income earned in a variety of countries but stashed in tax havens like Ireland, Singapore, the Cayman Islands, Guernsey, and the Isle of Man.[10]

But money is only one of three parts of the power equation. The second part is the lack of any restraint on its use for political donations and payment to lobbyists to promote a company's interests to U.S. political leaders. The third part of the equation is the company's right to sue the U.S. government in an independent court and, if it wins, stop the government from taking actions that might disadvantage the company. Under the Supreme Court's interpretation of the Constitution in the *Citizens United* case, the corporation has effectively the same rights as a human citizen of the United States. It can therefore spend as much as it likes on influencing politics in a variety of ways. In fact, however, the corporation is a super-citizen because it is richer than any normal citizen and effectively has eternal life. General Electric is 127 years old and still chugging. Ford Motor is 116 years old and still fully in the game. Unlike normal citizens, these corporations maintain permanent offices in Washington, DC, with staffs recruited from among former high officials, congresspersons, and congressional staffers. They have far, far more knowledge of and influence over government activity than any normal citizen. The reason U.S drug prices are many times those of any other country is the U.S. drug and medical company lobby. The reason American cars get the fewest miles per gallon of gasoline in the world is the auto industry lobby. The reason your gasoline contains corn-based ethanol that reduces its efficiency is the farm lobby. Effectively, the industry-focused lobbies buy the politicians and then write the laws.

I noted earlier that after a quarter century of taking the position that increasing earnings for shareholders was a CEO's only responsibility, the Business Roundtable has turned back to its old formulation. It now calls on CEOs to produce good products and to take care of workers, communities, and the country as well as shareholders. But after fifty years in which the students at leading business schools like Harvard, Wharton, and Stanford had "earnings for shareholders" drummed into them, it is not clear that the Roundtable's change of heart will affect the culture of many boardrooms. The U.S. Congress must ensure that it takes hold.

The fact is that a corporation cannot just establish itself. It must receive a charter from one of the states of the United States. By making the company a registered corporation, the state gives it something of great value—limited liability. A shareholder cannot be held personally liable for any of the corporation's debts, and without that guarantee, very few businesses would be able to find investors. The state grants this gift because it expects something in return: it anticipates that the corporation's activities will benefit the community. It doesn't grant the gift so that the corporation can park its cash in Ireland or the Cayman Islands to avoid taxes. It doesn't grant the gift so that the corporation can capture politicians and keep drug prices at scalper levels. But that is what has occurred.

It is therefore necessary to recharter the corporations. Any corporation with sales exceeding $1 billion and with 15 percent of its business generated abroad should, in addition to whatever state charter it has, be required as well to obtain a federal charter from the Department of Competitiveness. This charter will adopt the logic of Canada and will stipulate that the corporation is not a living person and not a citizen of the United States with the political rights of citizens. The corporation will not be permitted to make political donations or advertising of any sort, will not be permitted to hire former high-ranking officials as either lobbyists or executives, and will have only limited rights to sue the state and federal governments. In other words, it will not have greater rights than a citizen. Moreover, it will have a dual board of directors structure similar to companies in Germany. There will be a management board consisting of the key executives of the corporation, and a supervisory board on which some company executives will sit, but at least half of whose seats will be occupied by representatives of the company's workforce and of the public at large. Further, the corporation will be subject to severe punishment if it submits to demands of a foreign government that are contrary to the rights of American citizens regarding freedom of speech and religion and racial/ethnic equality. Any corporation that helps a foreign government exercise tyrannical power over its own people will be dissolved by the U.S. government.

A New American Labor Movement

American labor unions have extraordinary power compared to labor unions in many other free world nations, even though the percentage of workers those unions represent is mostly higher in other developed countries. The power U.S. labor unions have is the power of monopoly. For example, the United Auto Workers includes all the autoworkers at Ford, GM, and Chrysler. The union can decide at contract bargaining time to go on strike against only one of the companies, and the union members working at the other companies pay compensation to their fellow members who are on strike. A single company can't afford not to do a deal quickly, and once that deal is done, it is extended to the other companies. This system has decimated the U.S. auto industry by saddling it with higher labor costs than competing auto companies in Germany, Japan, Korea, and Mexico. Of course, Japanese and German producers have also opened factories in the United States, but they largely don't have union workforces. In a way, the U.S. union system has worked against itself.

Japan has no industry-wide unions. All its unions are company unions. There is a union of Toyota autoworkers and a union of Nissan autoworkers, and they are different organizations. All employees, except the key executives, are members of the union. They bargain with the executives (most of whom are former union members) and with the company's board of directors, which is mostly composed of its top executives.

The Germans have industry-wide unions, but all the unions and companies in an industry negotiate as a group. In the auto industry negotiations, Mercedes Benz, VW, and BMW executives all sit on one side of the bargaining table and the union representatives sit on the other side. If the union goes on strike, it must be a strike against all the companies at once.

Either system is superior to the U.S. system, and the United States should adopt one of them.

In sum, it is time for Americans and especially their leaders to realize they have been drawing down their inheritance from World War II and the Cold War for far too long. Now, they are once again back to the real nitty-gritty world of tough competition and constantly shifting power balances, a world in which there is little if any margin for error. The advantages of having the world's largest economy, of being the printer of the world's main reserve currency, and of maintaining the world's most advanced and widely spread military establishment will not be enough to save us from decline and to assure the independence and freedom of our sons and daughters. We can no longer make excuses. We must up our game.

Afterword: My Presidential
State of the Union Address

My fellow Americans and citizens of the free world, thank you for taking time tonight to hear me explain the fundamental reality of today's world that has caused me to announce the measures I have just made known to you. Thirty-odd years ago, in the wake of the collapse of the Soviet Union and the apparent turn of China onto the capitalist road, which it described as "socialism with Chinese characteristics," we and our allies engaged in what in hindsight looks like willful self-deception.

We thought we had reached "the end of history," that economic development would inevitably lead all countries to adopt free market economics, free trade, and free, rule-of-law democracy. We believed that free trade was always and everywhere a win-win proposition. Our economists even told us that unilateral free trade was better than no trade. We were told by our China experts that the Chinese Communist Party was releasing its iron grip on the Chinese economy and society, and that this loosening would inevitably continue. The Party's doctrine of "socialism with Chinese characteristics," they assured us, was just a euphemism for entrepreneurial capitalism. We thought the world was flat, that all global markets were coalescing into one common market whose benefits would be shared all. Our top business and Wall Street leaders told us that China was an El Dorado, not only for them but for all Americans. They invested heavily in telling us this story.

We believed it all and we acted on it. We welcomed China into the World Trade Organization, the International Monetary Fund, and into our own market. We encouraged our corporations to invest there, and even to move their production out of the United States to China. Our leaders told us this would be good not only for American and free world consumers but also for workers, who would find higher-paying jobs in the service industries. The result—5 million high-paying American manufacturing jobs were moved to China in the first decade of this century.

Virtually none of what we believed was true. Ralph Gomory and William Baumol, two very distinguished mathematicians and economists, demonstrated as early as 2001 that free trade is not always a win-win proposition. It is zero sum at least as often as it is win-win, perhaps more often. Moreover, the world is still round and even jagged. Countries with very different economic theories, policies, and interests interact in the real world, not in the make-believe world of econometric models. And China is not at all acting in accord with our forecasts of the 1990s.

It should have been clear to us in 2015, when the Chinese government announced its Made in China 2025 program aimed at achieving autarkic dominance in virtually all high-tech industries, that China had no intention of playing our kind of free trade game. It is abundantly clear today that China is dedicated to a highly state-guided economy that allows some market forces but that is permeated by Chinese Communist Party thinking and depends upon government intervention, subsidy, and suppression of true market information.

Even more important, it is now clear that the Chinese Communist Party is dedicated to much more than turning the Chinese economy into one that ranks among the world's leaders. For most of China's long history, it was the Middle Kingdom. Not only the world's biggest, most advanced economy, but its most powerful country, the imperial center that required payment of tribute from surrounding vassal states. Its ruler was the Son of Heaven who had authority over "all under Heaven." In a word, China was the "Ba," or great hegemon.

The recovery of this status is the objective of President Xi Jinping's Great Chinese Dream, or Rejuvenation of the Great Chinese People. China is an ancient civilization as well as the world's most populous country. It has a rich and proud history. Its effort to realize this dream would not be threatening if China operated under the rule of law, with substantial freedom of speech and tolerance of religions, ethnic minorities, and varying philosophies. The Chinese people themselves are not a threat to us or anyone else.

But the Chinese people do not run China. The Communist Party of China does. It recognizes no power above it and brooks no dissent below it. It has no tolerance for anything except the Party line, which it attempts with religious fervor to inculcate into the peoples under its domination. Nor does it limit its ambitions to China. It seeks to extend its power and influence throughout the world and establish the global dominance of authoritarian orders that will use every advanced technology to become equivalent to Big Brother in George Orwell's *1984*.

If you look closely, you can see virtually every day the increasing realization of this objective. The free world's airlines have all bowed to Beijing's command to rename their flights to Taipei. In the past, these flights were listed as, for example, San Francisco–Taipei, Taiwan. Now they have dropped the "Taiwan" in response to Beijing's objections and its implicit threat to suspend their flights to Chinese cities like Shanghai and Beijing. This is what United and every other free world airline is telling you when you book a flight to Taipei. This is what Daimler Benz is telling you when it apologizes to China for quoting the Dalai Lama in an ad that did not even air in China. As most of you know, the internet in China is censored. You can't Google anything. If you try looking for the Dalai Lama, or June 4, 1989, or any of a thousand other sensitive subjects, you won't find anything. It is not hard to imagine that as the power of the Chinese Communist Party/state expands, it will demand that the internet in countries closely tied by trade to China also be censored.

This Party/state and its doctrine are the biggest threat that the United States and the free world have ever faced.

The United States is a young country, only 244 years old. But it is also the westernmost extension of a Western civilization that is as old as China's. From the ancient Sumerians and Hammurabi's first known code of law through the Persians, Egyptians, Greeks, the Roman Empire, the Renaissance, the evolution of European technology, the Enlightenment, and the founding and development of the United States, this civilization has come to value the rule of law, freedom of thought and speech, freedom of belief, open political decision making, and truth.

As the leading representative of this ancient civilization, one completely dedicated to its values, the United States must, in league with all others holding similar values, face up to the threat posed by the Chinese Party/

state. The road will not be easy and may be very long. But we must walk it. To do so, we must find a greater unity among ourselves and with our friends abroad. The heads of U.S.-based corporations must think about what is good for America as well as what is good for their shareholders or for their companies' stock price. The heads of Wall Street banks must think about how wise it really is to sell shares in Chinese companies that can't be properly audited. Economists need to stop focusing so heavily on low prices for consumers and start thinking of how our country can produce more and higher-quality wealth. They must stop using fairy-tale assumptions in their econometric models to justify their preferred conclusions about free trade. Our universities need to remember that their main job is to educate Americans and keep them among the top thinkers in all fields. The heads of those universities need to stop thinking they are global CEOs and stop putting campuses in situations where they will be forced to compromise their values.

We all must stop thinking of China mainly as a source of inexpensive products and start wondering if we are feeding a machine that is increasingly threatening to ourselves and our values. We must recognize that we are in something much like the old Cold War. We of course do not want war, either hot or cold. But we must understand that the Chinese Party/state has effectively been acting as if it were at war with us. We must respond accordingly.

The good news is that we have done this before. We pulled ourselves out of the Civil War. Together with our allies, we won World War II and the Cold War. If we remain united and dedicated to one another and to our fundamental values, I have no doubt that we can successfully meet this challenge.

Thank you and good night.

Notes

Introduction

1. Francis Fukuyama, *The End of History and the Last Man* (1992; repr., London: Free Press, 2006).

2. U.S. embassy cable 176535, June 4, 1989, Wikileaks.

3. Eamonn Fingleton, *In the Jaws of the Dragon* (New York: St. Martin's, 2008), 190.

4. Robert Zoellick, "Whither China: From Membership to Responsibility?" Remarks to the National Committee on U.S.-China Relations, New York City, September 21, 2005, https://2001-2009.state.gov/s/d/former/zoellick/rem/53682.htm.

5. Office of the United States Trade Representative, "U.S.-China Trade Facts," accessed March 22, 2018, https://ustr.gov/countries-regions/china-mongolia-taiwan/peoples-republic-china; Robert E. Scott and Zane Mokhiber, *The China Toll Deepens* (Washington, DC: Economic Policy Institute, 2018).

6. Marites Danguilan Vitug, *Rock Solid: How the Philippines Won Its Maritime Case against China* (Bughaw, Philippines: Ateneo de Manila University Press, 2018), 7.

7. Ronsevert Ganan Almong, "It's Official: Xi Breaks Non-militarization Promise in Spratlys," *Diplomat,* December 16, 2016.

8. "Counterfeit Airforce," *Popular Mechanics,* September 19, 2018.

9. David Pilling, "No One Is Immune from Beijing's 'Gravity Machine,' " *Financial Times,* December 11, 2003.

10. Clive Hamilton, *Silent Invasion* (Melbourne: Hardie Grant, 2018), x.

11. Ibid., 2.

12. Ibid., 2–3.

13. Ibid., 3.

14. "Juncker Wants EU to Drop Unanimity," Radio Free Europe, September 12, 2018.

15. Pei Li and Adam Jourdan, "Mercedes-Benz Apologizes to Chinese for Quoting Dalai Lama," Reuters, February 6, 2018, https://www.reuters.com/article/us-mercedes-

benz-china-gaffe/mercedes-benz-apologizes-to-chinese-for-quoting-dalai-lama-idUSK-BN1FQ1FJ.

16. Mervyn Piesse, "Australia-China Trade Dispute: Has Australia Become Too Reliant on the Chinese Market?" *Future Directions International,* May 20, 2020.

17. Kurt Campbell, "The China Reckoning," *Foreign Affairs,* March/April 2018.

18. Josephine Ma, "Coronavirus: China's First Confirmed Covid-19 Case Traced Back to November 17," *South China Morning Post,* March 13, 2020.

1. Origins of the Chinese Dream

1. Steven Mosher, *Bully of Asia* (Washington, DC: Regnery, 2017), 34.

2. Orville Schell and John Delury, *China's Long March to the 21st Century* (New York: Random House, 2013), 20.

3. Zhengyuan Fu, *Autocratic Tradition and Chinese Politics* (Cambridge: Cambridge University Press, 1993).

4. Mosher, *Bully of Asia,* 11.

5. Ibid., 48.

6. Orville Schell and John Delury, *Wealth and Power* (New York: Random House, 2013), 17.

7. Ibid., 52, 53.

8. Ibid., 17.

9. Ibid., 25.

10. Ibid., 27.

11. Ibid., 117.

12. Ibid., 131.

13. Ibid., 186.

14. Ibid., 167.

15. Ibid., 210, 211.

16. Ibid., 202, 204.

17. Mao Zedong speech, September 21, 1949, Beijing, Chinese People's Consultative Congress.

2. The Party Is Like God

1. Orville Schell and John Delury, *Wealth and Power* (New York: Random House, 2013), 179.

2. Jung Chang and Jon Halliday, *Mao: The Unknown Story* (New York: Knopf, 2005), 243.

3. Ibid., 262.

4. Ibid., 320.

5. Ibid., 295.

6. Ibid., 296.

7. Ibid., 361.

8. U.S. embassy cable 176535, June 4, 1989, Wikileaks.

9. Kerry Brown, *China's Dream* (Medford, MA: Polity, 2018), 59.

10. Ibid.

11. David Barboza, "Billions in Hidden Riches for Family of Chinese Leader," *New York Times,* October 25, 2012.

12. Brown, *China's Dream,* 61.

13. Ibid.

14. Richard McGregor, *The Party* (London: Allen Lane, 2010), xx, xxi.

15. Ibid., 12, 13.

16. Ibid., 22.

17. Ibid., 24.

18. Ibid., 33.

19. Ibid., 41.

20. Ibid.

21. Peter Hartcher, "In China the Party Always Starts at the Top," June 8, 2010, Leader, www.theleader.com.au/story/88663/in-china-the-party-always-starts-at-the-top/.

22. McGregor, *The Party,* 42, 50, 56.

23. Ibid., 73.

24. Ibid., 75.

25. "Why Has China's Anti-corruption Rating Barely Budged Despite Thousands of Arrests?" *South China Morning Post,* February 23, 2018.

26. Nicholas Kristof, "China Takes on the Role of Enemy Number 1 for the West," New York Times, September 22, 1991.

27. Fabrice de Pierrebourg and Michel Juneau-Katsuya, *Nest of Spies: The Startling Truth about Foreign Agents in Canada* (New York: Harper Collins, 2009), 160–62.

28. Anne-Marie Brady, "Magic Weapons: China's Political Influence Activities under Xi Jinping" (paper presented at the conference "The Corrosion of Democracy under China's Global Influence," Arlington, VA, September 16–17, 2017); James Kynge, "China Market Opens to Overseas Investors," *Financial Times,* May 30, 2018; James Kynge, Lucy Hornby, and Jamil Anderlini, "Inside China's Secret 'Magic Weapon' for Worldwide Influence," *Financial Times,* October 26, 2017, https://www.ft.com/content/fb2b3934-b004-11e7-beba-5521c713abf4.

29. David Shambaugh, "China's Soft-Power Push: The Search for Respect," *Foreign Affairs,* July 2015, https://www.foreignaffairs.com/articles/china/2015-06-16/china-s-soft-power-push.

30. "Chinese Government Gave Money to Georgetown Student Group," *Foreign Policy,* February 14, 2018.

31. Eric Fish, "Caught in a Crossfire: Chinese Students Abroad and the Battle for Their Hearts," Supchina, January 18, 2018, https://supchina.com/2018/01/18/caught-in-a-crossfire-chinese-students-abroad-and-the-battle-for-their-hearts/.

32. Alexander Bowe, US-China Economic and Security Review Commission Report: *China's Overseas United Front Work: Background and Implications for the United States,* 12, August 24, 2018, https://www.uscc.gov/sites/default/files/Research/

China%27s%20Overseas%20United%20Front%20Work%20-%20Background%20and%20
Implications%20for%20US_final_0.pdf.

33. *Chinese Influence and American Interests* (Stanford: Stanford University, Hoover Institute, 2018), 1, 4, 5.

34. Ibid., 72.

35. Clive Hamilton, *Silent Invasion* (Melbourne: Hardie Grant, 2018), 1.

36. Ibid., 2.

37. Jonathan Manthorpe, *Claws of the Panda: Beijing's Campaign of Influence and Intimidation in Canada* (Toronto: Cormorant Books, 2019,), 40.

38. Hamilton, *Silent Invasion*, 2, 3.

39. Kynge, Hornby, and Anderlini, "Inside China's Secret 'Magic Weapon' for Worldwide Influence."

3. The Strategy

1. John Garnaut, "Engineers of the Soul," *Sinocism*, January 16, 2019.

2. Ibid.

3. Ibid.

4. Ibid., quoting Xi Jinping at an Australian government seminar in August 2017.

5. Ibid.

6. Verna Yu, "Veteran Chinese Journalist Gao Yu 'Had No Choice' but to Confess Guilt Before Early Release from Prison, Legal Experts Say," *South China Morning Post*, November 28, 2015.

7. Garnaut, "Engineers of the Soul."

8. Ibid.

9. Henry Sanderson and Michael Forsythe, *China's Superbank: Debt, Oil and Influence—How China Development Bank Is Rewriting the Rules of Finance* (Singapore: Bloomberg, 2013).

10. Henry He, *Dictionary of the Political Thought of the People's Republic of China* (New York: Routledge, 2016), 287.

11. "Historical GDP of China," Wikipedia, accessed May 10, 2020, wikipedia.org/wiki/Historical_GDP_of_China.

12. Jim McGrath, *Heartbeat* (New York: Scribner, 2001), 295–96 (speech by George H. W. Bush at Texas A&M University).

13. Congressional Research Service, "China's Economic Rise: History, Trends, Challenges, and Implications for the United States," 7, updated June 25, 2019, p. 7, www.everycrsreport.cm.

14. U.S. Department of Commerce, "Sources and Uses of Gross Savings, 1929–1970," series F552–65, p. 217.

15. https://medium.com/breakthrough-program-supply-chain-logistics/the-state-of-play-in-supply-chain-and-logistics. Data from *Trading Economics*. Chart from GS-Vlabs. *Trading Economics* provided average hourly manufacturing wages, which were converted to annual wages by assuming a constant forty-five-hour workweek and forty-eight weeks of work in a year. China's reported average annual manufacturing wages

were converted from Chinese yuan to U.S. dollars with the average conversion rate for each year from 1978 to 2017.

16. Congressional Research Service, "China's Economic Rise," 20.

17. Robert E. Scott and Zane Mokhiber, *The China Toll Deepens* (Washington, DC: Economic Policy Institute, 2018).

18. *U.S.-China Bilateral Trade Agreement and the Accession of China to the WTO: Hearing before the House of Representatives Committee on Ways and Means,* 106th Cong., 2nd sess., February 16, 2000.

19. Richard McGregor, *The Party* (London: Allen Lane, 2010), 43.

20. Andrew Szamosszegi and Cole Kyle, "An Analysis of State-Owned Enterprises and State Capitalism in China," U.S.-China Economic and Security Review Commission, Capital Trade Study, October 26, 2011, p 10, 16.

21. *OECD Investment News,* March 2008.

22. "China 2006–2010 Outbound Overseas Direct Investment Totals 216.6 Bln USD," Ministry of Commerce, Xinhua.net, December 27, 2010, http://www.fdi.gov.cn/.

23. 2010 Statistical Bulletin of China's Outward Foreign Direct Investment, 79, mofcom.gov.cn/hzs/accessory/.

24. Thilo Hanemann and Mikko Huotari, Rhodium Group Report—New Record Year for Chinese Outbound Investment in Europe, February 16, 2016; "China 2015 FDI Rises 6.4 Pct Despite Cooling Economy," Reuters, January 14, 2016, https://www.reuters.com/article/china-economy-foreign-investment-idUSB9N14V00 P20160114.

25. Echo Huang, "Chinese Foreign Direct Investment (FDI) in the US Rocketed to $45.6 Billion in 2016," "Who Is Great Again?" Chinese Investment in the US Skyrocketed Last Year," Quartz (QZ.com), January 3, 2017.

26. "Djibouti—China Naval Base," Global Security.org newsletter, February 6, 2018.

27. Tom Cotton and John Cornyn, "Keep the Chinese Government Away from 5G Technology," *Washington Post,* April 1, 2019.

28. Jan van der Made, "RFI: How Scary Is the Chinese Belt and Road Initiative?" March 4, 2019, Rfi/en/asia/pacific/20190402/-china's -belt-and-road-expose.

29. Philip Olterman, "Germany's China City: How Duisburg Became Xi Jinping's Gateway to Europe," *South China Morning Post,* August 9, 2018.

30. "Portugal: A China-Friendly EU Nation Driven by Need," March 12, 2019, www.dw.com.

31. Andre Tartar, Mira Rojanasakul, and Jeremy Scott Diamond, "How China Is Buying Its Way into Europe," *Bloomberg,* April 23, 2018.

32. Latin America Newsletters, Emerging Market Investors Association, "Panama Region: Rail Revival or Pipe Dream?" July 12, 2018, www.emia.org.

33. Miranda Green, "Solar Company Puts Hold on $20M US Investment Following New Tariff," *The Hill,* January 26, 2018.

34. 2017 USTR Report to Congress on China's WTO Compliance.

35. Ibid.

36. Karishma Vaswani, "Huawei: The Story of a Controversial Company," BBC, March 6, 2019.

37. William Holstein, *The New Art of War* (New York: Brick Tower, 2019), 41.

38. Ibid., 39.

39. Alex Hollings, "Counterfeit Air Power: Meet China's Copycat Air Force," *Popular Mechanics,* September 19, 2018.

4. The Threat

1. Adrian Zenz, Jamestown Foundation, China Brief, Internal Security, March 12, 2018.

2. Bill Gertz, "Chinese Spy Who Defected Tells All," *Washington Times,* March 19, 2009.

3. Chris Buckley and Paul Moser, "How China Uses High Tech Surveillance to Subdue Minorities," *New York Times,* May 22, 2019.

4. Javier Hernandez, "We're Almost Extinct," *New York Times,* July 12, 2019.

5. Ibid.

6. Colin Clark, " 'A Chinese Military That Is Active Everywhere': DIA China Military Power Report," Breaking Defense, January 16, 2019, https://breakingdefense.com/2019/01/a-chinese-military-that-is-active-everywhere-dia-china-military-power-report/.

7. State Council Information Office of the People's Republic of China, Beijing, "China's Military Strategy," May 2015.

8. Laura Zhou, "China Sends Troops to Military Base in Djibouti, Widening Reach across Indian Ocean," *South China Morning Post,* July 13, 2017.

9. Steven Lee Myers, "With Ships and Missiles, China Is Ready to Challenge U.S. Navy in Pacific," *New York Times,* August 29, 2018.

10. Hugh White, "Australia Must Prepare for Chinese Military Base in South Pacific," *Guardian,* July 14, 2019.

11. "Taiwan's Exports to Mainland up 6.3 Percent in 2018," Xinhua, January 7, 2019, www.xinhuanet.com.

12. "How Much Trade Transits the South China Sea?" ChinaPower, accessed June 3, 2020, Chinapower.csis.org/much-trade-transits-south-china-sea.

13. Humphrey Hawksley, *Asian Waters* (New York: Overlook, 2018), 50.

14. Ibid., 68.

15. Ibid., 69.

16. Ibid.

17. "Timeline: The Philippines-China Maritime Dispute," Rappler, July 12, 2016, https://www.rappler.com/world/regions/asia-pacific/139392-timeline-west-philippine-sea-dispute.

18. "Timeline of the South China Sea Dispute," Wikipedia, accessed May 10, 2020, en.wikipedia.org/wiki/Timeline_of_the_South_China_Sea_dispute.

19. Ibid.

20. Felicia Schwartz, "U.S. and China Conclude Annual Talks amid Tensions," *Wall Street Journal,* June 23, 2015.

21. Michael T. Klare, "The United States Is Already at War with China," *Nation,* February 18, 2019.

22. Uptin Saiid, "Here's Why the South China Sea Is Highly Contested," CNBC, February 7, 2018, https://www.cnbc.com/2018/02/07/heres-why-the-south-china-sea-is-highly-contested.html.

23. Daqing Yang, "Was There a 'Tacit Agreement' between China and Japan in 1972?" Wilson Center, March 27, 2017, www.wilsoncenter.org/blog-post/was-there-tacit-agreement-between-china-and-japan-1972.

24. Holly Ellyat, "Xi Calls Putin Best Friend," CNBC, June 6, 2019.

25. Jamei Tarabay, "As China Looms, Australia's Military Refocuses on Pacific Neighbors," *New York Times,* June 11, 2019.

26. Ewen Levick, "Is China Using Its South China Sea Strategy in the South Pacific?" RealClear Defense, June 18, 2019, www.realcleardefense.com/articles/2019/06/18/is_china_using_its_south_china_sea_strategy_in_the_south_pacific_114509.html.

27. Ibid.

28. Hannah Beech, "China Throttles River," *New York Times,* April 14, 2020, A19.

29. Ibid.

30. Ben Sharples, "Australian Coal Diverted from China," *Bloomberg,* March 19, 2019.

31. Farah Master, "Empty Hotels, Idle Boats: What Happens When a Pacific Island Upsets China," Reuters, August 19, 2018, https://www.reuters.com/article/us-pacific-china-palau-insight-idUSKBN1L4036.

32. Diego Torres, "Why the West Treats China with Kid Gloves," *Politico,* June 22, 2017.

33. Edward Wong, "Mongolia, with Deep Ties to Dalai Lama, Turns from Him toward China," *New York Times,* December 30, 2016.

34. "Norway, China Normalize Ties After Nobel Peace Prize Row," Reuters, December 19, 2016, www.reuters.com/article/us-norway-china/norway-china-normalize-ties-after-nobel-peace-prize-row-idUSKBN1480R4.

35. Josh Rogin, "How China Forces American Companies to Do Its Political Bidding," *Washington Post,* January 21, 2018.

36. Amy Qin and Audrey Carlsen, "How China Controls Hollywood Scripts," *New York Times,* November 19, 2018.

37. Clive Hamilton, *Silent Invasion* (Melbourne: Hardie Grant, 2018), 25.

38. James Jiann Hua To, *Qiaowu: Extra-territorial Politics for the Overseas Chinese* (Leiden: Koninklijke Brill, 2014).

39. Hamilton, *Silent Invasion,* 32.

40. Ibid., 33.

41. Ibid., 40.

42. Ibid., 43.

43. Ibid., 57.

44. Ibid., 66, 94.

45. Ibid., 72.

46. Ibid., 74.

47. Ibid., 77.

48. "Australia, NZ Face China's Influence," Council on Foreign Relations, December 2017, www.cfr.org.

49. Luke Henriques Gomes, "Nearly 80 Per Cent of Foreign Political Donations Come from China, Data Shows," New Daily, updated December 12, 2017, thenewdaily.com.au/news/national/2017/12/10/chinese-donations-australia/.

50. Ibid.

51. Hamilton, *Silent Invasion,* 84.

52. Ibid., 85.

53. Ibid., 111, 112.

54. Ibid., 159.

55. Ibid., 196, 197.

56. Daniel Hurst, "Australia Hails Global Support of Call for Investigation," *Telegraph,* May 18, 2020.

57. Elias Visontay, "After Barley What Next?" *Guardian,* May 19, 2020.

58. Jonathan Manthorpe, *Claws of the Panda: Beijing's Campaign of Influence and Intimidation in Canada* (Toronto: Cormorant Books, 2019), 6.

59. Ibid., 13, 16.

60. Ibid., 157, 158.

61. Ibid., 194.

62. Ibid., 219, 220.

63. Hoover Institution, *Chinese Influence & American Interests* (Stanford: Hoover Institution Press, 2018), 4.

64. Ibid.

65. Heather Somerville, "Technology News," Reuters, January 6, 2019, www.reuters.com.

66. Hoover Institution, *Chinese Influence & American Interests,* 5.

67. Ibid., 71–72.

68. For the phrase "useful idiots," see Wikipedia, accessed May 10, 2020, en.wikipedia.org/wiki/Useful idiot: "*Time* first used the phrase in January 1958, writing that some Italian Christian Democrats considered social activist Danilo Dolci a 'useful idiot' for Communist causes. It has since recurred in that periodical's articles."

5. How America Got Rich

1. Ha-Joon Chang, *Bad Samaritans: The Myth of Free Trade and the Secret of Capitalism* (New York: Bloomsbury, 2007), 44.

2. E. J. Hobsbawm, *Industry and Empire; From 1750 to the Present Day* (London: Penguin, 1990), 48.

3. Alfred E. Eckes Jr., *Opening America's Market: U.S. Foreign Trade Policy since 1776* (Chapel Hill: University of North Carolina Press, 1995), 2.

4. Ibid., 15.

5. Ibid., 16.

6. Ibid., 19.

7. Ibid. 20.

8. Ibid., 17.

9. Ibid., 21.

10. Ibid., 30.

11. Timothy J. Botti, *Envy of the World: A History of the U.S. Economy and Big Business* (New York: Algora, 2006), 92.

12. Doron Ben-Atar, *Trade Secrets* (New Haven: Yale University Press, 2004).

13. Louis D. Johnston and Samuel H. Williamson, "What Was the U.S. GDP Then?" Measuring Worth, accessed 3 June 2020, http://www.measuringworth.org/usgdp/.

14. Hobsbawm, *Industry and Empire*, 115.

15. Richard Franklin Bensel, *The Political Economy of American Industrialization, 1877–1900* (Cambridge: Cambridge University Press, 2000), 295.

16. Hobsbawm, *Industry and Empire*.

17. Aaron L. Friedberg, *The Weary Titan: Britain and the Experience of Relative Decline, 1895–1905* (Princeton: Princeton University Press, 1989), 26; Paul Kennedy, *The Rise and Fall of the Great Powers: Economic Change and Military Conflict from 1500 to 2000* (New York: Random House, 1988), 202.

18. Alfred E. Eckes Jr. and Thomas W. Zeiler, *Globalization and the American Century* (New York: Cambridge University Press, 2003).

19. Ibid., 45.

20. Robert Cohen, *America's Industrial Policy Successes: The Forgotten History of Picking Winners and Losers,* Economic Policy Institute Study Series (1990–91), 16.

21. Eckes and Zeiler, *Globalization and the American Century,* 50.

22. Ibid., 51.

23. Kennedy, *The Rise and Fall of the Great Powers,* 282.

24. Ibid., 329.

25. Eckes and Zeiler, *Globalization and the American Century,* 109.

26. Clyde Prestowitz, *The Betrayal of American Prosperity* (New York: Free Press, 2010), 72.

6. The False God

1. Trading Economics, "U.S. GDP Annual Growth Rate," www.Tradingeconomics.com/United-states/gdp-growth-annual; Stanford University, "U.S. Median Household Income, 1950–1990," https://web.stanford.edu/class/polisci120a/immigration/Median%20Household%20Income.pdf.

2. Bureau of Economic Analysis, U.S. Department of Commerce, "Gross Domestic Product by Industry Accounts, 1947–2008, www.bea.gov/industry/gpotables/gpo-list.cfm; Bureau of Labor Statistics, "Manufacturing as Percent of GDP, 1900–2018"; Bureau of Labor Statistics, "U.S. Manufacturing Employment, 1960–2012," www.data.bls.gov/timeseries/ces3000000001; Bureau of Labor Statistics, "Productivity Change in Nonfarm Business Sector, 1947–2018," www.bls.govopubnonfarm-business-sector-la.

3. Bureau of Labor Statistics, "Union Affiliation of Employed Wage and Salaried Workers by Occupation and Industry," www.bls.govunion2.nro.htm.

4. Alfred E. Eckes Jr., *Opening America's Market: U.S. Foreign Trade Policy since 1776* (Chapel Hill: University of North Carolina Press, 1995), 161.

5. Ibid., 158.

6. William Beaver, "Volkswagen's American Assembly Plant: Fahrvergnugen Was Not Enough," *Business Horizons,* November/December, 1992.

7. "Number of TV Households in America," Television History—The First 75 Years, http://www.tvhistory.tv/Annual_TV_Households50–78.jpg.

8. Eckes, *Opening America's Market,* 177, 179.

9. Brian Reinbold and Yi Wen, "Historical U.S. Trade Deficits," Economic Research, Federal Reserve Bank of St. Louis, May 17, 2019, https://research.stlouisfed.org/publications/economic-synopses/2019/05/17/historical-u-s-trade-deficits.

10. James McBride and Andrew Chatzky, "The US Trade Deficit: How Much Does It Matter?" Council on Foreign Relations, last updated March 8, 2019, https://www.cfr.org/backgrounder/us-trade-deficit-how-much-does-it-matter.

11. Alfred E. Eckes Jr. and Thomas W. Zeiler, *Globalization and the American Century* (New York: Cambridge University Press, 2003), 169.

12. Sertac Kayar, "Dollar Eases vs. Major Currencies After Trump's Tariff," Reuters, November 17, 2017.

13. Bureau of the Census, Department of Commerce, "Trade Deficit: Twenty Billion and Climbing," Census.gov foreign trade.

14. "U.S.-Japan Trade Accord," *Los Angeles Times,* June 21, 1995.

15. Clyde Prestowitz, *The Betrayal of American Prosperity* (New York: Free Press, 2010), 89.

16. Paul Krugman, *Strategic Trade Policy and International Economics* (Cambridge, MA: MIT Press, 1986).

17. Paul Krugman, "Is Free Trade Passé?" *Journal of Economic Perspectives* 1, no. 2 (1987): 132.

18. Ha-Joon Chang, *Bad Samaritans: The Myth of Free Trade and the Secret of Capitalism* (New York: Bloomsbury, 2007).

19. Laura Tyson, *Who's Bashing Whom? Trade Conflict in High Technology Industries* (Washington, DC: Peterson Institute, 1992).

20. Ralph Gomory and William Baumol, *Global Trade and Conflicting National Interests* (Cambridge, MA: MIT Press, 2001).

21. "How the West Got China Wrong," *Economist,* March 1, 2018

7. Blind Prophets, Tycoons, and Soothsayers

1. John Pomfret, *The Beautiful Country and the Middle Kingdom* (New York: Picardo, 2016), 43.

2. Anand Giridharadas, "JFK Faced India-China Dilemma," *New York Times,* August 26, 2005.

3. Richard Nixon, "Asia After Vietnam," *Foreign Affairs,* October 1967.

4. Pomfret, *The Beautiful Country and the Middle Kingdom,* 444.

5. Ibid., 452.

6. Ibid., 453.

7. Ibid., 450.

8. Ibid., 449.

9. Ibid., 455.

10. Ibid., 464.

11. Ibid., 467.

12. Ibid., 478.

13. Ibid., 479.

14. Ibid., 480.

15. Ibid., 486.

16. Kimberly Amadeo, "U.S. Trade Deficit with China and Why It's So High—The Real Reason Why American Jobs Are Going to China," *Balance,* February 26, 2020, www.thebalance.com/u-s-china-trade-deficit-causes-effects-and-solutions-3306277.

17. Pomfret, *The Beautiful Country and the Middle Kingdom,* 498.

18. Ibid., 502.

19. Ibid., 509.

20. Seth Faison, "Persistent Mystery: How Many Died in 1989," *New York Times,* June 4, 1999.

21. Pomfret, *The Beautiful Country and the Middle Kingdom,* 515.

22. Ibid., 518.

23. Presidential debate, *C-span,* October 15, 1992.

24. Pomfret, *The Beautiful Country and the Middle Kingdom,* 538.

25. William Safire, "The Biggest Vote," *New York Times,* May 18, 2000.

26. William Clinton, *My Life* (New York: Knopf, 2004).

27. "All Politics," CNN, June 11, 1998.

28. "Clinton's Words on China: Trade Is the Smart Thing," *New York Times,* March 9, 2000.

29. Pomfret, *The Beautiful Country and the Middle Kingdom,* 569.

30. Ibid., 570.

31. James Mann, *The China Fantasy* (New York: Penguin Books, 2007), 62, 63.

32. Pomfret, *The Beautiful Country and the Middle Kingdom,* 571.

33. Thomas Friedman, *The Lexus and the Olive Tree* (New York: Farrar, Straus and Giroux, 1999), 69, 71.

34. Ibid., 154, 336–37.

35. Pomfret, *The Beautiful Country and the Middle Kingdom,* 557.

36. Sandy Berger, "Foreign Policy for a Global Age," *Foreign Affairs,* November/December 2000.

37. Mann, *The China Fantasy,* 60–61.

38. Pomfret, *The Beautiful Country and the Middle Kingdom,* 592.

39. Gary J. Schmitt, "China Dream," *American Interest,* February 7, 2019.

40. "Unstoppable Momentum toward Democracy," *Telegraph,* September 7, 2005, 1.

41. Robert Zoellick address to the National Committee on US-China Relations, New York City, September 21, 2005.

42. Mann, *The China Fantasy,* 35–37.

43. Robert E. Scott, *The China Toll* (Washington, DC: Economic Policy Institute, 2012).

44. Mark Landler, *Alter Egos* (Raleigh, NC: TwoMorrow's Publishing, 2016).

45. Pomfret, *The Beautiful Country and the Middle Kingdom,* 624.

46. Ibid., 625.

47. "How the West Got China Wrong," *Economist,* March 1, 2018.

8. Lay of the Land

1. Paul Krugman, *Pop Internationalism* (Cambridge, MA: MIT Press 2009).

2. Alan Beattie, "Supply Chain Disruption," *Financial Times,* May 28, 2020.

3. Bret Stephens, "China and the Rhineland Moment," *New York Times,* May 30, 2020.

4. Jamie Smyth, "China-Australia War of Words Unnerves Business," *Financial Times,* May 27, 2020.

5. Lin Qiqing and Paul Mozur, "China Blocks American Books as Trade War Simmers," *New York Times,* December 27, 2019.

6. Zoey Ye Zhang, "China's SOE Reforms: What the Latest Round of Reforms Mean for the Market," China Briefing, May 29, 2019, https://www.china-briefing.com/news/chinas-soe-reform-process/.

7. "Beijing Plans to Restrict Visas for US Visitors with 'Anti-China' Links," CNBC, October 9, 2019, www.cnbc.com/2019/10/10/beijing-to-restrict-visas-for-us-visitors-with-anti-china-links.html.

8. Center for Strategic and International Studies, last updated May 14, 2020, Chinapower.csis.org/china-naval-modernization/.

9. Gregory Poling, "China's Hidden Navy: The Evidence Shows That Supposed Fishing Boats around Contested Islands Are Part of an Extensive Maritime Militia," *Foreign Policy,* June 25, 2019.

10. See data provided by the CEIC: www.ceicdata.com/en/indicator/united-states/gross-savings-rate; www.ceicdata.com/en/indicator/china/gross-savings-rate; www.ceicdata.com/en/indicator/japan/gross-savings-rate; www.ceicdata.com/en/indicator/germany/gross-savings-rate.

11. www.theglobaleconomy.com/USA/household_consumption/; tradingeconomics.com/china/household-final-consumption-expenditure-etc-percent-of-gdp-wb-data.html.

12. "Comparing United States and China by Economy," Statistics Times, August 2, 2019, http://statisticstimes.com/economy/united-states-vs-china-economy.php.

13. "China Seen Heading for Sub 6% Economic Growth," *Bloomberg,* September 2, 2019.

14. Li Jing, "Rising Sea Levels Set to Displace 45 Million People in Hong Kong, Shanghai and Tianjin if Earth Warms 4 Degrees from Climate Change," *South China Morning Post,* November 9, 2015.

15. Global Security Review, April 2018.

9. A Long Telegram

1. M. Taylor Fravel, J. Stapleton Roy, Michael D. Swaine, Susan A. Thornton, and Ezra Vogel, "China Is Not an Enemy," *Washington Post,* July 3, 2019.

2. "On Trade Reform and Future of Relations," interview with Charlene Barshefsky, *Insight: Journal of the American Chamber of Commerce of Shanghai,* January/February 2019.

3. "You Can't Contain China," *South China Morning Post,* January 14, 2019.

4. Asia Society, Task Force on U.S.-China Policy, "Course Correction: Toward an Effective and Sustainable China Policy," 7, February 12, 2019.

5. Ibid., 8.

6. Ibid.

7. Ibid., 18.

8. Ibid., 23.

9. Peter Navarro and Greg Autry, *Death by China: Confronting the Dragon—A Global Call to Action* (Upper Saddle River, NJ: Prentice Hall, 2011).

10. Dr. Christopher Ashley Ford, assistant secretary, Bureau of International Security and Nonproliferation, remarks made at the Multilateral Action on Sensitive Technologies (MAST) Conference, "Huawei and Its Siblings, the Chinese Tech Giants: National Security and Foreign Policy Implications," Loy Henderson Auditorium, U.S. Department of State, Washington, DC, September 11, 2019.

11. Kurt M. Campbell and Jake Sullivan, "Competition without Catastrophe: How America Can Both Challenge and Coexist with China," *Foreign Affairs,* September/October 2019.

12. Ibid., 105.

13. Stewart Paterson, *China, Trade and Power* (London: London Publishing Partnership, 2018), 84, 86–87.

14. See Sustainable Travel International, https://sustainabletravel.org/.

15. See EnergySage, Energysage.com.

10. The Plan for China

1. "Houston Rockets GM Morey Deletes Tweet about Hong Kong," CNBC, October 6, 2019.

2. Elizabeth Economy, *The Third Revolution—Xi Jinping and the New Chinese State* (Oxford: Oxford University Press, 2018).

3. "Apple Accedes to China's Despotic Demands," *Washington Post,* October 15, 2019.

4. "The NBA's New Normal in China," *Wall Street Journal,* October 25, 2019.

5. Christopher Balding, "One Good Reason to Delist Chinese Companies," *Bloomberg,* October 7, 2019.

6. Josh Rogin, "China Building Financial Leverage over All Americans," *Washington Post,* October 10, 2019.

7. Tobias Harris, " 'Quality Infrastructure': Japan's Robust Challenge to China's Belt and Road," War on the Rocks and the Stimson Center, April 9, 2019, https://

warontherocks.com/2019/04/quality-infrastructure-japans-robust-challenge-to-chinas-belt-and-road/.

11. The Plan for America

1. Jeffrey Mervis, "U.S. Lawmakers Unveil Bold Program," *Science*, May 26, 2020, 1.

2. See OECD savings rate data, 2015, at https://data.oecd.org/.

3. See OECD savings rate comparison data, 2017, at https://data.oecd.org/;data at GlobalEconomy.com, by country.

4. See China investment data at GlobalEconomy.com.

5. See http://uis.unesco.org/.

6. On R&D, see *American Institute of Physics Bulletin*, November 2016.

7. For life expectancy, see CIA, The World Factbook, https://www.cia.gov/library/publications/the-world-factbook/rankorder/2102rank.html.

8. For federal spending and debt, see Congressional Budget Office, "Updated Budget Projections, 2019–2029," May 2, 2019, https://www.cbo.gov/publication/55151.

9. "The Rich Really Pay Lower Taxes," *New York Times*, October 7, 2019.

10. "Apple's Cash Mountain," *Irish Times*, October 11, 2019.

Acknowledgments

I am deeply indebted to many, many people around the world who have given generously of their time, memory, and insights.

On the list of these people and institutions must first come my wife Carol, who, in addition to relieving me of most household and family responsibilities, has again proven to be an ideal researcher, editor, disciplinarian, and soul mate.

I am deeply indebted to Allan Song of the Smith Richardson Foundation for the very idea of writing the book in the first place. His initial call in February 2018 sparked the discussion leading to my proposal and, eventually, a very generous grant from the Smith Richardson Foundation to support the writing of the book. I must also thank Dan Dimicco, former CEO of Nucor Steel, for his kind recommendations.

I am also deeply indebted to my researcher in chief, Joel Fischl. A career foreign commercial service officer of the U.S. Department of Commerce and a Mandarin speaker with over twenty years of experience in Shanghai, Beijing, Hong Kong, Tokyo, and Manila, he went far, far beyond the call of duty in digging up contacts, old friends, experts, and difficult-to-find information. He was also extremely patient with me and managed to ride out all the rough spots with a combination of his vast network and knowledge and a truly exhilarating sense of humor.

I must give special thanks to my longtime assistant/publicist/political guide Kate Brown for her untiring assistance and guidance

My close friends and policy wonks, former assistant secretary of commerce Pat Mulloy, Mandarin Capital CEO Alberto Forchielli, Coalition for a Prosperous America fellow Jeff Ferry, Information Industry and Innovation Foundation president Rob Atkinson, former treasury assistant secretary George Tyler, and Wessel Group CEO Mike Wessel, were constant sources of information, contacts, critique, ideas, and encouragement. I must also thank my longtime friend, former college roommate, and debating partner William Krist.

Professor David Shambaugh at George Washington University has been extremely encouraging, generous with his time, and helpful in guiding my thinking and research directions. I must say the same for Admiral Dennis Blair, who generously advised on defense and foreign policy issues with China. Similarly, Professor Minxin Pei of the Claremont McKenna Colleges has been most encouraging and has provided great guidance on how to understand and analyze the Chinese Communist Party. Likewise, my longtime friend Ambassador Chas Freeman has, as always, proven to be an unending fount of knowledge, contacts, historical perspectives, and insider tales of the past fifty years of U.S.-China history. Ambassador Stapleton Roy was very generous with his insights and recommendations. I also want to thank my old friend Jung Chang, who first sparked my study of China with her book *Wild Swans* many years ago and whose biography of Mao is so completely revealing. Michael Pillsbury, former special assistant for Asian affairs to the secretary of defense and author of *The Hundred Year Marathon,* was generous with his time and insights, as was U.S. ambassador to the Philippines Sung Y. Kim. Richard McGregor, formerly with the *Financial Times* in Beijing and now a fellow at the Lowey Institute in Sydney, provided enormous insight into the Chinese Communist Party and the mindset of its key leaders. He was also extremely generous with his time. U.S. trade representative Robert Lighthizer, a longtime friend, provided insights from a career as a top trade negotiator, as did Richard McCormack of the U.S. Department of Commerce.

Old friend, China hand, and author of *The China Fantasy,* James Mann was both encouraging and helpful, as was my good friend Bob Davis of the *Wall Street Journal.* Former assistant secretary of state and current chairman of the Asia Group Kurt Campbell was generous with his time, as was Ely Rattner, the director of the Center for a New American Security. I am also indebted to Jim Waterman at the U.S. Chamber of Commerce. Old friend and fellow trade wonk Susan Rochford kindly read the manuscript and made many good suggestions, as did Don Lee of the *Los Angeles Times.* Longtime friend, advisor, and founding editor of the *American Prospect* Bob Kuttner provided continual support and editorial guidance, as did veteran trade negotiator and friend Maureen Smith. I must also thank my landlord and fellow Japan watcher Mindy Kotler. Denny Roy and Charles Morrison at the East West Center provided valuable and ongoing advice and critique. Ralph Cossa and Rear Admiral Robert Girrier were generous with their time and advice. I am also deeply indebted to Semiconductor Industry Association president John Neuffer and to Alan Turley, deputy assistant secretary of the U.S. Department of Commerce for China and Mongolia. I must also add that the president of GaveKal Dragon Economics, Arthur Kroeber, was generous with his time and suggestions. Ben Carliner of the EU Mission to the United States was his usual helpful self, as was Jeff Ferry of the Coalition for a Prosperous America.

In Hong Kong, I am deeply indebted to *Financial Times* correspondent Jamil Anderlini, whose understanding of modern China is exceptional. Louis Kuijs of Oxford Economics generously shared his deep insights into China's economic strategies. My longtime friends and free Hong Kong supporters former chief civil servant Anson Chan, United Democratic Party founder Martin Lee, and *Apple Daily* founder and publisher Jimmy Lai provided deep insights from their long experience. Sadly, Martin and Jimmy were recently arrested by the Hong Kong police under new Chinese Communist Party directorship for participating in pro-democracy demonstrations in August 2019. My friend and Hinrich Foundation founder and CEO Merle Hinrich was generous with his time, advice, and publicity support and introduced me to many valuable sources of information and analysis. Also very helpful was his chief of staff, Kathryn Diode. Senior foreign commercial service officer Jim Cunningham was generous with his time, insights, and suggestions as well. I also want to thank the members of the American Chamber of Commerce in Hong Kong, who welcomed me with a friendly and informative reception.

In Shanghai, I am deeply indebted to *New York Times* correspondent Keith Bradsher and to APCO Worldwide chairman and ultimate China expert Jim McGregor. The principal commercial officer at the U.S. Consulate in Shanghai, Jonathan Heimer, was very helpful, as was Consul General Sean Stein.

In Beijing, I am grateful to EU ambassador to China Nicolas Chapuis. I am deeply indebted to old friend and Peking University professor Michael Pettis, *Bloomberg* correspondent Michael Schuman, *Economist* bureau chief David Rennie, and *Financial Times* bureau chief Tom Mitchell. I am also greatly indebted to many people in China who for reasons of their own security asked not to be mentioned in this book. They have my constant gratitude and admiration.

Taiwan ambassador to the U.S. Stanley Kao was very helpful in arranging meetings for me in Taipei as well as in suggesting lines of inquiry. In Taipei, I am grateful to Raymond F. Green, deputy director of the American Institute in Taiwan, and to former director William Stanton for their insights and suggestions. I am also indebted to Taiwan foreign minister Joseph Wu, to Ketty Chen, vice president of the Taiwan Foundation for Democracy, and to the deputy minister of the Mainland Affairs Council, Chen Ming-chi, for their advice and insights. I also owe thanks to *Financial Times* Taiwan correspondent Kathrin Hille. Professor Syaru Shirley Lin and her husband Harry Harding, professor at the University of Virginia, were of immense assistance both in their substantive comments and in helping me get to the right people.

In Manila, I was fortunate to be able to have the advice and wisdom of the Philippines secretary of foreign affairs Teodoro L. Locsin and the undersecretary for foreign affairs Enrique A. Manalo as well as of Lucio Blanco Pitlo of the Asia Pacific Pathways to Progress Foundation and former undersecretary of finance Romy Bernardo. I am immensely grateful to Eva Antonio, who arranged many of my meetings and travel in Manila. Young reporter Gregg Yan was extremely helpful in explaining the slow death of the South China Sea. Journalist and author Marites Vitug was immensely helpful in her analysis of the present situation of the Philippines.

In Singapore, I am deeply indebted to the Foreign Ministry's most senior official, Bilahari Kauskan, and also to Ambassador and longtime prime ministerial advisor Tommy Koh. I must also thank Ong Keng Yong, executive deputy chairman of S. Rajaratnam University, for his insights and experienced views.

In Tokyo, I am deeply indebted to friend and analyst Hiromi Murakami, who worked closely with me in arranging and carrying out interviews. Kunihiko Miyake of the Canon Global Institute and a leading thinker on U.S.-Japan relations was generous with his time and advice. So was Jianrong Zhu, professor at Toyo Gakuen University and an expert on Chinese history and politics. Bonji Obara of the Sasakawa Peace Foundation and former defense ministry official was most helpful with regard to the security situation in East Asia. My friends Nobuo Tanaka, chairman of the Sasakawa Peace Foundation, and top Japan economist Richard Koo were extremely helpful with their analyses and advice. I am also deeply indebted to Admiral Umio Otsuka and former *New York Times* Tokyo correspondent Martin Fackler for their time and advice. University of Tokyo professor Akio Takahara provided many insights on Chinese politics, and Junhua Wu of the Japan Research Institute, George Washington University, and the Woodrow Wilson Center was most helpful in her analysis of the workings of the Chinese Communist Party. Hitoshi Tanaka, a distinguished retired Japanese diplomat and longtime friend, gave very helpful insights from his own experience. University of Tokyo professor Ryo Sahashi was most generous with his time and insights, as was Professor Narushige Michishita of the GRIPS institution. I am also grateful to Sasakawa Peace Foundation fellow Tsuneo Watanabe for his insights, and to Wu Junhua of the Japan Research Institute.

Last but far from least, I was very fortunate to have many friends and advisors in Australia. I am deeply indebted to my old neighbor and longtime friend Martin Adams for his advice and efforts in helping to organize my meetings. At RMIT University, Deputy Vice Chancellor Andrew MacIntyre was most helpful and also arranged a lunch at which I was able to obtain a wide variety of Australian views. Philipp Ivanov, CEO of the Asia Society of Australia, kindly provided many insights into Australia-China relations and arranged several excellent meetings for me. Clive Hamilton, author of *Silent Invasion,* a book about China's penetration of Australian politics and society, was generous with his time and insights. I am deeply indebted to John Garnaut, former China correspondent and Asia editor for *Fairfax News,* for his valuable insights and generosity with his time. Peter Hartcher of the *Sydney Morning Herald* has been a constant and inventive source, for which I am grateful. Warwick Smith, chairman of the Advisory Board of Stokes Australian Capital Equity and longtime China hand, was most generous with his time and advice. Strategic Forum chairman Ross Babbage provided insights and valuable historical knowledge. I am also indebted to Peter Jennings, executive director of the Australia Strategic Policy Institute, for his insights and suggestions.

In Europe, I am grateful for the insights and assistance of Alice Ekman, head of China research at the French Institute for International Relations, as well as to Volker Perthes, director of the German Institute for International Security Affairs. Robert Plachta and David Wilkens of the German embassy in Washington, DC, were quite helpful in arranging meetings for me in Germany. I am grateful to Pedro Velasco Martins and EU commissioner for trade Cecilia Malmström for their explanation of the EU's new perception of China as a strategic competitor. The Association of German Industries under President Dieter Kempf was also extremely helpful. I must also thank Ben Carliner of the EU embassy in Washington, DC, for his help in putting my European schedule together.

Index

academics and scholars: China's censorship of foreign, 124–25, 129; self-censorship and, 57, 130, 134

Adams, John, 145

Advanced Micro Devices (AMD), 171

adversarial trade, 178–81

advisory groups of former officials, 193,
207–8, 260

Africa: China's influence in, 79, 82, 133,
134, 230; OBOR project in, 8, 49, 80,
97. *See also specific countries*

African Growth and Opportunity Act
(AGOA), 82

African Union, 82

agriculture: Chinese liberalization of,
65; economies of scale in, 70–71;
Hamilton on, 144; Jefferson on, 142;
U.S. expansion of, 151–52, 164

Airbus, 176, 179, 180

Air Commerce Act (1927), 154

aircraft industry, 4, 29, 154, 157, 158

AISense, 130

Akio Morita, 172

Aksai Chin, India, 109

Albania, OBOR project in, 82

Albright, Madeleine and Albright
Group, 74, 207

Alexander, Bill, 192

Alexanderson alternator, 154

Alibaba, 29, 50, 259, 266

Alina Energy, 123–24

Allen & Unwin (publishing company),
7–8

Alliance Bernstein, 208

Amaya Naohiro, 169, 172, 176, 211

Amazon, 88–90, 243, 259

Amboyna Cay, 105

American Enterprise Institute, 178,
199

American International Group (AIG),
201–2

American Society of Civil Engineers,
285

American System of manufacturing, 144,
146, 147

Amnesty International Canada, 126

Anderson, Robert, 167

Angola, 82

Antwerp, Belgium, 83

Apple, 219, 255, 260–64, 279, 287

Argentina, 83

arms sales, 192–94

artificial intelligence, 29, 63, 93, 181,
228, 246, 255

abroad, 119, 122, 126, 129; free world coverage of China in, 129, 228; in Hong Kong, 53; overseas publications and, 119; in United States, 231
New Trade Theory, 175
New Zealand, 57, 58, 131–32
Nexen (oil and gas company), 127
Nigeria, 79, 82
Nixon, Richard, 100, 198
Nobel Peace Prize, 115–16, 212
Norsat International, 58, 126
Northern Expedition (1926), 33
Norway, 115–16
nuclear weapons, 126, 131, 158, 186–87, 194
nullification and impairment complaints, 242, 267
Nye, Joseph, 211

Obama, Barack, 5, 86, 103, 107, 212, 239–40
Office of Production Management (U.S.), 157
offshoring of jobs. See manufacturing
Ohlin, Bertil Gotthard, 162, 164
Okinawa, 107
One Belt One Road (OBOR) project, 8–9, 49, 80–84, 132–33, 229, 272
O'Neil, Jim, 84
Ontario Hydro, 126–27
open seas policies, 273–74
Operation Dove (drones), 93
Operation Sidewinder (secret report), 126
opium trade and Opium Wars, 18, 22–25, 185, 186
Organization Department (CCP), 44–45, 47–48, 51–52, 77–78
origins of Chinese dream. See Chinese dream
outsourcing. See manufacturing
Overseas Chinese Affairs Office, 55, 117–18, 126, 128
Oxenberg, Michael, 191

Pacific Railroad Act (1862), 147
Packer, James, 121
Paine, Thomas, 142
Pakistan, 194, 230
Palau, 114
Panama, 83–84
Panchen Lama, 224
pandemic. See coronavirus pandemic
Papua New Guinea, 110, 111
Parkinson, George, 148
Patent Act (1790) and patent law, 143, 148. See also intellectual property
Paterson, Stewart, 252
Paul (apostle), 36–37
Paulson, Henry, 203–5, 212
Payne, Marise, 131
Peng Dehuai, 36
penicillin, 158
People's Liberation Army (PLA): CCP served by, 42, 44; fishing vessels and, 111, 212; Huawei and, 49–50, 88; national security and, 95–98; organization and branches of, 96; Senkaku Islands and, 108; Taiwan Strait and, 101–2; Third Department of cyber espionage in, 124; Tiananmen Square massacre and, 42, 66, 95, 195; Unit 61398 cyberattacks by, 89–90; U.S. sales of arms to, 192
Perico Island, Panama, 83
Period of the Warring States (475–221 BC), 15
permanent normal trade relations with China, 200, 202
Perry, William, 192
personnel of CCP. See Organization Department
Peterson Institute, 178
Philippines: infrastructure investment in, 273; in neoclassical economic system, 164; offshoring production to, 262; South China Sea dispute and, 4–5, 102, 104–6, 112–13, 274